Leroy Ostransky is Professor of Music and Composer-in-Residence at the University of Puget Sound. He is the author of *The World of Music* (Prentice-Hall) and *The Anatomy of Jazz,* and has lectured on jazz at a number of the nation's leading universities.

see p 34 – check on metronome

3

LEROY OSTRANSKY

understanding
jazz

Prentice-Hall, Inc., *Englewood Cliffs*, N.J. 07632   A SPECTRUM BOOK

Library of Congress Cataloging in Publication Data

OSTRANSKY, LEROY.
   Understanding jazz.

   (A Spectrum Book)
   Bibliography: p.
   Includes index.
   1. Jazz music.   I. Title.
ML3561.J3093   781.5'7   77-969
ISBN 0-13-936542-7
ISBN 0-13-9365434-6 pbk.

To Natalie

© 1977 by Prentice-Hall, Inc.
Englewood Cliffs, New Jersey 07632

A Spectrum Book

10 9 8 7 6 5 4 3

Printed in the United States of America

Prentice-Hall International, Inc., *London*
Prentice-Hall of Australia Pty. Limited, *Sydney*
Prentice-Hall of Canada, Ltd., *Toronto*
Prentice-Hall of India Private Limited, *New Delhi*
Prentice-Hall of Japan, Inc., *Tokyo*
Prentice-Hall of Southeast Asia Pte. Ltd., *Singapore*
Whitehall Books Limited, Wellington, *New Zealand*

contents

preface

During my thirty years of teaching and lecturing about jazz, I have learned that for most students as well as for the public, the scope of jazz is, at the least, unsuspected. In this book I have tried in a nontechnical way to introduce students and the general reader to the scope of jazz, in one volume.

For some, jazz is musical excitement and propulsive rhythms; for others, soft lights and sweet music; for still others, it is the sound of love or hate or the way things used to be. Like other kinds of music, jazz encompasses all of these. Whether one likes or dislikes jazz does not call for analysis or comment; but to *understand* jazz, we have to know something about not only its musical nature, its principal exponents, and the jazz milieu but also its origins, its development, its styles, and how jazz was deeply affected by the most significant social, economic, and political events in American history.

Clearly, to accomplish all this in one volume, I have frequently had to use broad strokes, perhaps too broad and general for some tastes; to somewhat justify this, I trust I will be allowed to take refuge in the introductory nature of the book. For the interested reader, however, the bibliography at the end shows the sources I have used and also provides a sampling of books dealing at length with subjects I have only touched upon.

The origin of this book is *The Anatomy of Jazz,* originally published by the University of Washington Press in 1960, and reprinted by Greenwood Press in 1974. What began (I thought) as just a revised edition of *The Anatomy of Jazz* turned out to be, in fact, a new book. The *Anatomy* is a technical work, aimed at music theorists and classical music devotees, and ends with the state of jazz in the late fifties. This new book is nontechnical, aimed at all readers interested in appreciating or understanding jazz, or both, and discusses the jazz scene through the mid-seventies.

What I have tried to do is write a book that serves the same purpose, in words, that the Smithsonian Collection of Classic Jazz serves aurally. If you are especially interested in Bix Beiderbecke, say, you may feel that the Smithsonian Beiderbecke selections—two pieces—don't especially serve your purpose. Nor will what I have written on Beiderbecke serve your purpose. What you will want, of course, is Sudhalter and Evans' biography of Beiderbecke and a batch of Beiderbecke reissues, both of which are fortunately easy to come by. As I write this, in 1976, reissues of recordings by major and minor jazz masters of the past are being brought forth in numbers previously unheard of. Even record shops that once handled mainly Top 40 rock and pop records are now displaying jazz records for all to see, and happily there is something for nearly every taste.

Jazz in the mid-seventies is once more full of vigor and bounce, and appears ready to accommodate a generation raised on pop and rock and the Vietnam war. And these young people are showing mounting evidence of meeting older jazz buffs at least halfway. It is a wonderful time for jazz to once more become a young people's music.

acknowledgments

I wish to thank Doug Alvey for the use of his catalogues on electronic equipment and his essay on the synthesizer; Mark Clevenger for the use of his hillbilly jazz records; Kathie Eubanks for the use of her mainstream records; Woody Eversz for the use of his Miles Davis records; Mike Loomis for the general use of his jazz record collection; Marvin Van for the use of his Jazz Crusader collection; Ken Wiley for the use of his Bill Evans records; Elodie Vandevert for her research on the Creoles of New Orleans; and Steve Wehmhoff for the use of his jazz records of the seventies. I also wish to thank Martin Williams and J. R. Taylor of the Smithsonian and Sam Angeloff and Emmett Watson of the Seattle *Post-Intelligencer* for their good advice.

I wish to express my appreciation to Margaret Wilson for her help in typing the early chapters of the manuscript.

I am especially indebted to Desmond Taylor, Director of the Library at the University of Puget Sound, for his encouragement, helpful suggestions, and for his special effort in providing out-of-print jazz books and periodicals. I am further indebted to Mr. Taylor's staff—particularly to Bradley F. Millard, reference librarian, and Raimund E. Matthis, technical services librarian. I wish, too, to express my thanks to Sadie Uglow, and the staff of the Tacoma Public Library.

Finally, I wish to thank my daughter, Sonya, for her considerable help with the research for jazz as protest.

I wish to express acknowledgment and thanks to the publishers and authors who have granted permission to use the following:

Acknowledgments

Winthrop Sargeant, author, for material from *Jazz: Hot and Hybrid.*

Excerpts from *The Jazz Makers,* edited by Nat Shapiro and Nat Hentoff, are reprinted by permission of Holt, Rinehart and Winston, Publishers. Copyright © 1957 by Nat Shapiro and Nat Hentoff.

Excerpts from *Jazz: A People's Music,* by Sidney Finkelstein, are used by permission of Lyle Stuart, Inc.

Excerpts from *A History of Jazz in America,* by Barry Ulanov, are used by permission of The Viking Press, Inc. Copyright © 1955, 1957 by Barry Ulanov.

Excerpts from Marshall Stearns, *The Story of Jazz* are used by permission of Oxford University Press.

Excerpts from *Hear Me Talkin' to Ya,* edited by Nat Shapiro and Nat Hentoff, are used by permission of Holt, Rinehart and Winston, Publishers. Copyright © 1955 by Nat Shapiro and Nat Hentoff.

Excerpts from *American Jazz Music,* by Wilder Hobson, are used by permission of W. W. Norton & Company, Inc. Copyright 1939 by W. W. Norton & Company, Inc. Copyright renewed 1967 by Wilder Hobson.

Excerpts from *Jazz, from the Congo to the Metropolitan,* by Robert Goffin, are used by permission of Doubleday & Company, Inc.

Excerpts from *Jazz: Its Evolution and Essence,* by Andre Hodeir, are reprinted by permission of Grove Press, Inc. Copyright © 1956 by Grove Press, Inc.

Excerpts from *His Eye Is on the Sparrow,* by Ethel Waters and Charles Samuels, are used by permission of Doubleday & Company, Inc. and McIntosh, McKee & Dodds, Inc. Copyright 1950, 1951 by Ethel Waters and Charles Samuels.

Excerpts from *Mister Jelly Roll,* by Alan Lomax, are used by permission of Hawthorn Books, Inc.

Excerpts from *Shining Trumpets: A History of Jazz,* 2nd ed. revised and enlarged, by Rudi Blesh, are used by permission of Alfred A. Knopf, Inc. Copyright 1946 © 1958 by Alfred A. Knopf, Inc.

Excerpts from *Jazzmen,* by Frederic Ramsey, Jr. and Charles Edward

Smith, are used by permission of Harcourt Brace Jovanovich, Inc. and Sedgwick & Jackson Ltd.

The excerpt from *The Heart of Jazz,* by W. L. Grossman and J. W. Farrell, is used by permission of New York University Press. © 1956 by New York University.

Material from *A Pictorial History of Jazz,* by Orrin Keepnews and Bill Grauer, Jr. (new edition revised by Orrin Keepnews) is used by permission of Crown Publishers, Inc. © 1966 by Orrin Keepnews and Jane Grauer.

Excerpts from *The Kingdom of Swing,* by Benny Goodman and Irving Kolodin, are used by permission of Stackpole Books.

The excerpt from "Jazzmen in City Still Battle Myths," by George Goodman, Jr., is used by permission of The New York Times. © 1975 by The New York Times Company.

The photograph of Thelonious Monk is used by courtesy of Fantasy/Prestige/Milestone Records.

The photograph of the Fletcher Henderson Orchestra is used by permission of Culver Pictures.

The photograph of Dizzy Gillespie is used by courtesy of Polydor Incorporated.

The photograph of Duke Ellington is used by courtesy of James. J. Kriegsmann Studios, New York, N.Y.

The photograph of Benny Goodman is used by courtesy of Benny Goodman.

The photograph of the Modern Jazz Quartet is used by courtesy of Atlantic Records.

The photograph of Cecil Taylor is used by courtesy of Arista Records. Photo by Mary-Lou Webb/Arista Records.

The photograph of Bill Evans is used by courtesy of Helen Keane Artist's Management, New York, N.Y.

It is . . . our responsibility to help the students see the music of any given period in the light of its own social, political and cultural climate; to understand that the esthetic laws and technical considerations of one period cannot be superimposed upon another; to make known to the student the varying convictions of leading musicians, both past and present, in order to help him make his own judgments; to learn that art is not concerned with conformity; to equip the student to deal with the novel without ridicule or fear of its strangeness, yet without being impressed by sheer novelty, and with the ability to probe the depths of the unfamiliar.

The Juilliard Report
on Teaching the Literature and Materials of Music, 1953

I

some
early difficulties

(Overleaf) *King Oliver and his Creole Jazz Band: 1923. This is the greatest of all the jazz organizations of the early and middle twenties and one of the very greatest of all time. It is this group which recorded the Okeh Mabel's Dream, a copy of which was sold at auction last year for ninety dollars! Front center is Louis Armstrong, posing with a slide trumpet. Others, left to right: Honore Dutrey, Baby Dodds, King Oliver, Lil Hardin Armstrong, Bill Johnson, Johnny Dodds. Photo by Bill Johnson, posed with banjo but actually the bass man.*

THE HISTORY OF JAZZ STYLES started with the New Orleans style in the late 1890s. Since then, the history of jazz and its performers have been given a fair amount of serious attention. Until relatively recently, however, analysis of the styles of jazz, as music, have been given little serious or systematic thought. The prime reason for this may be found in the analyses and evaluations made by jazz writters who apparently had difficulty in making themselves understood. The language of jazz was coined, for the most part, by jazz musicians with little regard for the written word, or by well-meaning writers with little technical knowledge of music in general, or—worst of all—by a small but influential school of semiliterate enthusiasts whose main interest seemed to lie not in furthering jazz itself, but in merchandising the adjuncts of jazz: records, horns, bop berets, and tired stock arrangements. Aimed at adolescents and jungle intellects, the language of this last group jangled with nouns and verbs that carried little meaning and adjectives that, while barely descriptive, were on the whole redundant. Unable to make even an attempt at straightforward musical analysis (or, for that matter, to write a straightforward sentence), they adopted a gibbering prose calculated to hide the thinness of their analysis and evaluation.

With the establishment in 1934 of *Down Beat,* a jazz magazine, there appeared to be hope for serious discussion of the subject. But this was a hope soon betrayed, for the editors aimed their publication at adolescent jazz fans and conceived their function to be that of serving the jazz industry as movie magazines served Hollywood. Until the swing era, during the middle and late thirties, there was little mention of jazz in popular magazines of national circulation, and whatever notice jazz received in the daily press was—its scantiness notwithstanding—pejorative and a little absurd. Jazz buffs therefore welcomed the new publication sight unseen, only to find its critical writing a disappointment. Serious jazz students, who had little to choose from among the writing on jazz before *Down Beat,* soon learned not to expect much of *Down Beat* either.

Although the quality of its writing and criticism was greatly improved from the 1960s on, in its youth it lacked seriousness and depth. Nat Hentoff, a former associate editor of *Down Beat,* summed up the magazine's first twenty-five years of publication when he said, in the March 15, 1958, issue of *Nation: "Down Beat* is especially shallow and is apparently geared for less advanced high school sophomores. . . . Critical and historical jazz writing does appear to be slowly improving, but fervid amateurism is apt to be predominant for some time, because the fan-writer is well entrenched. As long as *Down Beat* remains the 'bible' of the field, the writing will be of a caliber more appropriate to revealed religion than to responsible criticism." [1]

Because of their inability to write on jazz as music, writers for most of the popular jazz journals turned their hands to grinding out deadline record reviews and uncovering sensational biographical data that were then translated into trite but shocking headlines; or they concocted diffuse sophomoric think-pieces intended to show why the jazz musician is a nice guy or a bad guy or simply a misunderstood guy who never got the breaks until the writer discovered him in a tired but happy moment.

The language problem was one thing, but wrong-headed intolerance was another. As late as the mid-fifties there was a tendency among jazz writers to look down upon anyone who didn't "dig" jazz. Their attitude toward the uninitiated layperson was often one of indifference. But their attitude toward classical musicians was one of intolerance—not just a passive intolerance, but an active one. In its most primitive form, this intolerance manifested itself in simple name-calling; in a somewhat higher form it appeared in the condescension apparent in the following *Down Beat* items. The first compares the musical intelligence of the classical musician to that of the jazzman.

CAT ON KEYS

New York—Drummer Osie Johnson was telling of the time a group of classical musicians were gathered in a jazzman's home, and the latter put some Charlie Parker records on the phonograph.

After a few seconds, one of the classical men protested: "Come on now, fix the machine. That motor's obviously going too fast. Nobody can play that many notes so fast." The jazzman took great and obvious delight in proving that there was nothing at all wrong with the machine.[2]

The second is a three-column headline of an article on recording studios which reminds its readers: "Classics Recorders Just Discovering Something Jazz Fans Found Out Early." [3]

Square or classical musicians, finding themselves patronized by the self-appointed defenders of jazz, were unlikely to seek to overcome their feeling of alienation from jazz. The tone of *Down Beat* helped cement many of the so-called squares into four-square blocks of antagonism toward all jazz. It is a happy circumstance that many serious musicians were nonetheless able to disregard the rather obvious insinuations of petty jazz writers who, to retaliate for fancied snubs, attacked with their fists flying in the name of defending jazz. There were many first-rate muscians who believed it was possible, and even desirable, to study, understand and enjoy the work of Armstrong as well as the work of Bach, the work of Mozart as well as the work of Thelonious Monk. Such musicians may have been amused at the ineptness of undistinguished jazz reporters, but they were less likely to be amused when a critic of André Hodeir's reputation and sensitivity asked, in his *Jazz: Its Evolution and Essence,* a question such as this: "Isn't it true that those who prefer the Beethoven work [*Ninth Symphony*] confess implicitly their inability to understand Stravinsky's masterpiece [*The Rite of Spring*]?" [4]

If Hodeir meant to imply by his question that there were musicians who preferred Beethoven to Stravinsky, or that there were musicians who believed there was something unnatural about any music that was not German, then he should have said so. No one would have questioned this. If, however, his question was to be taken at face value, it would have seemed to indicate an inability on Hodeir's part to recognize the distinctions between comprehension, appreciation, and enjoyment. A respectable number of classical musicians understood (and understand) fully the nature of Stravinsky's work, but nevertheless prefer Beethoven's *Ninth Symphony* to Stravinsky's *The Rite of Spring* —and if not Beethoven's *Ninth,* then a Bach suite perhaps, or a Mozart divertimento, a Schubert song, a Chopin etude. Moreover, there can be no doubt that many musicians, and laypersons as well, not only did not prefer *The Rite of Spring* but did not understand it; neither is there any doubt, in my mind at least, that there were (and are) a good many who preferred Beethoven's *Ninth* and didn't understand *it,* either. The fact remains that it is not necessary to understand a work in order to like it; or, to put it another way: a musician may have a comprehensive understanding and appreciation of a work—jazz or otherwise—without liking it. The failure to understand this principle—perhaps the guiding principle in critical evaluation—was part of the reason for the apparent schism between some well-known jazz critics and contemporary classical musicians who evinced an interest in jazz.

In the late forties jazz reached an important stage in its growth.

It finally attracted a number of people of literary taste and musical perception, and this favorable climate has been maintained. Jazz still needs the aid and interest of historians, theorists, performers, composers, estheticians—anyone willing to lend support, knowledge, and experience to the task of establishing jazz as a significant part of music. Jazz is an important branch of music, of American music especially; as such, it must be allowed to flourish, cultivated by respectful consideration and intensive study. Much has been already done toward this goal: the inauguration of jazz study groups and institutes, for example, and the recognition of jazz as a subject for study in institutions of higher learning. Of the highest significance, also, is the probing look backward by people of appropriate intellectual habits, people who feel the compulsion to take the study of jazz out of the shadows of semiliterateness and anti-intellectualism and place it in the light of serious and searching study.

Jazz at last became respectable. But in order to understand the origins of its present-day problems—semantic and otherwise—it is necessary to survey, however briefly, early jazz criticism. As long ago as 1946, in *Jazz: Hot and Hybrid,* Winthrop Sargeant wrote: "There has been a great deal of dubious and highly confusing writing around the subject of jazz. Probably no musical movement in history has been made the subject of more leaky speculation. . . ." [5] Many critics have since echoed, in more or less detail, Sargeant's view. In order to show the scope of the work still to be done, I have listed the following representative statements, which, I believe, still pose the most important problems faced by jazz writers and theorists. Morroe Berger, a Columbia University fellow in sociology, wrote, in 1946, in Ralph de Toledano's *Frontiers of Jazz:* "The origins of jazz and the story of its spread, as well as the careers of its players . . . are significant, also, for the problems of the origins and diffusion of culture, and racial interaction, which involved other arts as well as some sciences." [6]

In 1955 Keepnews and Grauer, in *A Pictorial History of Jazz,* commented on the growing importance and complexities of jazz in America: "Perhaps the truest measure of the validity of jazz is that it can be all things to all men: a mild form of amusement; an emotional or an intellectual stimulant; an art form; a social commentary; a cult; something to like, love, or even hate for a wide variety of esthetic, emotional or social reasons. . . . And thus it is a fit subject for all the analysis, history, biography, criticism, and written what-have-you that has been built up alongside it." [7]

In 1956 Jacques Barzun, in *Music in American Life,* emphasized the difficulty we are concerned with: "It [jazz] ranks with sports and philately as the realm of the self-made expert and of the controversialist as well, for musicology has not yet settled all the historical, stylistic, and biographical problems that have been raised about it." [8]

In 1957 Shapiro and Hentoff summed up the question in *The Jazz Makers:* "Since jazz musicians are notoriously inarticulate verbally, a good deal of analytical and creative writing about jazz during the past three decades has been speculative, fanciful, romantic and wrong." [9]

Shapiro and Hentoff's statement brings us back to the semantic problem. It is sometimes easy for us to forget how new the language of jazz is, and quite frequently how subjective the meanings are of even its established terminology—such vague and enigmatic designations as Dixieland, bop, cool, progressive, and the New Thing. To say nothing of "jazz."

Although the word "Jazz" was undoubtedly in use for a good many years before 1914, it was not until then, according to Nick La Rocca, founder of the Original Dixieland Jazz Band, that "jazz" appeared in an advertisement. "The Original Dixieland Jazz Band," he said, "was the first band in the world to be called a Jazz Band. Our first billing was in the year of 1914, month of March, place Boosters Club, Chicago, Illinois, Manager Harry James." Two years later *Variety* said, "Chicago has added another innovation to its list of discoveries in the so-called 'Jazz Bands.'" According to Slonimsky's *Music since 1900,* this may be the first mention of the word "jazz" in print. A year after the *Variety* item appeared, the Victor Company issued the world's first jazz record (March 1917) with the Original Dixieland Jazz Band playing "Livery Stable Blues" and "Dixieland Jass Band One-Step." An advertisement in the Victor catalogue said, "Spell it Jass, Jas, Jaz or Jazz—nothing can spoil a Jass band." A year later, the Columbia Phonograph Company issued *its* first jazz record, "Darktown Strutters Ball" and "Indiana," played by the original Dixieland Jass Band.[10]

Conjecture on the derivation of the word "jazz" (or "jass") has ranged widely. The term has been variously considered as a corruption of "Charles" by way of "Chas," "jass," "jazz"; a diminution of *"jaser,"* that is, to exhilarate; and some linguistic scholars claim to have traced its origins to West Africa. In the early days of jazz writing, it may have seemed more profitable to seek the linguistic origins of jazz than to try to define it. Once it was out of its infancy, however, little could be said of its linguistic origins that had not been said before, and critics—the apt and inept alike—set about defining, or not defining, jazz.

Many of those attempting to define jazz took advantage of the elusiveness of the term by using jazz as a spring-board for sociological, psychological, and anthropological speculations, without once recognizing that jazz is music; nevertheless, many of these early critics have made some contribution to the understanding of jazz. Before we attempt to search out the musical aspects of jazz, it might be well to acknowledge the work of those social critics who had a hand in creating the image of jazz still dominant in the minds of many people. These are the critics who have, in the main, produced the miasmatic atmosphere in which jazzmen often have had to perform. These are the critics who have stamped their opinions and attitudes upon the jazz-uninformed reading public and have made it difficult, and sometimes impossible, to convince the uninitiated of the worth of jazz, or to persuade them to accept the understanding of jazz as a serious and worthy enterprise.

For the social critics of jazz and the people they have influenced, the years between 1920 and 1929 were the crucial years, the years when all good men strode onto the field of Armageddon, pen in hand, to conquer the evil forces of jazz. It is therefore natural to search for the corpus of social criticism of jazz in the writings of Jazz Age critics—not because its critics were unmusical (or, in some cases, not even American), but because their criticism reflects the literate viewpoint of sincere writers and jazz-innocent readers at the time when first impressions of jazz were being formed.

In 1920 Harold Spender, a representative critic of American mores and author of *A Briton in America,* was led to believe that many of the jazz tunes he had heard were African in origin. This caused him painful concern. If we were not careful, American musical tradition might be "submerged by the aboriginal music of the negro," and, if we insisted on stomping along such "semibarbaric paths," heaven knows where we would end up.[11] But Harold Spender, the Englishman, was a mild fellow indeed compared with a critic whom I shall call "The Amazing American." That author, who preferred to remain nameless, wrote a provocative study ingeniously entitled "The Amazing American," quoted in G. H. Knoles' *The Jazz Age Revisited,* in which, his lack of comprehension not deterring him a bit, he spoke of jazz, among other evils. The place of America in the future spiritual scheme of things was, he opined, assured. Any nation capable of producing the "nigger minstrel, rag-time music and the tango dance," was close to the bottom. His indictment of jazz, however, is spiritless compared to his brilliantly indiscriminating castigation of American culture in general. In 1925 he wrote:

> In deathless page, in song, in art, America has contributed but little to the world's treasury. If that land were to cease to be to-morrow, its most flattering epitaph would be the sign of the dollar chiselled in the stone. . . . It is a land of flesh-pots, with no great national aim speaking through a national art. . . . The general attitude of the American mind is in deadly opposition to culture.[12]

Outbursts of this sort were not uncommon even among authors who signed their work. At about the same time, the distinguished writer Aldous Huxley had a go at us. He said much the same thing as the others, but with more style. Here, in jazz prose, is a sample from his book, *Jesting Pilate: An Intellectual Holiday:*

> Jazz it up, jazz it up. Keep moving. Step on the gas. Say it with dancing. The Charleston, the Baptists. Radios and Revivals. Uplift and Gilda Gray. The pipe organ, the nigger with the saxophone, the Giant Marimbaphone. Hymns and the movies and Irving Berlin. Petting Parties and the First Free United Episcopal Methodist Church. Jazz it up![13]

If laid end to end, all the jazz-inspired, pointed-finger, stream-of-licentiousness pieces of the twenties on the debilitating effects of wine, women, and jazz would span the distance from New Orleans to New York—by way of Memphis, Kansas City, and Chicago—and back again. Jazz, for critics in the twenties, was a social manifestation, not a musical one. For anyone interested in jazz as music, the critical climate promised little sunshine.

The slow progress in jazz analysis was probably due chiefly to the confusion of jazz with commercial popular music. It is scarcely credible nowadays that certain writers of the Jazz Age were unable to recognize that jazz is a manner of performance rather than a collection of Tin Pan Alley tunes. Nevertheless, such was the case, and this confusion resulted in establishing men like Paul Whiteman, George Gershwin, and Irving Berlin at the top of the jazz hierarchy. By now, of course, their place in jazz is clear; their place in popular music even clearer. But in the twenties the confusion—even in the minds of otherwise acute writers—enabled Whiteman to attain the unchallenged position of King of Jazz.

For the general public the songs of Berlin and Gershwin, as played by the Whiteman band, had enough characteristics in common with whatever fragments of jazz they knew to seem to be much the same thing. Those who heard genuine jazz occasionally—the music of Armstrong, say, or Fletcher Henderson—heard these men and their groups play tunes with the same titles used by Whiteman, and they naturally assumed that what they were hearing was, simply, a poor version of Whiteman's music. To their conditioned ears, Whiteman's "jazz" was smoother, richer, cleaner, and more civilized. In 1926, at the height of the confusion, Henry O. Osgood wrote *So This Is Jazz*, a book Whitney Balliett has happily described as "a triumphant and fascinating failure." In this work Osgood showed how it was possible to write a book on jazz without actually considering the black's position in jazz. Here is the premise on which Osgood's book was based:

> Nowhere have I gone into detail about negro jazz bands. There are so many good ones, it would be hard to pick out a few for special men-

tion. None of them, however, are as good as the best white bands, and very rarely are their best players as good as the best white virtuosos.[14]

Osgood was not alone in his beliefs; other, more astute writers than he made the same mistakes. In 1923, Gilbert Seldes, then a brilliant young critic with unrestrained interests and perpetually *au courant,* set about answering another critic who believed that jazz was on the way out. "Jazz, for me," Seldes wrote, in *Dial,* August 1923, "isn't a last feverish excitement, a spasm of energy before death. It is the normal development of our resources, the expected, and wonderful, arrival of America at a point of creative intensity." [15]

Now, that was an enthusiastic, patriotic, moving, even poetic statement, except for one thing: Seldes had little notion of what jazz was in 1923. He made the fashionable mistake of thinking that certain pieces of sheet music were jazz—good or bad—and others were not; that certain songwriters were better jazz composers than other songwriters; and that the notated melodic, harmonic, and rhythmic structure of a piece of music determined its jazz quality. Seldes is a good man to have on your side in any literary battle, but in 1923 he was not writing about jazz; he was writing about popular music. He was not yet aware that the jazz quality of a piece is determined by the manner in which it is played. Jazz is not a piece called "Tiger Rag," "St. Louis Blues," "Wang Wang Blues," or "Yes We Have No Bananas." The title determines nothing. Seldes, apparently unaware of this, made an extraordinary effort to show that Irving Berlin was a great jazz composer. "Mr. Berlin's masterpieces . . . in jazz," he wrote in the same article, "are 'Everybody Step' and 'Pack Up Your Sins.' " "Berlin's work," he added, "is musically interesting, and that means it has a chance to survive. I have no such confidence in 'Dardanella' or 'Chicago.' " [16]

Seldes then went on to distinguish between white jazz and black jazz, and it is here that he missed the riverboat entirely. About the future of American music, he wrote, "I say the negro is not our salvation because with all my feelings for his desirable indifference to our set of conventions about emotional decency, I am on the side of civilization." [17] Words like these from a man of Seldes' unquestionable intellect and sensitivity helped delay the unprejudiced, thoroughgoing analysis of jazz a good many years. As long as critics of Seldes' caliber and reputation continued to write about "emotional decency" and whatever it is that is not "on the side of civilization," jazz continued to seek its laurels along skid road.

In 1929, or shortly before the release of Ellington's "Wall Street Wail," P. F. Laubenstein, a serious music critic, made an attempt to present the prevailing position of jazz in an essay in the *Musical Quarterly*. Trying hard to be objective—but not always succeeding—Laubenstein was not especially sympathetic to jazz. His essay did, however, summarize certain significant aspects of jazz and recognized certain problems of the future at a time when many hoped that jazz had no future. Here, from "Jazz—Debit and Credit," is Laubenstein's summation:

> Indeed, many of its contemporaries there be who execrate the "stuff" as inebriate, doggerel, degenerate, ghoulish, vulturine, etc. *ad infinitum.* . . . Its enthusiastic devotees see in its local generation and popular cultivation the very best attestation of its truly representative American character. . . . Those holding a middle ground discover in it some elements of permanent value and certain developments which must be counted as real contributions toward the progress of music.[18]

Critical onslaughts in books, journals, and magazines were, of course, the bulk of jazz criticism. In addition, the daily press, acting as if it were woefully certain that jazz would flourish under any circumstances, offered little sympathy or understanding. Until the early sixties jazz news consisted mostly of unfavorable criticisms by names in the news and self-styled watch and ward societies. The subject of jazz, with its popular connotations, could usually be counted on to make provocative and lively news copy. What the general reader read in the newspapers about jazz was what he wanted to believe; and what the press published reflected his opinion. He knew nothing about jazz as music, but he had a firm opinion that the men and women of jazz were degenerate and unwholesome. The average reader received (and still receives) great comfort in believing that there were people to whom he could feel superior. And much feature writing was intended to reinforce the reader's opinions. With few exceptions, it is not an easy task to find a news item of the twenties on jazz that does not speak of jazz with tongue in cheek, as a kind of drollery always good for a chuckle, if not a laugh. Overseas items, from France particularly, were always welcome and in the twenties were usually offered with heavy-handed merriment. The following headlines from the *New York Times* reflect the general public's attitude toward jazz in the Jazz Age:

> Fails to Stop Jazz, Is Arrested Later [July 7, 1922]
>
> French Police Stop Jazz Band Burial; Dead Man Wanted It in Procession, but the Mourners Were Foxtrotting [October 18, 1923]
>
> France Orders Our Jazz Players Expelled [May 31, 1924]
>
> Isadora Duncan Plans Greek Temple for Nice; She Is Reported to Have Bought the Theatre Promenade des Anglais to Fight Jazz [May 1, 1925]
>
> Ford Wars on Jazz; Gives Party for Old Time Dances, Seeking to Revive Their Popularity [July 12, 1925]
>
> American Dancer Jazzing the "Marseillaise" Angers Friendly Audience in Paris Music Hall [January 31, 1926]
>
> Church Jazz Wedding Utilizes Saxophone [November 14 1926]

Damrosch Assails Jazz [April 17, 1928]
French Find Our Jazz Too Soul-Disturbing [February 3, 1929]

From these headlines, it would seem that nobody in the twenties dared say a kind word for jazz. By the thirties, however, the jazz initiate could sense that some changes would be made. The Roosevelt administration's early efforts to lift the nation out of the Big Depression looked as if they would work, and everything, jazz included, suddenly seemed brighter and more useful. Many intellectuals sought, and found, rewards in studying America's popular culture, and folk songs and jazz came in for a good share of the spotlight.

In 1933, the repeal of Prohibition and the subsequent opening of many nightclubs and dance halls led to the employment of more jazz musicians and to a wider audience for jazz. It is possible also that the general unrest caused by events in Europe helped create a small musical nationalism, much of which may well have been fostered by the reports in the daily press of various actions and pronouncements against jazz in European countries. On March 15, 1933, the National Socialist head of the Berlin Rundfunk forbade the broadcasting of "Negro jazz," and on January 7, 1934, a headline in the *New York Times* read: "Ban against Jazz Sought in Ireland." (A week before, an Irish anti-jazz group had paraded in Mohall, Ireland, with banners and posters bearing the slogan "Down with Jazz and Paganism." The unruly anti-jazzists had been aroused by the actions of their finance minister, Seán MacEntee, who had stood by while jazz bands broadcast their wares over the state broadcasting system.) On October 12, 1935, Eugen Hadamowski, director of the German broadcasting system, issued an order banning broadcasts of jazz in order, as he put it, "to do away with the last remnants of the culture-Bolshevistic Jew." [19]

16

By the time these items appeared in the press, the swing era was underway; swing—or jazz—was beginning to enjoy unprecedented popularity in the United States, and Hadamowski was no longer talking about the music of a handful of people, but the music of millions.

Once swing as a popular movement surged forward and Americans learned that other nations saw jazz as a threat to their way of life, many began to see in jazz a symbol of their own freedom, and foreign pronouncements condemning jazz became something to ridicule and defy. There were no great public refutations or demonstrations, of course (unless one so considers the crowds flocking to the New York Paramount Theater, Randall's Island, and Carnegie Hall swing concerts), and the thought that jazz was a symbol of anything was for the most part left unsaid. Altogether, though, there was increasing public support for jazz as something American. And this was all to the good. Pronouncements like those issued by the Nazis may not have sent anyone into a fit of righteous rage, but perhaps such items made it possible for people—some of them public figures—to feel less queasy about defending jazz, in whatever aspect.

In the late thirties, swing burst forth and reached all parts of the nation. Radio and admen—agencies responsible for much of swing's growth—were becoming powerful and influential; a shrewd promotion of swing, big white bands in particular (with Benny Goodman's name leading the rest), resulted in making swing a suitable, if controversial, topic for conversation however genteel. Since respected figures occasionally spoke up for swing, tongue-in-cheek press notices diminished (to increase again after World War II, with Dizzy Gillespie and his early high jinks) and became serious, objective, and sometimes even sympathetic reports. And on May 5, 1937, the *New York Times* reported that "Dr. Carleton Sprague Smith, head of the Music Division of the N.Y. Public Library, championed 'swing' music tonight, terming it an 'appropriate' musical expression which must receive serious consideration."

During this same period, however, the opposite point of view continued to be expressed with varying degrees of violence. The president of the Dancing Teachers Business Association, for example, in a talk to his associates reported by the *New York Times* on July 7, 1938, said that swing music was a "degenerated form of jazz," and its devotees were "unfortunate victims of economic instability." He went on to predict hopefully that "the popularity of swing will fade with the return of economic stability." Furthermore, if people wished to dance, there were plenty of suitable and proper tangos, rumbas, and waltzes. On May 22, 1938, an exhibition of "degenerate music" opened in Düsseldorf. Nazi Germany wished to prevent the spread of jazz and atonal music—"the microbes of musical decomposition"—and to wipe out all music that showed "Marxist, Bolshevistic, Jewish, or any other un-German tendencies." [20] And, finally, Dr. Harry D. Gideonse, then head of the economics and social science department of Barnard College, stated in the *New York Times* of November 2, 1938, "Swing is musical Hitlerism."

Altogether, it is not difficult to understand why so little serious work on jazz was accomplished in the twenties and thirties. Add the confusions, misunderstandings, disagreements, and misconceptions of those sincerely interested in jazz to the rantings and bitterness of those opposed to jazz, and you have the main reason why jazz analysis was delayed until we were well into the swing era. By the middle forties, serious attempts to analyze jazz as music became more frequent. Most critics began to recognize the need for emphasizing proper jazz analysis and evaluation and de-emphasizing the social import of jazz; attempts to tie jazz in with sociology became less and less rewarding, until jazz as a social issue was raised in the sixties and seventies. Freed of its social shackles, jazz in the forties finally became a fit subject for serious study, and students of jazz were now able to ask, "What is jazz?"

2

toward a definition of jazz

DESPITE SEMANTIC DIFFICULTIES AND THE HOSTILE SOCIAL ATMOSPHERE, there were many serious, if unfruitful, attempts at formulating a definition of jazz, especially after World War II. Critics, historians, theorists, composers, and performers took a crack at it. Some began by saying that jazz was something indefinable and then went on to attempt a definition; others offered short, all-encompassing definitions of jazz that upon examinaton turned out to be just as valid for much of the classical music of the eighteenth and nineteenth centuries. Still others have maintained that the truth about jazz is to be found in defining what jazz does, rather than by defining what it is. Finally, there have been critical examinations of jazz by those who believe jazz to be an important aspect of twentieth-century music, deserving its own definition in musical terms.

The discussion that follows does not include all the definitions of jazz or swing, or even the greater part of them, but those given are representative of the various kinds of definitions that have been given in the past. In the process of evolving a satisfactory definition of jazz, writers seem to have agreed only that jazz is music; but there are among them writers who, while they believe that jazz is music, see it not as one aspect of all music, but rather as a separate and distinct art—despite its musical content. Nevertheless, as will appear, most writers have been able to find certain broad areas of agreement.

(Before we go on to examine the various definitions of jazz, it is necessary to recognize the important influence of the swing era on all subsequent jazz criticism and explication. From the beginning of the swing era, the question "What is swing?" was asked over and over by a public determined to keep asking the question regardless of the number or quality of the answers it got. When the questions and answers finally subsided, it seemed that the question "What is swing?"

could not be answered properly without first defining jazz. It was soon plain to almost everyone concerned that "swing" appeared to be another word for "jazz," and therefore many critics used the terms "swing" and "jazz" practically interchangeably. Except where it is stated otherwise, this holds true for all subsequent quotations.)

When Sidney Finkelstein wrote, "Jazz is a flow of motion in music guided by the most conscious skill, taste, artistry and intelligence," [1] he was stating, however felicitously, that jazz is created the same way as other music. His statement is as true of Tchaikovsky's *Nutcracker Suite* as it is of Ellington's "Mood Indigo," leading one to ask: Doesn't jazz have any *special* qualities? André Hodeir, one of the most astute of jazz analysts, pointed out that jazz is "perhaps essentially the Negro interpretation of elements borrowed from other music." [2] It is difficult to argue with "perhaps " and "essentially." Nevertheless, it seems necessary to ask whether jazz may suffer certain nonblack "interpretations."

Definition by metaphor is a delight to read, and frequently illuminates a dark corner. Classical composer Charles Ives, writing about ragtime in 1920, said it "is something like wearing a derby hat on the back of the head, a shuffling lilt of a happy soul just out of a Baptist Church in old Alabama." (In answer to those who believed that jazz was America's ruination, he went on to say: "Ragtime has its possibilities. But it does not 'represent the American nation' any more than some fine old senators represent it.") During World War I, the French composer Erik Satie said, "What I love about jazz is that it's 'blue' and you don't care." [3] Since then, Satie's and Ives' definitions have been, in effect, repeated countless times. Definitions by metaphor are, of course, esthetic ones. They are more usually made by the relatively inarticulate, but sometimes more poetic, jazz performer than by the more (one would think) articulate classical composer. Esthetic definitions of jazz by jazzmen may be found in most books on jazz, and they are all trying to say what jazz drummer Chick Webb said: "It's like lovin' a gal, and havin' a fight, and then seein' her again." [4] Jazzmen and classical composers alike will no doubt continue to make esthetic definitions. The elusiveness of jazz invites emotionally conceived definitions, and composers—even those accustomed to handling the musical materials of jazz—may surely be permitted a colorful phrase or two. André Hodeir, in *Jazz: Its Evolution and Essence*, explains why definitions by metaphor will continue to be with us: "No common definition of this music has been reached. It resists dictionary definition, and its musicians splutter nervously and take refuge in the colorful ambiguities of its argot." [5]

George Gershwin, in a definition neither colorful nor profound, said, "Jazz is music; it uses the same notes Bach used." [6] Although few serious jazz critics credit Gershwin with any contribution to jazz, to the general public—the European public particularly—he is *the* jazz composer. In any case, I do not believe it would be improper to say that jazz did more for Gershwin than Gershwin did for jazz. Although the fashion of coupling Bach's name with jazz has long since become a commonplace for certain jazz intellectuals, Gershwin's statement has no intellectual overtones. He would have been just as happy to say that jazz used the same notes Josquin des Près (1450–1521) used. His statement was intended to show only that jazz can be notated. In 1933, when Gershwin made his statement, the question of "improvised" jazz versus "notated" jazz was being explored, and the answer to this question was important to Gershwin's reputation as a composer of jazz. A few years later, with the coming of the swing era, the gist of Gershwin's statement was to have many defenders.

UNDERSTANDING JAZZ

In the late thirties, defining jazz became more difficult for some and easier for others. Those who had never attempted to define jazz now found it easy and convenient to say, "Jazz is swing." This was also true of many who had previously had difficulty defining jazz. For one group, swing became a branch or at least an offshoot of jazz; for another, swing had roots of its own. The fact is, neither the word "swing" itself, nor the controversy it initiated, was new. The swing public (and happily the general public) carefully and solemnly listened to jazz sinners and evangelists alike. Paul Whiteman said, "Swing is, after all, nothing more than good old jazz," and Cootie Williams said, "There is no difference between jazz and swing."

For Fletcher Henderson (whose swing arrangements had much to do with launching the swing era) the difference was technical. His view was that swing involved premeditation while jazz was spontaneous, although both drew from the same source.[7] Wilder Hobson, in his early study, *American Jazz Music*, presented another aspect of the problem: " 'Swing' has often been spoken of as if it were an absolute quality—either a band swings or it does not, etc. But 'swing' will be present to some degree wherever a momentum is built up in suspended rhythms. In other words, it is not confined to jazz. It may, for instance, be in ragtime, Schumann's syncopations, Astaire's tappings." [8]

Another point of view implied that swing was not only different from jazz, but was somehow better. In the *New Republic* of January 29, 1936, Frank Norris said, "Swing is to jazz what the poetic quality is to verse"; another journalist, Gama Gilbert, in a piece entitled "Swing: What Is It?" in the *New York Times* of September 5, 1937, said, "Unlike ordinary jazz, it [swing] is a creative process necessarily engendered in a state of highest emotional excitement." And Virgil Thomson, writing in *Modern Music* in 1936, interposed the power of his reputation into the general debate by presenting "swing-music" with a definition all its own. "Swing-music," he wrote, "is a form of two-step in which the rhythm is expressed quantitatively by instruments of no fixed intonation, the melodic, harmonic, and purely percussive elements being freed thereby to improvise in free polyphonic style." [9]

The foregoing remarks, by critics with amateur jazz standing, received little attention from the forces who considered themselves the true jazz polemicists. These embattled few managed to create an air of hostility that has not yet been dissipated. On one side stood the traditionalists: the defenders of true jazz (also variously known as real jazz, hot jazz, old-time jazz. genuine jazz, and of course traditional jazz). Opposing the traditionalists were the modernists or, as they have been called, the progressives. In any event, the engagement that followed only intensified the confusion and disagreement and led bewilderingly to an impasse not yet unblocked. The crux of this disagreement—perhaps the most profound of all disagreements among the critics of jazz—was made clear by Barry Ulanov. In *A History of Jazz in America*, he said:

> Confusion surrounded the use of the two terms "swing" and "jazz" as soon as swing became popularly accepted. There was one school of thought, of which critic Robert Goffin was the most rabid exponent, that believed "swing" denoted the commercialization and prostitution of real jazz, that it had partly supplanted jazz, and that it consisted only of written arrangements played by big bands, whereas jazz consisted only of improvised music played by small bands. . . .[10]

Although they were hard pressed to define jazz, the Goffinites stood for "pure" jazz. They might have disagreed among themselves on a definition of jazz, but it was nevertheless obvious to them that swing

27

was not true jazz. Such a controversy could not be resolved satisfactorily for all concerned as long as the arguments of both sides continued to be delivered with inflammatory words. For the "mechanized orchestration" and "prefabricated phrases" of swing, the Goffinites offered "collective improvisation," "a general trance," and "spontaneous fancy." They refused to accept the "artificial dynamism" of swing as a substitute for the "spirit of pure jazz." All in all, they saw swing as an enfeebling influence, an intellectually contrived music that debased the emotionally conceived true jazz; they therefore stood opposed to swing, or anything else inclined to diminish the pure, real, hot, traditional jazz. They were not opposed to swing as such, but the idea that swing could pass itself off as jazz was quite another thing. Goffin, himself, stated their final position in *Jazz, from the Congo to the Metropolitan:* "Jazz has passed from the state of pure improvisation into that of swing, which might be called an intellectual construction assisted by solos. Some prefer one format, some the other; those who are sufficiently objective can like both kinds, taking into full consideration the respective differences of evolution and atmosphere." [11]

In recent years, the great majority of writers have agreed that swing was jazz. My own position (stated more fully at the end of this chapter) is that jazz is a generic term, swing a specific term with considerable overtones; in short, one meaning of swing is that it is a style of jazz whose characteristics were formed mainly between 1935 and 1945. This leads us back to the persistent question: What is jazz?

Until the mid-fifties, those who attempted jazz definitions were too often subjectively involved in controversy and were more concerned with proving the validity of their position than with fashioning a definition of jazz suitable for all. Prescience is not often a trait of the traditionalists' makeup, and they saw little need to look for the future directions of jazz. In any case, of those who attempted definitions early in jazz history (and in seeking jazz definitions the thirties and early forties may be considered early history), too many afterward felt compelled to view the jazz scene in the light of their own definitions. By starting with meager historic and stylistic data, they inadvertently maneuvered themselves into a position of trying to justify their sincere but inadequate definitions; by cutting corners sharply, they were able to measure the contemporary jazz scene to their satisfaction—but with a yardstick short of standard. The fact is that in order to formulate proper standards in jazz—or, for that matter, in any art—one must have the benefit of historical and stylistic perspective; that is, one must be able to see the parts in relation to each other.

Although relatively little time has passed since those early attempts at defining jazz, the wide dissemination and proliferation of jazz since the thirties make those early efforts seem quite remote in time. Therefore, definitions of jazz by critics who are flexible enough to keep up with the changing scene and to accept the jazz of *all* periods as worthy of study, and who believe jazz has a future as well as a past, seem to have greater validity (and certainly wider application) than the limited definitions of the jazz pioneers. For an inclusive definition of jazz, therefore, we must look to the work of those writers who have had the advantage of historical hindsight as well as literary and musical perception.

For this reason, I have selected various definitions and qualifying remarks put forward by Paul Eduard Miller, Barry Ulanov, Marshall Stearns, and André Hodeir. It has also seemed necessary to include Hodeir's statement on the conditions for the production of swing, because he considers swing to be an indispensable element in all jazz. (We will return to this question in the concluding paragraphs of this chapter.) There were, of course, other definitions and remarks worthy of inclusion in this group; I believe, however, that the subsequent analyses and resulting concordances will encompass the sense—if not the words—of those omitted. Here, then, are the opening arguments.

In Paul Eduard Miller's "An Analysis of the Art of Jazz," in *Esquire's 1946 Jazz Book*, he said that "jazz must be approached as music, and not as a *type* of music distinct from all others. . . ."

> [He said], . . . there exists a qualitative difference, technically, between jazz and classic. Jazz differs from classic in the following characteristics: (1) *Rhythm*. A rigid 4/4 beat (occasionally 2/4 or 8/8) combined with polyrhythms, or cross-rhythms more commonly known as syncopation, and the use of free rubato. (2) *Harmony*. The blues triad (dominant, sub-dominant, tonic), which has been intermixed with harmonies stemming from European traditions, including polyphony and polytonality. (3) *Figurations*. Refers chiefly to suspensions, afterbeats, passing tones and melodic intervals. Since the use of figurations results in a mixture of concords and discords, this accounts for the disregard of the so-called pure tone and the subsequent utilization of what has come to be known as jazz intonation.[12]

From Barry Ulanov's *A History of Jazz in America:*

> [Jazz] is a new music of a certain distinct rhythmic and melodic character, one that constantly involves improvisation . . . on the spot. In the course of creating jazz, a melody or its underlying chords may be altered. The rhythmic valuations of notes may be lengthened or shortened according to a regular scheme, syncopated or not, or there may be no consistent pattern of rhythmic variations so long as a steady beat remains implicit or explicit. The beat is usually four quarter-notes to the bar, serving as a solid rhythmic base for the improvisation of soloists or groups playing eight or twelve measures, or some multiple or dividend thereof.[13]

From Marshall Stearns' *The Story of Jazz:*

Like any other dynamic art the special qualities of jazz cannot be described in a few words. The history of jazz may be told, its technical characteristics may be grasped, and the response it evokes in various individuals may be analyzed. But a definition of jazz in the most complete sense—how and why it communicates satisfying human emotions —can never be fully formulated. . . . we may define jazz tentatively as a *semi-improvisational American music distinguished by an immediacy of communication, an expressiveness characteristic of the free use of the human voice, and a complex flowing rhythm; it is the result of a three hundred years' blending in the United States of the European and West African musical traditions; and its predominant components are European harmony, Euro-African melody, and African rhythm.*[14]

From André Hodeir's *Jazz: Its Evolution and Essence:*

There would seem to be five optimal conditions for the production of swing. (I couldn't deny the theoretical possibility of swing's resulting from others, though I have never seen this happen.) They are:

1. the right infrastructure;
2. the right superstructure;
3. getting the notes and accents in the right places;
4. relaxation;
5. vital drive.

The first three are technical in nature and can be understood rationally; the last two, which are psychophysical, must be grasped intuitively. Only the second (and, to a lesser degree, the first) has to do with what is properly referred to as musical conception. . . .[15]

We may start by considering the moot points. Miller sees jazz as music, as a musical style containing primarily the same definable elements that are found in art music of the past. Ulanov's "new music" falls into a somewhat narrower category because it is not clear whether he means "new music" to serve as a synonym for "modern music" or perhaps "contemporary music," or whether "new music" is simply being used loosely to distinguish it from "old music." In any case, he wrote his book in 1952, and perhaps by "new" he meant simply that the music was not classical.

Stearns saw jazz as a separate and distinct art. It seems to me that Stearns' definition implies that he was more concerned with having jazz *judged* by separate and distinct standards than he was in building a case for jazz as a separate and distinct art. If the implication exists only in my mind, the question must be raised: What is jazz to be separate and distinct *from*? Stearns' statement that the how and why of jazz communicaion can never be fully formulated was an important one, as was his concern with "expressiveness"; but in these, his position was no different from Miller's when Miller said that technical definitions "do not tell us everything"; or from Hodeir's when he said that the last two of his conditions for swing—"relaxation" and "vital drive"—were psychophysical and "must be grasped intuitively."

The question of improvisation will be discussed more fully in the chapter on that subject. For the present, it is sufficient to say that Miller did not believe improvisation to be "an essential and distinctive characteristic of jazz." [16] He believed that improvisation, properly executed, may affect the relative excellence of a jazz work, but not its essential jazz nature. Stearns' term, "semi-improvisation," was apparently an effort to find a term to settle the difference between "free" improvisation and big-band jazz, and perhaps concede something to "head arrangements" (pre-arranged verbal agreements among jazz musicians, usually in small and medium-sized groups, as to who will do what at which point; the arrangement is agreed upon only moments before the actual performance). On the place of improvisation in jazz, Stearns disagreed with Miller. To Stearns, but not to Miller, improvisation was a basic characteristic of jazz and the essence of creativity in jazz; it was the primary basis for judging excellence because, as Stearns put it, "it is utterly impossible to conceal the *quality* of your improvisation in jazz, where you are judged on the spot by your peers." [17]

Hodeir is inclined to agree with Stearns; he believes free improvisation to be synonymous with creative performance. There is, however, conscious or subconscious thought controlling the improvisation, and the quality of improvisation depends on the performer's depth of thought. When a performer's fingers simply " 'recite' a lesson they have learned . . . there is no reason to talk about creation." [18] It is not unlikely that Miller, Stearns, and Hodeir would all have accepted Ulanov's "improvisation of a minor sort" and "of a major sort" without necessarily accepting his qualifying remarks. In any case, it is reasonably certain that all four would have agreed that first-rate jazz has usually contained an abundance of first-rate improvisation—major or minor, creative or derivative.

The question of rhythm is an unruly one. Miller apparently regarded as the *sine qua non* the maintenance of a rigid duple meter, simple (1–2) or compound (1–2–3–4) against which were heard syncopation and "free" rubato. The classical term "rubato" means the player has the freedom to go a little faster here, a little slower there— a freedom to vary the speed, even from one measure to another. (Unless by "free" rubato Miller meant the "full" rubato of classical composers—a rubato degenerating into a tempo without any metrical pulse at all, and something practically unknown in jazz before the fifties, except in the last two or three measures of a piece—then "free" appears to be redundant.) Miller's "rigid beat" became Ulanov's "steady beat"; and for Ulanov the beat could have been implicit (that is, "felt" instead of being heard), an important distinction for understanding jazz of a much later time, certain third-stream pieces, for example. Ulanov's conception of duple meter, however ("four quarter-notes to the bar"), was somewhat narrower than Miller's. Stearns, by requiring a "complex flowing rhythm," not only took in Miller's and Ulanov's requirements, but indicated, it seems to me, a tolerance of future rhythmic possibilities in jazz; his "African rhythm" as a predominant jazz component seems, however, to have extolled rhythmic characteristics belonging not to jazz in general but to several specific styles of jazz.

Hodeir's "right infrastructure" is, in brief, the same simple and compound duple meter required by Miller and Ulanov, but in a "right" tempo. "Tempos at which swing is possible," Hodeir claims, "range from about 54 quarter notes a minute to about 360." [19] He believes that a medium tempo—168 quarter notes a minute—is properly called the "swing tempo," and that a certain balanced relationship is necessary between theme and tempo. His "right superstructure" is essentially the favorable employment of the rhythmic disagreement or dislocation of the melodic rhythm with the metrical accents—again, simply a type of syncopation. Hodeir's third requirement—"getting the notes and accents in the right places"—deals first with the question of the proper placement of syncopated notes, and then with the necessity, in ensemble playing, for the subordination of the individual to the group. On this latter point, there seems little need for discussion; on the question of where to place syncopated notes, however, I believe Hodeir has fallen into error as a result of failing to distinguish between the general characteristics of jazz and specific characteristics of certain styles.

In music, theory follows practice. It is not the analyst's job to point

out, as Hodeir does, what he considers to be faulty syncopations in
the work of Johnny Dodds and Kid Ory. "One of the oldtimers' most
common weaknesses," he writes, "results from their playing syncopated notes prematurely, in moderate tempos, on the second third of
the beat. This 'corny' syncopation is a carry-over from the polka-style.
Rhythmically, the effect is deplorable. . . ." [20] Now, whether the
effect is deplorable or not is a matter of taste, not of analysis, and I
am not taking issue with Hodeir's taste. I simply contend that the
proper analysis needs first to be centered on style. On certain levels
of analysis, music is seldom judged as good or bad, right or wrong;
either a piece of music is stylistically consistent or it is not. The
musical style of a period is created by the composers and performers
of the period, and when an analyst says that something is deplorable
he, in effect, chastens the creators of the music for not doing in their
time what the analyst believes they should have done. (A related
example of this practice is strikingly evident in the case of music historian Willi Apel who, knowing that baroque composers used the
terms "chaconne" and "passacaglia" as titles of compositions interchangeably and indiscriminately, nevertheless classified certain cha-
connes as passacaglias and vice versa, implying that baroque composers would have done the same if they had known better.)

On the question of harmony in jazz, Miller, Ulanov, Stearns, and
Hodeir all agree that its basis is in European harmony. Miller spoke
of the "blues triad" but went on to show that the primary triads grew
into chords of larger proportions and have themselves merged with
a greater harmonic complex. Ulanov seemed to imply, by omission,
that he believed the harmonic language of jazz in general was not
substantially different from that of music in general. Hodeir tells us
what the harmonic language of jazz was in 1957, when he wrote his
book. "To sum up," he wrote, "jazz musicians have no special reason

35

for taking pride in an harmonic language that, besides being easily acquired, does not really belong to them but rather to a 'light harmony' that North America borrowed from decadent Debussyism." (Debussy was especially fond of triads with an added tone, augmented chords, and chords moving in parallel motion.) [21]

Turning to the question of melody, I must assume that Miller's "figurations" referred, generally, to melodic tones and, specifically, to their harmonic or nonharmonic functions. (Certain of Miller's terms are endowed with a fuzzy quality that makes his intention difficult to determine. Figuration, for example, usually has a straightforward meaning: it refers to the employment and repetition of stereotyped figures; and in this sense one may reasonably speak of certain kinds of florid riffs, say, as being figural. Miller's grouping together of the nonharmonic tones, the suspension and passing tone, in the same breath, so to speak, with "afterbeat"—a term that is common to rhythm, not melody—is particularly confusing. It is possible that he is referring to an unresolved nonharmonic tone that falls on an unaccented beat, or part of a beat. In any event, it is perplexing language to deal with.) When Miller spoke of the difference between jazz and classical music, he seemed to include as "classical music" all art music of the past; if this is the sense in which he uses it, then his reference to "figurations" does not show any disparity between the "figurations" of jazz and those of classical music.

Ulanov spoke of "a certain distinct rhythmic and melodic character," which seemed inclusive enough. Stearns' "Euro-African melody," however, was more inclusive. There is no question that the unaccompanied melodies in which jazz has its roots had *their* roots in African melody; the move away from unaccompanied melody resulted (in art music as well as in jazz) in the harmonically conceived melody, and this type of melody is European. In a harmonically conceived melody the composer *starts* with certain harmonies, that is, certain chords, then writes a melody that will *fit* the chords. The original chords then become the harmonic accompaniment.

Improvisation, rhythm, harmony, melody—these are the ingredients of jazz that serious jazz writers have treated at great length. These elements of jazz have been considered the basic ones. But in recent years, on a broader base of criticism, jazz has been increasingly referred to certain other aspects of art music—intonation, form, style, tension and release, for example—and it is with these that we are presently concerned. Miller, Ulanov, Stearns, and Hodeir all have dealt with one or more of these aspects of jazz (with certain ones more thoroughly than others, of course), and it seems proper to explore these views, however briefly, before going on to the final summation.

Ulanov evidently felt the need to include a word on form in his definition. His "eight or twelve measures, or some multiple or dividend thereof" has certainly been a structural unit in jazz forms—the twelve measures for blues, and the eight measures for most other tunes. Stearns believed that jazz form has been restricted by the requirements of improvisation. "As long as improvisation is a vital element in jazz," he wrote, "the blues will probably be the prime form for its expression." [22] When Hodeir says, "The only structure in jazz is the theme and variations, which is the simplest of all and the one best adapted to improvisation," [23] one hopes that he is talking not about the theme and variations as a form (despite the strong implication) but about the technique of variation. The theme and variations, as well as the passacaglia, chaconne, and others, are individual structures in a category of classical music structures known as variation form. The technique of variation is essentially the basis for much of the art music composed in the past five centuries—jazz included. If

Hodeir insists that the theme and variations (one specific architectural idea) is the *only* structure in jazz, this would at once disallow the contrapuntal forms that have engaged the attention of many first-rate jazzmen, the Modern Jazz Quartet, for example. At any rate, both Sterns and Hodeir based their statements on the significance of improvisation, and we have come full circle again—improvisation being the key word. We return to improvisation in Chapter 3; for the present, however, we must go on.

Miller's statement, "Since the use of figurations results in a mixture of concords and discords, this accounts for the disregard of the so-called pure tone and the subsequent utilization of what has come to be known as jazz intonation," deserves further exploration. First, the use of figurations (suspensions, "afterbeats," and passing tones) does *not* result in a mixture of concords and discords. The use of nonharmonic tones results only in discord—to use Miller's term. To put it technically, the use of nonharmonic tones results in harmonic dissonance. The terms "concord" and "discord" have more currency with estheticians than with analysts; concord and discord have connotations of pleasantness and unpleasantness, whereas consonance and dissonance mean resolved and unresolved, and imply relief from tension, and tension. Furthermore, if Miller's figurations *did* result in a mixture, there is no reason to believe that this would account for the "disregard of the so-called pure tone." Approached from any angle, the logic is faulty.

Then again, it is not clear whether by "pure tone" Miller was referring to pitch or to tone quality. On the outside chance that he was speaking of tone quality, it would seem that the question is not one of disregard of pure tone, but rather one of special regard for a distinctive tone. No jazz performer, to my knowledge, has been penalized for trying to play with a "pure tone"—provided he was playing good jazz. The saxophone tone of Coleman Hawkins has been described as rich, and Benny Goodman's clarinet tone as legitimate. Surely the position of these two jazz performers (doubtless there were others) has not suffered because of their enduring success in producing rich, romantic, legitimate tones. Their position is due to the jazz that flowed out of their horns, and not from any arbitrary regard or disregard for tone. The position in jazz of men like Pee Wee Russell, Dizzy Gillespie, John Coltrane, Miles Davis, Stan Getz, Paul Desmond, and others will ultimately depend not upon the degree of their regard or disregard for pure tone, but upon the jazz they will have created. The search for distinctive tone and "new" sounds—while necessary to the growth and development of jazz—is an inadequate substitute for rhythmic, melodic, and harmonic creativity. The unusual electronic musical sounds and textures that became available in the sixties and seventies were fertile ground and worth exploring, but they are not uniquely the province of jazz. No performer's ultimate position in jazz is delimited by the quality of his tone.

Much more important to the future of jazz is the matter of tension and release. On this, Hodeir said that "jazz consists essentially of *an inseparable but extremely variable mixture of relaxation and tension.*" [24] This is an aspect of jazz that needs to be studied to gain insight not only into the creation of jazz but also into the subjective process of evaluating it. For Hodeir, relaxation is as indispensable to swing as swing is to jazz. However, one feels the need for an expansion of the discussion of tension and release in jazz; rhythmic tension and release must be studied in conjunction with melodic, harmonic, coloristic, textural, structural, and directional tension and release—in short, everything about a piece of music that is capable of creating within the listener feelings of tension and release from tension.

In this chapter, along with what I hope has been a partial disentangling of terminology, I have attempted to clarify what I believe needed clarifying. It would not be strange if, for some, I have beclouded what at first sight seemed clear enough. The language of jazz, like jazz itself, grows rapidly. Whitney Balliett said, "Because of its nature and the speed with which the music has developed, writing about jazz is, of course, somewhat like trying to photograph a jet plane with a Brownie." To photograph jazz on the run requires, first, a technical and linguistic ability to make it sit still. The definition that follows will be, I hope, a first step toward keeping it from darting away too often. The statement is intended to be neither complete nor even composite. It is simply intended to sum up what Miller, Ulanov, Stearns, and Hodeir have said, to express certain of my own conclusions, and to serve as a point of departure for Chapter 3.

Here, then, is the working definition: Jazz is the comprehensive name for a variety of specific musical styles generally characterized by attempts at creative improvisation on a given theme (melodic or harmonic), over a foundation of complex, steadily flowing rhythm (melodic or percussive) and European harmonies; although the various styles of jazz may on occasion overlap, a style is distinguished from other styles by a preponderance of those specific qualities peculiar to each style.

As a corollary to the process of attempting to define jazz, it is necessary to discuss, however briefly, the intangible quality sometimes called swing. The most flexible word in the jazz lexicon is "swing." It may be used as a verb (swing high, swing low); as a common noun (it don't mean a thing if you ain't got that swing); as a proper noun (Goodman's band played Swing); and as an adjective (what is the swing experience?). Jazz people have been much taken with trying to define this elusive quality, but their attempts have generally been unsuccesful or, at least, not very convincing. The principal reason for this, I believe, is that they saw swing as a *rhythmic* quality and assumed that by a painstaking rhythmic analysis of a number of pieces and a subsequent ordering of characteristics, the problem would somehow solve itself. We know now that the problem did not solve itself. It has become apparent that no amount of technical rhythmic analysis, even by established authorities, can bring us any closer to *defining* what swing is, to answering the simple question of what makes a piece swing for one person and not for another. Swing, in my view, is not just a rhythmic problem, but also involves experience. We *experience* swing, and for the purpose of clarity, and its meaning in our present discussion, we will think of swing as the swing experience.

"Meaning," Albert Upton wrote in his *Design for Thinking*, "is always a matter of relation. Nothing ever means itself alone; it can only be meaningful to somebody about something else. Meaning, then, is simply a function of the cortex in action; it is what goes on in the brain when it makes a thing or connection between two or more things." In order to have a relation, you must have, Upton added, "a thing, a relation, and another thing. The meaning of one of them is determined by your momentary awareness of the other two." [25] Swing is an essential part of jazz, and can be defined only in relation to whatever else it is that brings about the jazz experience. If we do not understand the function of swing, and how it works on us, we cannot then be certain of the function of any other part of jazz.

Richard A. Waterman stated the case clearly, as long ago as 1962, when he wrote, in the *Journal of Ethnomusicology,* "Let us hope that sometime soon, someone . . . will turn his attention to an analysis of the mechanisms by which jazz, supported perhaps by cultural understandings and psychological sets, establishes itself as a musical medium communicating, through its quality of *swinging* [my italics], a predominant effect, that of euphoria. Until this is done, jazz will resist definition." [26]

Although jazz writers, critics, historians, and sociologists have offered a seemingly endless number of definitions of jazz throughout its history, why, we may ask, has no one ever offered a single definition of jazz that was satisfactory to all? Why has no single definition clarified what jazz has that gives its listeners the "jazz" feeling? Perhaps one reason is that jazz has not just one meaning but many; jazz can mean distinctly different things to different people; further, jazz can mean different things to the same people at different times. The question leads to greater complications when we become aware that some may perceive jazz simply as music, with its appropriate harmonies, melodies, and rhythms (a group I believe to be in the smallest minority). A much larger group may associate jazz with the trappings and ambience of a certain environment—nightclubs, say, or dance halls; or a specific street or neighborhood in a particular city; or smoky rooms, the clink of glasses, after-hours laughter, sex, whatever is illicit, whatever seems forbidden. And still others may associate jazz with freedom, or protest, or belonging to this or that in- or out-group, or with simply thumbing one's nose at the Establishment.

I would suggest that the way each of us responds to jazz (and therefore what jazz means to us) depends upon a combination or intermingling of two things: first, the circumstances "outside" ourselves—that is, the social setting, the place, and the kind of jazz we're listening to at a particular time in our lives. Second, what is happening "inside" ourselves—our state of mind at the moment, our frame of reference, our drives, goals, purposes, wishes, appetites, and what there is on the "outside" that denies or grants them to us. If we wish to understand our personal relation to jazz (and how it may relate to us) we should ask ourselves: Are we taken with jazz as music, or with the *idea* of jazz, or both? Do we prefer new things to old things, action to contemplation, predictability to surprise? Clearly, no one can answer these questions for someone else; and there may even be difficulty in attempting to answer these questions for ourselves. Nevertheless, if we are to raise the question of why this or that jazz piece "swings" for one person and doesn't swing for another, the answer must be sought in the various "inside" and "outside" factors that influence our lives.

3

understanding
improvisation

(Overleaf) *Ornette Coleman*

LUDWIG WITTGENSTEIN (1889–1951) WAS A PHILOSOPHER who devoted much of his life to a scrupulous study of language as we actually use it. He believed that much philosophical confusion could be avoided by not attempting to make pat definitions for even the most seemingly simple things. Morton White, in his book *The Age of Analysis*, tells us that Wittgenstein contended "that to understand a word is to be able to use it in accord with customary social practice," and that Wittgenstein's most famous slogan was, "The meaning is the use." Wittgenstein, himself, put it this way:

> Consider for example the proceedings that we call "games." I mean board-games, card-games, ball-games, Olympic games, and so on. What is common to them all?—Don't say: "There *must* be something common, or they would not be called 'games' "—but *look and see* whether there is anything common to all.—For if you look at them you will not see something that is common to *all* but similarities, relationships, and a whole series of them at that.[1]

Difficulties in understanding improvisation arise from the fact that there are different kinds of improvisation; it is, therefore, not enough to offer a pat description of improvisation. What we are seeking is rather an understanding of improvisation as it has been practiced in performance. A dictionary definition—"to compose on the spur of the moment"—tells us only part of the story; "composing and performing simultaneously" tells us still another part of the story. We have also heard frequent references to "free" improvisation and to "collective" improvisation. In addition, every jazzman knows what he means by improvisation, and every writer knows what *he* means, and the result is, of course, an involved combination of meanings leading to unnecessary disagreements and puzzlements.

Jerry Coker, in his excellent study, *Improvising Jazz,* tells us, "Five factors are chiefly responsible for the outcome of the jazz player's improvisation: intuition, intellect, emotion, sense of pitch, and habit. His intuition is responsible for the bulk of his originality; his emotion determines the mood; his intellect helps him to plan the technical problems and, with intuition, to develop the melodic form; his sense of pitch transforms heard or imagined pitches into letter names and fingerings; his playing habits enable his fingers to quickly find certain established pitch patterns." [2]

Basically, there would seem to be two kinds of improvisation: free and controlled. However, to a degree the "free" has controls, and the "controlled" has certain freedoms, and these facts lead us back to Wittgenstein's statement that "we see a complicated network of similarities overlapping and crisscrossing: sometimes overall similarities, sometimes similarities of detail."

Moreover, surrounding the entire question are the value judgments of individuals—and rightly so. When a young child sits at the keyboard and indulges his right to play with the keys, producing haphazard tunes and chords on the spur of the moment, there is no doubt that he is "freely" improvising, unhampered by previously conceived harmonic, melodic, rhythmic, or structural concepts. There are, nevertheless, certain controls. His legs may be too short to reach the sustaining pedal (and this will lessen the possibility of his playing legato —smoothly—even if he knew what this meant), his fingers may be too short or too weak, or his span may be too narrow for octaves and tenths. Briefly, the child's playing, extemporaneous or otherwise, is controlled by physical limitations that result in technical limitations, not to mention artistic limitations. But, one may ask, what happens when free improvisation is undertaken by a mature performer with relatively no physical or technical limitations? Roy Eldridge, when asked about free improvisation, said: "Clyde Hart and I made a record like that once. We decided in front that there'd be no regular chords, we'd announce no keys, stick to no progressions. Only once I fell into a minor key; the rest was free, just blowing." [3]

When Eldridge "fell into a minor key" he was being controlled by his memory, by the ability of his fingers involuntarily to press down valves in combinations long since automatic, by labial convolutions repeated a hundred thousand times. When he says, "The rest was free," he means free only of certain restrictions—the restriction of a fixed form, perhaps, or of previously established harmonic patterns. The fact is, completely free improvisation is possible only when the creative processes, so to speak, are able to function without the aid of manuscript or memory. Free improvisation bears the same relation to jazz that so-called automatic writing does to prose. Paradoxically, both techniques may be acquired to a high degree by "practicing." Willi Apel has called free improvisation "a 'soapbubble' phenomenon the evanescent nature of which defies documentation and detailed description." We may nevertheless use the term "free" as long as we understand that it indicates a striving on the part of the jazzman to play outside the bounds of his conscious memory.

On the other hand, controlled improvisation, or improvisation on "given" musical materials, is relatively easier to understand. Its *raison d'être* is as old as music itself. In the beginning, music was largely improvisatory, largely supplied on the spur of the moment by primitive folk to accompany the functions of everyday living—work, play, war, love, and worship. Music was not separate from, nor was it simply an adjunct to, these activities; it was rather the force by which were communicated the special, often magical, relationships of man to nature and man to man. The improvised dance music, work songs, war songs, dream songs, love songs, and children's songs of primitive and agrarian societies are more significant to the rise and development of jazz improvisation than the highly civilized, notated complexities of, say, Stravinsky's *The Rite of Spring.*

The thread leading from early improvisations to jazz improvisations is a long one and not easily traced; there are entanglements all along the way. A part of primitive (folk) music becomes civilized (art) music and is notated; improvisations are then based on notated music; notated music becomes "frozen" improvisations; and so on through the Middle Ages, the Renaissance, and the baroque period, right up to the present, when, in jazz, the entire process seems to be repeated all over again. Nevertheless, if we are to have a broader understanding of the meaning and function of improvisation in our own time, it is necessary to show the evolution of improvisation, however briefly. And it seems proper here to begin with the words of Béla Bartók, from his definitive study on folk music. In *Hungarian Folk Music* he wrote:

> Performance by peasants, exactly as performance by a great artist, includes a good deal that is almost extemporization; for instance, . . . surface alterations and slight rhythmic alterations; at times the pitch (or perhaps even the note itself) will be changed. . . . It is obvious, indeed, that no essential alteration of a musical element can come from one individual peasant. And there can be no doubt that with peasants who people one geographical unit, living close to one another and speaking the same language, this tendency to alter, in consequence of the affinities between the mental disposition of individuals, works in one way, in the same general direction. It is thus that the birth of a homogeneous musical style becomes possible.[4]

What Bartók said of peasant societies holds for higher cultures as well. Two thousand years ago the practice of improvisation among the Greeks was widespread. The bases for their improvisations were called *nomoi,* or what we might call "stock melodies"—a collection of tunes known by all musicians. During the Middle Ages, singers improvised countermelodies against a given melody usually written in a large choir book that all the singers could view simultaneously; some of the singers sang the notated tune while others ornamented the tune according to the prevailing style. There were certain rules to go by—when to use octaves and fifths, special uses of contrary motion, and so on—but no doubt many of the rules were broken in actual performance. Concerning the use of instruments, we know from paintings and manuscripts of the period that during the fourteenth century certain instruments—the drone, for example—were widely used, yet we find written music without parts for these instruments. This would indicate that, whenever improvisation flourishes, the written composition often contains only the skeletal form of the performed composition.[5]

In the early Renaissance, improvisation was such an integral part of the practice of performance that the theorist Tinctoris (*ca.* 1435–1511) felt it necessary to say that counterpoint (which at the time was synonymous with composition) "is not only a generic term, embracing both improvisation . . . and written music . . . but also a specific term, used as a synonym for 'improvisation.' "[6] The score of the first genuine *ballet de cour,* 1581, contains in places only two outer parts to be used as instrumental accompaniment to vocal music —a clear indication that the performers were expected to fill in, or improvise, the accompaniment. And five centuries before the rise of San Francisco's beat generation, the practice of reciting cellar poetry to an improvised musical accompaniment was a commonplace. There is also an abundance of evidence that dance tunes, the *basse danse* particularly (a French court dance of the Renaissance), were played "straight" by some instruments while others improvised around the melody.

Renaissance organists had their own version of the "cutting" contest. In the mid-sixteenth century improvising contests were quite common, especially in Italy, and often were the sole basis for selecting job applicants. The ability to improvise in a fugal style (several melodies going at the same time) was a standard requirement for all appointments to organ positions, and the ability to improvise certain compositions was particularly important in the free-for-all competitions. Most of the composing of the sixteenth-century organist was therefore accomplished during actual performance.

A hundred years later (1600–1750) improvisation had become one of the cornerstones of baroque performance. Melodies called "grounds" became the basis for much baroque improvisation (as they did for jazz-pop-rock groups in the sixties and seventies); "continued" grounds became the basis for extended works. The thorough-bass technique—a method in which bass notes only were shown, with symbols indicating the proper harmonies—characterized baroque performance. Melodies were improvised upon in various ways; an organist and violist, for example, would offer a performance in which the violist was free to improvise upon the bass line, or melody, ornamenting it without changing its essential contour; or the violist would create new melodies against the bass line, the organist meanwhile improvising on the fixed harmonies, and so on. In his masterful and lucid study, *Music in the Baroque Era,* Manfred Bukofzer illuminates certain aspects of baroque musical practice that, in many ways, are analogous to jazz in the twentieth century.[7]

From .Bukofzer's study we may conclude that manuscripts and printed scores of the baroque give us only the vaguest notion of how the music sounded in actual performance. The composer considered his written score as an outline to be interpreted, in full, by the performer—the composer quite often serving both functions. Many scores were little more than what today's jazzmen call "lead sheets" (a portion of a lead sheet may be seen in Chapter 4). Great improvisation was considered one of the highest forms of musical art, and the ability to improvise, a performer's crowning artistic asset.

After J. S. Bach's time, however, the art of improvisation, as an essential part of the practice of performance, went steadily downhill. This is not to say that after Bach improvising stopped. It did, however, become a special, rather than a customary, part of a musical performance. History is full of the improvising exploits of Mozart, Beethoven, Paganini, Liszt, and other giants after Bach, but these distinctions are conferred as something apart from their ability to create written compositions; their improvisations became a matter of technical prowess.

As we move into the nineteenth century we find Beethoven, possibly the most gifted and creative of the romantic improvisers, more concerned with getting his ideas on paper than with amazing his audiences with his keyboard fireworks. He worried whether his dynamic signs, the symbols for the degrees of loudness and softness, were where they should be; he fussed over the expression marks, tempo indications, and the hundreds of Italian phrases that are intended to illustrate his intentions. But of Beethoven as a performer his pupil Czerny said: "His improvisations were most beautiful and striking. In whatever company he might chance to be he knew how to produce such an effect upon every hearer that frequently not an eye remained dry and many would break out into loud sobs. . . ." [8]

Despite Beethoven's and other composers' concern with the notated composition, improvisation continued to remain a high point of most popular concerts. Such composers as Liszt, Paganini, Mendelssohn, and, later, Franck and Saint-Saëns, made the most of their improvising abilities, and the stories of their prowess have been recorded in many sources. For example, from Casimir Wierzynski's *The Life and Death of Chopin* we learn that during a Vienna concert in 1829 Chopin was given a motif (a fragment of melody) from a current popular opera to improvise upon, and, since the second half of his concert was called *Freie Fantasie*, he proceeded to treat the motif with fantastic variations; as an added gesture, he managed to work in the Polish drinking song, "Hops," no doubt further intoxicating his audience.[9]

At the same time Chopin was playing variations on "Hops" in Vienna, blacks in the American South were making a music partly their own and partly derived from whatever their musical environment happened to be. For present purposes, it is only necessary to point out that, especially from the mid-nineteenth century on, the improvisation of untrained musicians was influenced by that of trained musicians who, in turn, adopted some of the devices of untrained musicians. There is little question that during this period both kinds of musicians existed alongside each other and influenced each other. In the South after the Civil War there were field hands who improvised on homemade instruments, and other freedmen in the cities who improvised on "legitimate" instruments. Many big-city bandsmen—right up to the 1920s—knew as little about reading music as their field-hand contemporaries. But a great many of the military bandsmen had training of one kind or another, and eventually these happy few were responsible for the subsequent rise and development of jazz improvisation.

From *Hear Me Talkin' to Ya*, Nat Shapiro and Nat Hentoff's first-rate collection of reminiscences of jazzmen and their intimates, it is relatively easy to determine the influence of "readers" on "non-readers." Here are several excerpts from jazzmen born close enough to the beginning to have recollections of it still.

Alphonse Picou, born in 1878, was an important early New Orleans clarinetist who was able to read music; about 1895, after taking lessons for eighteen months, he was asked to play with a band, and he recalls: "That particular style of music was very new to me. I think it was impossible to me! It seemed a sort of style of playing without notes." [10]

Bunk Johnson, born in 1879, a New Orleans cornetist who enjoyed a brief revival in the forties, recalls the Buddy Bolden band of 1895–96: "Now here is the thing that made King Bolden's band the first band to play jazz. It was because they could not read at all." [11]

Edmond Hall, born in 1901, self-taught and generally regarded as one of the best of the New Orleans clarinetists, recalls: "In the early days of brass bands, in the 'nineties and even before, the music was mostly written—I mean in the kind of band my father played in. As time went on there was more improvising."[12]

Buster Bailey, born in 1902, one of the important early jazz clarinetists who did not come out of New Orleans, recalls:

> We were playing in Memphis at the same time they were playing in Storyville in New Orleans. The difference was that the New Orleans bands did more improvising. Ours were more the note variety. We played from the sheets.[13]

Early jazzmen—and, for that matter, a good many later ones—had little intellectual awareness of what was coming out of their instruments. They played, as so many of them have put it, what they "felt," but the resulting improvisation was controlled by their technical ability to play their instruments, their musical environment, and their musical knowledge in general. Much of what they knew they learned by imitation and rote, as is true of all early music; much of their jazz was the result of what "lay under their hands"—intervals, scales, and arpeggios (the notes of a chord played one tone after another) natural to the horn, the keyboard, the fingerboard, and, for drummers, combinations of rudimentary rhythmic patterns. The result, however commonplace the materials, was nonetheless exciting.

Just as the performer in the seventeenth and eighteenth centuries created his everyday improvisations on a given bass, so does the jazzman create on given material. In the early days of jazz he improvised on a given melody and, as his musical knowledge increased, on given harmonies. The structural design of his improvised creation was, of necessity, simple—square phrases in an easy-to-remember two- or three-part form able to serve as a framework around a qualified use of the primary triads (the simplest three-note chords, such as CEG, FAC, GBD) and a few other chords mostly of dominant function. Two-, four-, and eight-bar phrases were the order of the day, and the bar line was never more tyrannical. This kind of basic structure, however, was necessary if the jazzmen were to play in ensemble or to alternate solos: the structure had to be simple enough to require little concentration; the harmonic progressions had to seem inevitable—that is, be the fundamental harmonic progressions of traditional eighteenth-century music. The meter—perhaps under the influence of the military band music most early jazzmen grew up with—was invariably duple.

The twelve-bar structure known as the "blues" is easily the favorite form of jazzmen, followed closely by the thirty-two-bar AABA form of the popular song. (From the sixties on, the AABA appeared considerably less frequently, and all new forms, though still in sections, were much looser.) A glance at the following example of a blues form makes its structure clear:

The basic twelve-bar blues form

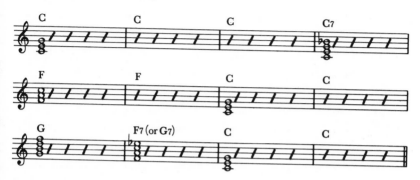

Each of the diagonal lines represents a quarter-note, or one beat; the letter symbols C, F, and G ^{7} stand for tonic (I), subdominant (IV), and dominant (V), in the key of C major. Depending on the jazz style of the improviser, other chords may be substituted for certain of the basic ones. The harmonic progressions and harmonies (what jazz musicians call "the changes") implied in improvised melodies are one part of what characterizes a style. It is therefore necessary to point out that the "basic" harmonic progressions shown above are not likely to appear in just that way, except perhaps in early blues improvisations and in the work of later jazzmen intent on imitating the early style. For the present, it seems sufficient to say that the twelve-bar blues structure is the jazzman's basic frame of reference.

The thirty-two-bar AABA form of the popular song has few basic harmonic patterns; the harmonies and their progressions vary according to the jazz style. Because the so-called standard tunes on which most improvising is done were originally written against simple triads (three-note chords) and various chords of the seventh (four-note chords), these simple chords, despite their eventual harmonic expansion, may be considered the "fundamental" chords of a given tune, and they may be seen on almost any piece of popular sheet music.

Whatever else it may be called, improvisation is variation; the technique of variation is the essential substance of jazz improvisation, as well as of all music. Jazz improvisation consists almost entirely of creating new melodic patterns to "fit" a given harmonic foundation that, except in the case of the basic blues formula, usually has a melody of its own; while the harmonic foundation remains fixed, the original melody is varied. The performer may vary the melody only slightly—changing a note here, a rhythm there—or he may change it considerably, adding and subtracting musical elements, but keeping the musical character and outline of the original melody still recognizable; finally, the variation will be based solely on the chord changes and there will be little reference to the original tune.

Hodeir, on this subject, distinguishes between what he calls a "theme phrase" and a "variation phrase." "The *theme phrase*," he writes, "is more stripped, less diffuse, because it has less ornament than the variation phrase." He goes on to say that the variation phrase may be further divided "into two principal types, the *paraphrase* and the *chorus phrase*. The first retains definite melodic affinities with the theme phrase from which it springs; the second, which is a kind of free variation, gets away from it completely. . . ." [14]

Improvisation, then, consists of performing variations on a theme —and the theme may be either a melodic subject or a harmonic progression (or, under certain circumstances, a rhythmic pattern); it may consist of any of these singly or in any combination. Robert U. Nelson, in his first-rate study *The Technique of Variation,* discusses the "song variation"—a structure common to the baroque period—which bears certain relationships to jazz improvisation. The following description sounds much like what the jazzman sets out to accomplish with an improvised solo. Nelson writes:

. . . the theme is followed by a moderate number of units, set off by cadences, which are arranged more or less progressively according to their rhythmic animation and degree of figural elaboration. The growth in animation is not always steady, being interrupted from time to time by a return to quieter rhythms, yet by and large there is a noticeable increase in activity from the beginning of a set to the end. . . . The component variations keep unchanged the main outlines of the given subject, above all its structure, its tonality, and generally its meter and chief harmonic outlines.[15]

Thus jazz performers build up their own extended, improvised solos: improvisations begin with little or no variation on a melodic subject and, as the performers warm to their job, progress to more elaborate melodic variation until finally the melody is completely abandoned for the harmonic variation. In both the thirty-two-bar form and the basic blues, the performer strives to achieve a balance of rhythmic tension and release as prescribed by the song variation. Above all, the first-rate jazz performer strives to create within the limitations of the style he chooses to work in. Held within the boundaries of a few chords, his imagination soars to melodic heights, driven by the energetic rhythmic force that has given the best jazz its characteristic vitality. The harmonic formulas of jazz improvisation are undoubtedly simple, but then so are the basic formulas for Bach's *Goldberg Variations* and Beethoven's *Diabelli Variations*.

Two jazz musicians with about the same musical knowledge, early training, and environment are likely to react to a given set of chords with a similar stylistic interpretation; their individual playing styles and techniques may be quite unlike, but their performances will be similar in style and spirit. The virtuoso jazzmen—men like Louis Armstrong, Benny Goodman, and Charlie Parker—were great because they explored the limitations of the jazz styles they worked in and found ways to turn the limitations to their advantage, always with stylistic consistency. The great jazzman is not born a mature artist; his art evolves. He has transitional periods, of course, during which he is trying to find his means of expression; his greatness comes when he has found what he sought and the means of communicating it through his playing—even when he himself continues the search, unaware of his discovery. The stylistic consistency I am speaking of is manifested most clearly after the discovery is made. It is obviously difficult to evaluate jazz improvisation when it is still in the formative period. We must, therefore, look for the characteristic improvisation of the great jazzman when he is at the peak of his improvisational—that is, creative—powers, and not in periods of evolution or decline.

As we have pointed out earlier, the possibility of completely uncontrolled improvisation is remote. How then, we may ask, do jazz performers create significant new compositions on the spur of the moment? The answer is that they do not. That is, they do not compose on the spur of the moment; their significant improvisations are the result of long practice and experience. In the course of years of listening, absorbing, analyzing, and imitating the work of his predecessors and contemporaries (and even his own work), the jazz performer builds up a stock of musical material. He modifies and adapts, to his individual conception of jazz, melodic fragments, rhythmic patterns, and even entire phrases he has heard and admired. All these memories and impressions are assimilated and transformed into music that is fresh, and often, when it is coupled with the spirit of spontaneity, music that is new. The performer's task is to organize his material—however spontaneous his performance may seem—in such a way as to make it appear that the material is, in truth, his own. A phrase he happened upon earlier, consisting of melodic fragments partly under his hand and partly, perhaps, the result of accident, is repeated for a month or a year as well as he can remember it. Then it is further modified in the solitude of individual practice and under the stimulation of rehearsals and public performances until, one evening, it bursts forth apparently new-born.

Ironically enough, it is in the few moments of improvisation, when the improvisers actually are not immediately aware of what they are doing, that something apparently spontaneous is likely to occur. Early moments in improvising sessions usually consist of each performer's blowing himself out, so to speak—ridding himself of those musical ideas close to the surface of his memory, those that come to mind too easily and too readily. As the session progresses, however, and if the performer has any regard for his colleagues' opinion of him, he feels compelled to reach out, or perhaps inward. In such moments great jazz may be born.

Since the early days of jazz, performers have made considerable efforts to explain what they and their colleagues were trying to accomplish in their improvisations. For the most part, their remarks have been colorful but not very enlightening. It nevertheless seems worthwhile to look briefly at some of the statements attributed, in Shapiro and Hentoff's invaluable collection, *Hear Me Talkin' to Ya,* to jazzmen who spent a good part of their lives working toward a barely perceived, often intangible goal: the creation of significant improvisation. Johnny St. Cyr, representing the view of many early jazzmen, said: "A jazz musician have to be a working class of man. . . . The more enthusiastic his audience is, why, the more spirit the working man's got to play. And with your natural feelings that way, you never make the same thing twice. Every time you play a tune, new ideas come to mind and you slip that on in." [16] Mutt Carey, another pioneer of New Orleans jazz, recalls what he felt after hearing

Armstrong perform before the first World War: "Louis sings just like he plays. I think Louis proves the idea and theory which holds that if you can't sing it, you can't play it. When I'm improvising, I'm singing in my mind. I sing what I feel and then try to reproduce it on the horn." [17] Armstrong was, of course, a jazz phenomenon. He has been quoted, imitated, and, in certain jazz circles, revered. Armstrong at his best was magnificent, and much of what has been said about him was undoubtedly warranted.

Miles Davis, who studied at the Juilliard School of Music, when asked about improvising the blues, told Eric Larrabee in *Harper's* of May 1958: "You don't learn to play the blues. You just play. I don't even think of harmony. It just comes. You learn where to put notes so they'll sound right. You just don't do it because it's a funny chord." Despite Davis' assertion that "it just comes," the limitations on improvisation are severe. The performer must accept the discipline of melodic, harmonic, rhythmic, and structural limitations—in short, stylistic limitations—if he is to create significant improvisations. When the performer is not bound by stylistic limitations, his improvisations become sketchy and sporadic, he shows flashes of creativity, he plays an interesting measure or two here and there, but his creation suffers in its total impact. The best improvisation, like the best notated music, comes to the listener as an organized pattern, a unified structure. Music, improvised or written, if it is to be art, must have direction and purpose; one must be able to search for and find the same qualities in jazz improvisation that one would expect to find in the best calculated, notated music. Considering the severe limitations upon the performer, it is remarkable how many fine and sensitive improvisations have been created over the years.

The evaluation of improvisation and other aspects of jazz does not appear to me to be as controversial as certain of the traditionalists would have it. The problems of evaluation are thorny enough without complicating the issues with such questions as "Is oldtime jazz better than current jazz?" There is as little point to such a question as there is to the question of who is the better composer, Tchaikovsky or Ravel. Both questions are based on a false premise. Composers and their music are properly evaluated only in the setting and spirit of their own time; serious evaluators and critics ought not to be permitted to impose the limitations or freedoms of one period on another. Nevertheless, this is exactly what traditionalists and progressives alike have done in the controversy over the relative merits of notated and improvised jazz. Those who see collective improvisation as the foundation of all jazz are understandably nonplussed when asked to evaluate, for example, Fletcher Henderson's or Benny Goodman's version of "The King Porter Stomp." Those who by some obscure reasoning hold that chords of the eleventh are more musical than chords of the seventh are equally nonplussed when asked to evaluate, for example, Bunk Johnson's solo on the "Saints." The rationale of critics on both sides of the fence is largely fanciful and irrelevant.

As soon as jazzmen learned how to read, the traditionalist view held, jazz started downhill. Since the basis of jazz is, or ought to be, collective improvisation, their argument went, individual improvisation leads to inflated egos and undisciplined freedom, which, in turn, deny the value of the musical teamwork essential to the true jazz. In the mid-forties, the traditionalists considered the relatively short life of swing and the groping for new jazz styles sufficient proof of the inadequacy of solo improvisation to contribute anything to jazz; on the other hand, the resurgence of the New Orleans, or Dixieland, style in 1946 was offered as evidence that true jazz will prevail.

The progressives, advocates of solo improvisation (with or without the accompaniment of the big band), took little stock in the foregoing views. They saw little difference in the kind of individuality required for collective and for solo improvisation; they made a strong point of holding up to ridicule the traditional jazzman's meager musical resources and technical deficiencies; they claimed that their kind of jazz required infinitely more skill, knowledge, and profundity —more art, if you will—to perform. Further, the progressives believed that the large ensemble, with its arrangements and solo performers, served to unify and display significant characteristics of style; that the big band gave satisfactory form to what the individual or small group initiated; that the big band worked toward financial security for the jazzman since it provided more opportunities for playing, through which jazz would be brought more forcibly to the attention of the general public; and that all these factors would result in a wider acceptance of jazz. The unprecedented activity during the swing era when, for the first time, jazz and popular music were almost synonymous, was considered by the progressives as sufficient evidence of swing's contribution to jazz. (In the sixties and seventies, similarly structured arguments went on between conservatives and the avant-garde.)

There is much to say for the attitude of both sides. Each side, in its way, saw itself as a defender of jazz; this, in itself, was a good thing. A part of what each side stood for was true. But the traditionalist needs to know that collective improvisation at one time *was* the basis of jazz but only during a particular period; and the progressive needs to recognize that during a particular period the basis of jazz may very well be collective improvisation. Both sides need to know that creativity in jazz must be measured according to the musical and technical means available to the creators; that jazzmen are not to be devalued because certain means are not available to them in their time. The art of Giotto is not better than the art of Picasso; the Colosseum is not a better example of architecture than the Houston Astrodome;

the music of Mozart is not better than the music of Debussy. The critic may, for purposes of guiding the reader, show relationships between two periods in art, two periods in music, or when necessary between one period in art and another in music. He may compare techniques and materials; he may not, however, concoct an arbitrary scale of values. He may prefer romantic music to baroque music, or Dixieland to "the new thing," but he must make clear that this is not a value judgment; it is a matter of taste and preference.

How, we may properly ask, does one evaluate that part of jazz which is written and not improvised? Most critics would agree, I believe, that when a soloist or even a group of soloists is improvising, one or more instruments are providing a background against which the improvised solo is heard. Are we then to assume that the soloist is playing jazz and the accompanist is not? Or that the whole is not jazz if any of its parts is notated and played as written? If this should prove to be the case, then much that has passed for jazz would have to be discounted.

Without doubt improvisation is not the sole element in jazz, but it is an integral one, and the value of the accompaniment must be assessed according to the manner in which it acts upon improvisation —that is, whether it impels or restrains improvisation. Arranged jazz is only as important as the solos it frames, and unless it does frame one significant solo, at least, it is pseudo-jazz. A background or, for that matter, a foreground, may move with rocking-chair relaxation or swing high and mighty with jetlike force, but without the excitement of solo jazz it will not get off the ground. The qualities of drive, relaxation, and swing in written jazz need to be judged according to their effect on the soloist, and, just as a solo can be ill-conceived, so can a background. According to Ethel Waters, the drive she needs to move her forward comes in great part from what she hears in her accompaniment. In her autobiography she writes:

> I kept having arguments with Fletcher Henderson about the way he was playing my accompaniments. Fletcher, though a fine arranger and a brilliant band leader, leans more to the classical side. On that tour Fletcher wouldn't give me what I call "the damn-it-to-hell bass," that chump-chump that real jazz needs.[19]

Good jazz needs solid support whether it comes from a wire brush accompaniment of indeterminate pitch or from eight brass rocking a C major chord.

It seems that certain jazz soloists do feel a great need for the "proper" accompaniment, while others are relatively unaffected. (It is difficult to imagine, for example, that the accompaniments provided for Armstrong solos in the early thirties on such records as "I Surrender Dear," "Them There Eyes," "Confessin'," and "Basin Street Blues" held him back in any way, or that they provided him with much stimulation. However, it may be that Armstrong's style—one of sticking close to the melody and, in blues, close to the basic blues material—did not require much support and stimulation from outside himself.) There is certainly a relationship between a performer's technical ability and the kind of background he requires for solo work. For example, numerous instances have been mentioned of the importance of the lead cornet in New Orleans style: of the importance to the improviser of having the tune where he could hear it constantly. On the other hand, a bop improviser would no doubt feel somewhat constricted in his playing if he had the tune impressed upon him all the time; more than likely he would be more responsive—that is, more stimulated to get off—to a rich harmonic background and stimulating rhythmic punctuation.

Furthermore, there is a relationship between the kind of background a performer requires and the degree of intellectuality with which he approaches his solo. Armstrong, for example, never one for being concerned with misses and near-misses, required only a steady two or four; emotional stimulation he apparently found within himself. Armstrong created with a full awareness of his technical limitations. Armstrong played what he felt was right, and it was right just because it pushed at the bounds of his technical and emotional capacity; and, in his genre, Armstrong was as hard to beat as Charlie Parker was in his. Technical limitations do not limit one's creative ability; they do limit the possibilities of creating in a particular style. Charlie Parker, at the peak of his work, would probably have been as much hampered by a New Orleans style background as Armstrong would have been by a bop ensemble.

Certain early jazzmen and critics believed that too much technical facility and musicianship were detrimental to a jazzman's ability to create significant improvisation, and they were right for their time and for the jazz styles they represented. During the late fifties, however, one wondered at Dave Brubeck's curious attack on technique: "It's a very strange thing the way I feel about technique and creativity," he said to Ralph Gleason, "the idea is that when you have real clean technique and you pride yourself with it and you have certain standards that have to come to what you want technically, you're gonna cut off creativity. . . ." [20] Brubeck's statement would have sounded more objective if one knew he had not been concerned with answering those critics who wished he had greater technical facility. Brubeck's error was his failure to recognize that, in the past, he had accomplished quite a lot considering his technical limitations, because technical deficiencies did not hamper him in the jazz style in which he chose to work. His early works deserve credit and admiration, and these he received in abundance. In a jazz style, however, where a high degree of technical proficiency is an established prerequisite to improvising and creating, it is foolish to ask what one must do first in order to create in that style.

A first-rate performer in one jazz style is not necessarily a first-rate performer in another style; he may, in fact, be quite impotent in a style not his own. This is not to say that a performer may not attempt a style not his own; if he does, however, his listeners should not expect to hear first-rate jazz on order. Chances are that what they hear will range anywhere from mediocre to poor, stylistically speaking. There is no question that there are people who rejoice in hearing certain jazz styles rather than others; these are the listeners most likely to confuse style with quality. For them, any quality of jazz-rock, say, is better or has more value or is more significant than, say, any quality of Dixieland; the fact is that examples of artistically superior, mediocre, and poor jazz can be found in all styles, and the acceptance of this simple proposition is indispensable to the making of proper jazz evaluations.

It may be useful here to point up the difference in the restrictions on an improviser during the period of the 78 rpm recording and the subsequent changes brought about by the advent of the $33\frac{1}{3}$ rpm, so-called lp, recording. The recording time for the standard ten-inch 78 was about $3\frac{1}{2}$ minutes, which not only eventually controlled the musical form in which band arrangements were cast, but rigidly prescribed the duration of solo improvisations. When an improvisation is limited to, say, one minute, the jazzman's intention is seriously circumscribed by that duration. The best jazzmen, of course, had a constant awareness of this point. Given 5, 10, or 15 minutes to speak their piece on the $33\frac{1}{3}$ rpm recording changed their intention, and their musical goals became somewhat different. In this respect, we may note that had performers like John Coltrane, Ornette Coleman, and those who became attached to the "free-jazz" movement, been required to play within the confines of the 78 rpm recording, they would certainly have suffered a lack of breathing space. And in this regard, we are able to see how technological advances can bring about artistic change.

It is important that we know the style of a jazz work, but once we know what the style is, it is more important to determine the general level of performance, the soloist's apparent intent, and whether artistic communication has been effected. Only the experienced and analytical listener can determine the degree of artistic success reached by the performer. Anyone, however, may say without compunction what he or she *likes*. The analyst has the task of separating the artistic from the inartistic, the experimental from the commercial. He acts as a conscience for those who, once they discover what they believe to be a successful formula, exploit it for all it is worth; he exposes vulgarity, sentimentality, speciosity, and pretentiousness. The analyst attempts to relate technique and depth of feeling. He is constantly aware of Frank Lloyd Wright's "excess never to be mistaken for exuberance," aware that "creative" implies exuberance and spontaneity.

Because of the nature of jazz improvisation, there is much difference of opinion as to what makes significant improvisation. There is one point, however, on which most analysts agree: improvisation, to be significant, must contain the unexpected; it must produce the feeling of excitement and exhilaration that comes from the illusion of spontaneity, and the sound of surprise. When Bix Beiderbecke, the near-legendary jazz cornetist of the twenties, took a chorus, the audience was curious about what he was going to do next. And Milt Hinton says that Dizzy Gillespie's music was exciting for him because he tried to do things he couldn't. Aaron Copland summed up the case, in

Composers on Music, when he said, "When you improvise, it is axiomatic that you take risks and can't foretell results." [21]

What distinguishes superior creative musicians from the mediocre ones of all periods is the manner in which they create resolutions—a resolution being a breaking of tension—and to create resolutions it is necessary to set up tension, or irresolutions. This perhaps oversimplified statement summarizes the process of creation, which must be understood if its products are to be judged properly. In order to understand what the jazz creator is attempting to resolve, one must determine his intent; knowing the creator's purpose makes it easier to evaluate the end result. Poor and mediocre jazzmen will impose problems on themselves, problems of resolution whose answers are already evident in the irresolutions they set up. Poor and mediocre jazzmen fretfully pursue resolutions that, when accomplished, surprise no one but themselves; their resolutions seem not so much inevitable as commonplace. Jazzmen in these categories often do not understand that the quality of their jazz will depend not on any resolution, however elaborate, but rather on the inherent intricacy of the irresolution. The answer to two plus two is four, and finding a way to solve this by calculus does not make the problem more profound. The first-rate jazzman sets himself difficult examinations. He is not looking for easy solutions, quick formulas, or back-of-the-book answers. Although he is vitally concerned with solving the problem of creativity, he knows that technique and method of operation are the important factors through which he may achieve his end. The approach that engenders comfort and security is not his. He knows that the intangible qualities of imagination, intuition, and inspiration are in part the result of experience and knowledge, and that only through a delicately balanced organization of all these qualities will the spirit of creativity manifest itself.

the musical elements of jazz

(Overleaf) *Fletcher Henderson and his orchestra: 1924. Left to right: Howard Scott, Coleman Hawkins (seated on floor), Louis Armstrong, Charlie Dixon (above bass saxophone), Fletcher Henderson, Kaiser Marshall, Buster Bailey, Elmer Chambers, Charlie Green, Bobbie Escudero (seated on floor), and Don Redman*

A JAZZ PERFORMER USUALLY IMPROVISES ON GIVEN MATERIAL, and, while it may be extremely difficult to show an exact written version of the improvisation itself, it is relatively easy to show a written version of the given material. Jazz consists of musical sounds, and the basic elements of music—rhythm, melody, harmony—are shown in jazz in essentially the same way as in other music. The problems of symbolizing musical sounds are therefore not unique to jazz, but are present in all music. The symbol of a musical sound—that is, a note—is not the sound itself but merely the representation of the sound. While the note indicates duration (how long it is to be held) and pitch (highness or lowness), it seldom provides for either intensity or timbre (the quality, or tone color, of a sound); if one wishes to indicate degrees of loudness or softness, additional symbols are necessary. Even so, there is no assurance that the composer's sign for "very soft" (*pp*) will not be interpreted—at least to the composer's way of thinking—as "loud"; for that matter, there is no assurance that the indicated pitch will be sounded exactly. Microtonic deviations from pitch are a commonplace; furthermore, in times past, instruments were tuned higher in the United States than they were in Europe.

The problem of notating the jazz solo does not lie in the technical deficiency of the composer, as some critics believe, nor is it impossible to solve, as others believe; rather, the difficulty lies with the insufficiency of notational symbols. Those who have attempted to notate a composition of large proportions, in whatever musical style, will know that a constant effort to represent what is in the mind's ear with inadequate symbols invariably leads to frustration. There can have been few composers in the history of music who have not at one time or another felt this frustration and known the gross inefficiency of musical symbols. Nevertheless, composers continue to labor over their work and manage to communicate to the performer, with the performer's help, of course, more than the written page indicates. The evolution of this means of communication is a long one, and it may be useful here to summarize how it came about.

From the earliest times, there have been many different systems of writing down music. Not all these systems, of course, had equal currency, and not all played a role in the evolution of our present system, but many of them did. Our modern system very likely has its basis in the symbols used in Greek and Jewish speech recitations of the second century B.C. These symbols, known generically as ekphonetic notation, were for the most part short diagonal lines whose direction indicated whether the speaker was to raise his voice or lower it. (Present-day singers of Jewish chant still use ekphonetic signs.) About the sixth century, the ekphonetic notation grew into a system of signs known as neumes, symbols that expressed—though not very clearly—the general outlines of a melody. Neumes, however, represented neither pitch nor duration; a vocalist delivered his chant in the same rhythm he would use for speaking prose. For the performer, neumes were really mnemonic devices; he learned his music by rote, and neumes helped him to remember approximately how the tunes went so that he was able to hand down the oral tradition to the next generation. Later, attempts were made to clarify the vagueness of neumes by adding letters to the symbols (letter notation had been in use since the early Greeks), and, in about the ninth century, additional help came from the use of a horizontal colored line. Eventually two lines were adopted for writing music on, but only the space between the lines was used. The staff lines increased until the theorist-monk Guido d'Arezzo, in the eleventh century, introduced the four-line staff, alternating black lines with the colored lines of his predecessors, and called the four lines (from the bottom line up) *f a c e*. When it became necessary to show higher or lower pitches, he merely added new lines.

SOME DEVELOPMENTS IN NOTATION

Ekphonetic notation (second century)

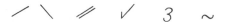

Signs like these appeared over a text to be sung. Essentially memory aids, they helped the singer to recall whether the melody was to be turned, vibrated, moved up or down.

Neumes (sixth century on)

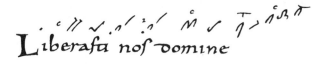

These signs provided a general outline of the melody. Later, letter names of the tones were added to clarify the pitch.

Staff

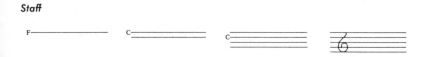

Lines increased from one to two and, in the eleventh century, to four. The five-line staff did not come into use until the thirteenth century.

The clef sign shows where a particular pitch is located, usually **F**, **C**, or **G**.

Square notation (twelfth century on)

White mensural notation (mid-thirteenth century)

Mensural means rhythmically measured, as opposed to Gregorian chant, which was sung relatively freely, or in an unmeasured style.

Black mensural notation (late thirteenth-century on)

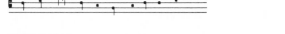

Modern equivalent

Lute tablature (around sixteenth century)

Tablatures show the player on what strings and frets to place the fingers, and what rhythms to use. The six lines represent the six strings; the numbers refer to the frets; the zero indicates the open string.

Modern guitar tablature

The black dots show where the fingers are to be placed. The letters are the names of the open strings and are commonly omited.

Some standard signs

Measure 1: *f* is an abbreviation of *forte*, which means "loud"; the contracting lines stand for *decrescendo*, which means "gradually softer." Measure 2: *p* is an abbreviation of *piano*, which means "soft." Measure 3: *mf* is an abbreviation of *mezzo-forte*, which means "medium loud"; the curved line is called a "slur" and requires these notes to be played *legato*, or smoothly, without break between notes. Measure 4: this is an accent sign, meaning the tone is to be sounded with a special emphasis. Measure 5: *mp* is an abbreviation of *mezzo-piano*, which means "medium soft"; *rit.* is an abbreviation of *ritardando*, which means "slowing down"; the dots over the last two notes are signs for *staccato*, which means the notes are to be played very short,

with rests between the sounds. Measure 6: a *crescendo* sign, which means "gradually louder."

A jazz lead sheet

The letters and numbers represent chords used to harmonize the melody. A chord remains in effect until the new one is shown.

By the end of the thirteenth century the five-line staff was widely used; the neumes had acquired a square shape and definite rhythmic values based on the repetition of simple ternary metrical patterns; indicating pitch was no longer a problem. Square notation developed into what is known as white mensural notation (larger note values became white shapes instead of black shapes), a system that was established around 1250 by the theorist Franco of Cologne and flourished until the seventeenth century. Franco's system set up a flexible time relationship between note values much like that of our present system. (There were still certain differences from our modern system. While our undotted note is equal to two notes of the next smaller value, in mensural notation certain notes are equal to three of the next value.) Around 1320 Philippe de Vitry, sometimes called the "father of modern notation," developed the principle of binary rhythm, giving it equal importance with ternary rhythm. Later, black mensural notation superseded the white, and the system, in essence, became our modern one. In his definitive volume on notation, Apel writes that "the development of notation from 1100 to 1600 is characterized by a gradual simplification and rationalization, by steps leading from extremely vague notions to the laws and principles prevailing in our days." [1]

It has already been stated that there were other notational systems besides the ones mentioned. For example, the development of systems of tablatures—the notation for solo keyboard and lute music that corresponds in some degree to the guitar and ukelele symbols found in much sheet music of the 1920s—was concomitant with mensural notation. Not until some fifteenth- and sixteenth-century keyboard tablatures are bar lines evident, and then they are inconsistently used and are apparently a matter of convenience in reading rather than a symbol to be placed after each repeated number of definite beats. (This function of the bar line has been adopted by most twentieth-century composers who do not favor the system of changing meters; performers of contemporary music have long since learned to ignore the bar line except as an orientation point and a convenience in counting measures.) The use of the bar line, together with the tie, which appeared first in a sixtenth-century keyboard score, mark the principal distinctions between mensural notation and modern notation. By J. S. Bach's time, a number of dynamic signs and tempo indications were widely used; by Mozart's time, the signs for various kinds of staccato and legato were well established. Small changes and additions continued to be made through the nineteenth century up to our own time, and even if one looks at scores by such contemporary composers as Cage and Stockhausen, there is little reason to believe that our present-day notation is the end of notation's evolution.

In the past, systems of notation have had to conform to composers' needs, and, when the needs could not be met, the system was altered to fit. There is a definite need for more serious and concerted effort to adapt our modern system of notation to the needs of jazz if jazz is to be notated properly. However, the imposition of special signs and symbols on jazz will not in itself be enough, as long as jazzmen continue to believe that what they improvise cannot be written down. This will be particularly true as long as reading music is considered a lesser accomplishment than improvising it. Practically speaking, we must admit the likelihood that jazz will always have two types of jazzmen: those who believe a serviceable jazz notation can be evolved, and those who either do not believe it or are indifferent to the problem. It is my belief that a jazz notation will evolve that will serve jazz-oriented performers as well as classical notation serves performers of classical music. Furthermore, this evolution has been proceeding quite rapidly in the past forty years; many more musicians who ordinarily function outside the jazz scene have become aware of the practice of jazz performance, and it is the combined knowledge of notation and performance practice, not notation by itself, that brings about truthful interpretations of the composer's intent. (This point is of great significance, and we shall have to take a closer look at it further on.)

Let us see briefly which elements of jazz lend themselves readily to our present system of notation and which do not. Of the so-called special effects of jazz the most notable are the glissando, the growl of brass instruments, the fluttertongue of both brass and reeds, absence or exaggeration of vibrato, and slighty flatted notes. (The use of special mutes, while peculiar to jazz, is not a notational problem.) Standard notation provides serviceable symbols for the glissando, fluttertongue, and vibrato. What notation does not provide for is the degree to which these are to be used. The glissando, for example, indicates only a sliding up or sliding down; when the glissando is not immediately followed by another tone, there is no indication where the glissando is to end, or for that matter how rapidly or slowly it is to be effected.

Knowing how these things are done is a matter of knowing the practice of performance. For a musician technically familiar with the practice of a given jazz style, "smearing" a tone, for example, is no problem. If a special kind of glissando symbol is meaningless to a technically proficient nonjazz musician, so may Bartók's notational symbol for playing notes flat be meaningless to the jazz musician. And, even if both musicians understand the significance of the symbols, they must know their use in performance if they are to effect them with the proper style. Further, academically trained musicians do not generally know the meanings of such written indications as "smear," "growl," "bend," and others, not because they are technically incapable of performing them but because they are unfamiliar, first, with the indications and, second, with the proper manner of executing them. Because many nonjazz performers are not willing to devote the necessary time and practice to acquire a sense of jazz style does not mean they are incapable of doing so. (Not all nonjazz musicians are willing to devote the necessary time and practice to acquire a sense of Renaissance style either; it is a matter of preference.) Acquiring a "feel" for playing jazz is possible for any technically proficient musician who is willing to work at it; given the proper musical and social environment and study, any academically trained musician can learn to perform creditable jazz.

In some ways the problem of notating jazz effects that concern pitch appears less formidable when approached through the notation of folk music, rather than art music. The reason for this is that, while the flatting of certain tones in jazz is usually related to a preconceived harmonic basis, the off-pitch tones of folk music may be looked at for themselves; folk music is conceived as melody without harmony. In folk song, despite the arbitrary major-minor basis by which most of us understandably relate all music, there is no harmonic conflict. Harmonic conflict is not an essential factor in folk song.

Béla Bartók, who probably did as much as anyone in an attempt to notate special musical sounds and effects, recorded thousands of folk tunes on wax cylinders, after which he attempted to set them down on paper. It would seem that the special symbols Bartók had to create to realize even an approximation of the actual recorded performance might well be given further consideration by those who feel the necessity for notating improvised jazz melodies. The reader interested in *seeing* such characteristic jazz sounds as the glissando—sliding up to and away from tones—the smear, the growl, the blue tones and half tones, and a host of other graphic representations, is directed to Bartók's definitive *Hungarian Folk Music*.[2] (*Down Beat*, read by many aspiring jazz performers, has through the years published hundreds of notated examples of solo improvisations.)

If one insists upon saying, "Jazz is invariably in duple meter," or, "Jazz can also be made to swing in ternary rhythm," one runs the risk of confusing the measure of the music with the 4/4, 3/4, or 2/4 time indicated in the signature; one also runs the risk of confusing bar lines perhaps intended only as orientation symbols with bar lines intended as measuring posts. Without question, music of certain periods—from Bach to Brahms—used the bar line as an aid in indicating weak and strong beats. In such music the preponderance of strong accents is in agreement with the meter. In 4/4 time, for example, the strong accents in the music usually fall on the strong first and third beats, and the weak accents on the weak second and fourth beats, and, since the bar line is used to measure off every four beats, it is proper in this style to give more stress to the beat immediately after the bar line and less to the beat immediately before the bar line. However, much twentieth-century music, as we have already stated, is not controlled by the bar line, to understand the meter of such music one cannot simply count bar lines or take time signatures at face value. One must measure the music, its strong and weak accents, its entire rhythmic structure.

It is the element of rhythm and the performer's manner of interpreting rhythmic indications that help distinguish jazz from other music. If we are to follow the evolution of the rhythmic characteristics of jazz, we may consider the general conclusion that rhythm, at the outset, was strict and steady, consisted chiefly of equal values, and had its basis in the motions of dancing. When it became necessary to sing, the simple dance rhythms were adapted to the rhythm of words. In the third stage—a return to the dance—the complicated rhythms derived from words were imposed on dance tunes, making the rhythms of the final stage considerably more complex than those of the first stage.[3]

Most observers would agree that the evolution of jazz styles was accompanied by increasingly complex rhythms. One has only to compare characteristic New Orleans rhythms with characteristic "new thing" rhythms to recognize the degree of rhythmic complexity that separates the two. Nevertheless, there is a rhythmic drive and vitality common to the best jazz that forces one to seek for some rhythmic device by which all jazz could be characterized. Many who have tried to isolate such a device have done so in vain, for the answer is not to be found in the repetition of particular rhythmic patterns or in the variation of others. Certain writers have searched for answers in Freud; others have tried West Africa; still others have speculated on "psychic tension" and "personal magnetism." If there is an answer to the secret of rhythmic vitality, I believe it lies in a remote region of the listener's mind and is activated only when the listener receives and understands the consummated intention of a jazz performer.

It seems certain that one part of the secret of rhythmic drive concerns the rhythmic element known as syncopation. Much has been written on syncopation, mostly on its effect on the listener; here we are concerned, rather, with the manner in which it may be used. Walter Piston, in his *Harmony,* writes, "Syncopation implies a well-established rhythmic pulse, the effect being based on a dislocation of that pulse by giving a strong accent where one is not expected, and suppressing the normal accent of the pulse." [4] Jazz has been concerned principally with this simple syncopation—a disagreement between the melodic rhythm and the established pulse.

There is another kind of rhythm to be considered, what is called harmonic rhythm. When a harmony, say, a C major chord, is the basis for one measure in 4/4 time, we say that the chord has a harmonic rhythm of four beats, usually shown as a whole note. If there is a new chord every two beats, say, the harmonic rhythm may be shown as half-notes. And so on. In addition to the regularly stated pulse accompanying most jazz, at least through the fifties, the harmonic rhythm was in agreement with the meter. That is, the chord changes generally came in the rhythmically strong places—at the beginning of a measure or on a strong beat within the measure. On the other hand, little attention has been paid to the theoretical possibilities of having syncopation result from a manipulation of the harmonic rhythm—that is, having the chord changes come in places that disagree with the established pulse.

As long as the harmonic progressions of blues—rhythmically the most rigid—dominated jazz performance, there was little room for exploring syncopation based on the dislocation of the harmonic rhythm. The blues progression, and progressions in the standard tunes of the twenties and thirties, with their important root changes agreeing with the meter, required almost total concentration on the rhythm of the melody. By the forties and fifties, however, as jazz players began working with thematic material in which the important changes did not necessarily coincide with the normal accent of the pulse, syncopations based on dislocation of the harmonic rhythm had a greater opportunity to develop and expand. The principle of simple syncopation, coming as a result of single tones accenting weak beats or weak parts of beats against an established pulse, could now be expanded to a syncopation coming as a result of strong harmonic changes falling on weak beats or weak parts of beats against a melody whose rhythm agrees with the established pulse.

Composers who feel that binary rhythm (*one*-two or *one*-two-*three*-four) in jazz may have outlived its usefulness, that binary rhythm restricts jazz, and that new time signatures are necessary if jazz is to continue to grow may do well to put aside temporarily their concern with 3/4, 5/4, 7/4, and other time signatures and concentrate their efforts on the potentialities of syncopation through harmonic rhythm. In exploring the possibilities of harmonic rhythm, it is likely they will find that much that previously received little consideration can be done in binary rhythm.

In some respects, rhythmic complexities have not had as much fascination for jazzmen, particularly during the first fifty years of jazz, as have harmonic complexities. But, before we turn to the harmonies of jazz in the twentieth century, it might be proper to consider briefly the evolution of traditional harmony, since it is from this that jazz harmony has been derived. The basis of harmony is the scale. From the scale are derived intervals that, when sounded in combination simultaneously, result in chords. Harmony, sometimes called "vertical" music, is a much later development in music than counterpoint, or "horizontal" music; the system of traditional harmony as we know it is in fact an outgrowth of counterpoint, as is our tertian system of building chords. (Tertian means, in part, the building of chords using the interval of a third as the basic unit of construction; starting with the note C, for example, and adding a third, E, to it, and adding a third, G, to the E, makes the major chord C E G.) We shall see that the harmonies of jazz have their models in the harmonies of the past, from the tenth century to the twentieth.

The evolution of harmony may be divided into three periods: from 900 to 1450, when harmony was the result of contrapuntal writing; from 1450 to 1900, when harmony consisted of pre-established combinations of sound; and from 1900 to the present, when systems of harmony other than tertian were evolved. The three periods may be called pre-tertian, tertian, and post-tertian. Discussion of the techniques of the post-tertian period will be found in the last two chapters; for the present we shall concern ourselves with the two earlier periods.

In pre-tertian days a system of scales called modes was used as a basis for the composition of solo vocal melodies; when one voice was joined by another part, vocal or instrumental, the result was certain "acceptable" harmonic intervals. By the end of the pre-tertian period there was a wide use of three-part counterpoint that frequently produced an effect not unlike that of the consecutive minor triads with added seventh, a sound much favored by many jazzmen in the fifties and sixties.

Around 1450, in the early tertian period, composition in more than three parts was so widespread that the modal scales, originally conceived for the solo voice, no longer served this purpose. When the theorist Glareanus published his book, *Dodecachordon,* in 1547, he added four modes to the eight then current. They were (and still are) called: Dorian, Phrygian, Lydian, Mixolydian, Aeolian, Ionian, Hypodorian, Hypophrygian, Hypolydian, Hypomixolydian, Hypoaeolian, and Hypoionian. These modes were eventually replaced by two of the modes, the major and minor, which correspond to the Ionian and Aeolian modes, and composers became more concerned with vertical combinations of sounds. (In the late fifties and sixties, jazz composers working with minor blues found themselves composing in one of the old modes.)

The basis of modern harmonic theory was formulated by Jean Philippe Rameau in his *Traité de l'harmonie,* published in 1722. In this remarkable treatise, Rameau recognized the necessity for a strong tonal center, presented a theory of chord inversions, and made out the case for tertian harmony. Whereas composers for five centuries previous had heard harmony as the result of combined melodies, Rameau contended that melody was derived from harmony. With Rameau's system well established, gradually there was a complete transition from modal writing to tonal writing. The nineteenth century saw composers working, first, to expand tonality, and in the end seeking to avoid it. The romantic period, characterized by the late work of Beethoven and such harmonic styles as are found in the compositions of Chopin, Wagner, Franck, Strauss, and Debussy, was the culmination of the system developed by Rameau. As we move away from the romantic period into the twentieth century we discover, among certain composers and theorists, a widespread movement to disestablish—perhaps we should say further disestablish—Rameau's system of functional harmony. It is therefore rather ironic that many jazzmen who consider jazz to be "new" music and classical music to be "old" music choose to remain harmonically in the last quarter of the nineteenth century, with an occasional exploratory dip into modal harmonies.

The harmonies of early jazz are much the same as those found in a large number of eighteenth-century dances and nineteenth-century evangelical hymns. The early jazzplayer accepted the harmonies of his musical environment and went on to develop what he was mainly concerned with: melody and rhythm. Since the development of any art proceeds slowly, it is no surprise to find that most jazzmen still rate harmony after melody and rhythm. They are concerned with harmony, but not in the same creative sense that they are concerned with melody and rhythm. Aside from harmony's function as a base for their improvisation, most jazzmen believe that harmony serves best when it is strengthening and maintaining the key they are playing in.

Except for relatively few jazzmen, the approach to jazz harmony has been naive in the extreme. After years of hard use by jazz composers, the primary triads, diminished seventh chords, and various chords of the seventh were expanded into a "modern" jazz harmony that is still being purveyed in little pamphlets at anywhere from two to five dollars each. (These works, originally available in the early fifties, are unfortunately still in stock in some music stores during the seventies, and can be quite misleading to aspiring students.) For example, Johnny Warrington's twenty-four-page *Modern Harmony* (published in 1948 by Bregman, Vocco, and Conn) informs the anxious student about the whole-tone scale and its augmented chords; chords with added notes ("Adding notes to major and dominant seventh chords provides one of the most modern devices in scoring for large dance bands"); parallelism; the modes ("The six principal Greek modal scales form the basis of our present-day harmony. The purpose of this study is to show how they can be applied in a modern manner"). The last statement is followed by a two-page study. The remaining sixteen pages cover, in the language of the author's subject headings: "Superstructure Chords," "Contrapuntal Writing," "The Minor Dominant Seventh Chord," "Impressionistic Motion of Chords," "Chromatic Alteration of Scale Chords," "False Progression of Dominant Chords," "Tonic Harmonization of Scales," "Free Chords," "Dissonant Seventh Chords," "Chord Substitutions," "Complete Modern Reharmonization."

Until one thinks about it, there seems little harm in this sort of thing, but its pretentiousness is certain to repel some students and discourage others. It is true that the author is not a jazz composer, and his pamphlet does not emphasize any appeal it may have for jazz students. But what innocent jazz student would not be attracted by its title? There are too many pamphlets of this kind. Perhaps some of them serve a good purpose, but one wishes that their authors had more regard for the printed word. It is one thing for a jazzman to be inarticulate—he has tradition on his side—but an inarticulate author writing a jazz teaching manual is quite another thing. Usually the musical examples are clear enough, and if the student can avoid reading the text he is less likely to be confused. A good example of ambiguous language and confused terminology, in an otherwise quite clear musical context, can be seen in Van Alexander's *The Be-bop Style,* published in 1949 by Criterion Music Corporation with endorsements attributed to Pete Rugolo, Miles Davis, Babs Gonzales, and Tadd Dameron. On page 2 Alexander writes:

Be-bop may be analyzed by these steps:

1. The melodic framework (tune) which helps determine the character, mood, and tempo.

2. The harmonic sequences, which give the key to the improvisation.

3. The rhythmic pattern of the original theme sets the new structure. While bebop is basically four, it is usually an implied beat and is usually sparked with counter rhythms by the piano and bass. It is also colored by sporadic beats and chords.

4. The instrumentation of the performers, which determine the color.

Probably the worst confusion of terms arises out of step number two. Obviously what is meant is not "the harmonic sequences," but the harmonic *progressions;* and to use "key," a term of technical significance, in a loose, popular sense, can only heighten the confusion. (If the ultraconservatism of jazz harmony could be attributed to any single compositional device, the sequence would surely rate as high as any. The sequence, not a bad thing in itself, is too often the method taught by the pamphlets in question. Given a one- or two-bar cliché, the unimaginative composer or performer is led to believe it will gain in strength if repeated two, three, and even more times at different pitch levels. The compilers of these works were apparently unaware that a mere change of pitch or key does not enrich what may be, at best, a banal motive.)

The study of harmonic practice is the study of consonance (release from tension) and dissonance (tension). It is necessary to remember that these qualities are relative—what is dissonant in one musical style may be consonant in another. Furthermore, the question of consonance and dissonance seems to depend as much on the harmonic conditioning and experience of the listener as on scientific analysis. For most listeners, an interval of a third or a sixth is more consonant —more "pleasant," as they would put it—than an interval of a fourth or a fifth; yet, in the earliest periods of music history, fourths and fifths were considered consonant, and not until the fourteenth century were thirds so considered. Consonance and dissonance are determined by context.

In short, even among the traditionally acknowledged dissonances, there are *degrees* of dissonance. And, if there are degrees of dissonance, there may be degrees of consonance. According to one's experience, then, resolutions may be heard as a lesser degree of consonance or a lesser degree of dissonance. Prearranged combinations of sound (chords) are not intended to stand by themselves, but rather are conceived by most jazzmen as a foundation on which to build melodies, and, when melodies are not made up entirely of chord tones, their disagreement with the harmony must be justified according to the harmonic style of a particular jazz period. Walter Piston, in his *Harmony*, puts it this way:

> The question of deciding whether a tone is a chord factor or a nonharmonic tone comes often to the fore in the study of harmony. More important than the decision of this question is the appreciation of both sides of the issue. Let us repeat that all chords are the product of the momentary coincidence of melodic parts. A vertical cross-section of the music at a given instant is undeniably a chord, but we notice that some of these chords are constantly recurring under different conditions whereas others seem to depend on some other simpler chord for their existence.[5]

Before going on, it may be helpful here to show the most common chords and symbols, as the jazzman sees them. The lowest note in each instance is middle C; the "m" stands for minor; the numbers stand for intervals; the + stands for augmented, and the [0] for diminished. The sounds can easily be tried out at the keyboard, even by nonperformers.

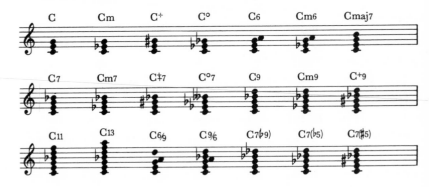

Chords, as we know, are derived from scales, and scales are arbitrary successions of horizontal intervals. It has been the practice during the history of tonal music to select one scale tone, called the tonic, or first degree, and to use it as a base to which all the other tones must find relationship. When this is accomplished according to prescribed rules, tonality is established—that is, the music has a tonal center and a key. While scales may be constructed on any number of tones in any intervallic relationship, only three of the scales that have come down to us have had wide and important use: the pentatonic (a five-tone scale), the diatonic (a seven-tone scale), and the chromatic (a twelve-tone scale). And, of course, the modal scales. A form of the diatonic is the basis for most jazz through the sixties. In addition, early jazz theorists spoke of a "blues scale," shown below.

The "blues scale" is a reasonable enough term for this scale, but in addition the minor third degree and minor seventh degree, shown

in the illustration, are often referred to as "blue notes," a less happy term. Marshall Stearns, in an attempt to merge the blue note and the blues scale, refers to them in combination as "blue tonality." [6] The blues scale, as we have mentioned, may be a reasonable term, but it is not a correct one. It is not truly a special ten-tone scale, as some writers have suggested, or even a nine-tone scale. If we accept the harmonic practice of composers in the past, it becomes evident that, in the blues scale, we are dealing with a simple diatonic scale, subject to the same harmonic and melodic manipulations as any diatonic scale. The problem posed by the blues scale is based, I believe, on the seemingly ambiguous intervals between the C, or root, and the third and seventh scale degrees.

It is easy to lose sight of the fact that the practice of jazz preceded the construction of the blues scale. Early jazz players probably saw little distinction between major and minor modes and used the major and minor thirds interchangeably. In any event, if the blues scale needs further to be characterized, it would not be improper to refer to it as being in the major-minor mode, or, more simply, bi-modal.

5

understanding
style

IN SOMETHING LIKE EIGHTY YEARS, jazz has divided itself into four significant periods encompassing a number of styles. A full understanding of the evolution of jazz from 1900 to the present time is possible only through a careful analysis of the characteristic style in each period. Jazz, as well as all other music, can only be properly understood in relation to its historical and stylistic development. We might add that one cannot understand the development of a style unless one is willing to study the various theoretical aspects of jazz, or at least to be aware of their existence. Theory attempts to provide the technical reasons for music's sounding as it does, and helps illuminate the fundamental qualities that characterize a musical style. Those who wish simply to enjoy jazz, their favorite jazzmen playing their favorite pieces, may of course continue to do so without compunction. The study of theory, however, is essential to those who wish to understand the musical history of jazz or any other music.

A musical period may extend over many years, or even centuries, and during one period there may be numerous changes in the music, the manner in which it is played, and so forth. How, then, is it decided when one period ends and another begins? In the broadest view the periods were distinguished when the music being composed and performed was so "new" that current writers and critics apparently felt compelled to say so. This wholesale critical phenomenon, in classical music, occurred once every three hundred years, starting with Guido d'Arezzo's introduction of the four-line staff in the year 1000. Approximately three hundred years later, composers thought of their music as new and music before 1300 as old (*ars nova* as against *ars antiqua*). Around 1600, Italian composers, prompted in part by the title of a published volume of music called *Nuove musiche*, broke from the traditional "old" music and went on to compose thousands of "new" operas, oratorios, and cantatas that are now considered old by those who around 1900 decided that old music had had its day, particularly old romantic music. About 1925, or about the time Louis Armstrong was contemplating something "new," someone in Germany designated the period from 1900 to that time as the period of *Neue Musik*. And so it goes.

To regard the eighty-year history of jazz as a miniature history of music in general is, of course, an oversimplification. It is true that jazz, like classical music, has gone through a number of "periods" in its relatively short span, but only time can tell whether the various kinds of jazz represent true periods or are only a number of jazz styles that may in the future all turn out to belong to one or two periods.

Each of the so-called new-music periods may be considered a musical and historical point of departure. Each new-music period fostered lesser periods—identified mainly by terms borrowed from poetry, painting, and architecture—which, in turn, resulted in an array of musical styles, many of which are still practiced, at least in part. For our purposes the periods of music may be enumerated as follows: the Middle Ages (600–1450), the Renaissance (1450–1600), the Baroque era (1600–1750), the Classic era (1750–1825), the Romantic era (1825–1900), the Modern era (1900–   ). As we know, each period embraced many styles, and jazz has come under certain influences from a number of them, particularly the harmonic and contrapuntal style of the baroque period as characterized by the music of J. S. Bach, and the impressionistic style of the romantic period as characterized by the music of Debussy. The special influences of various periods and styles on jazz will be discussed more specifically in the chapters devoted to each jazz period. For the present, we need only discuss briefly what we shall call the four main jazz periods.

Until time has made sharper distinctions among jazz styles and periods, we prefer to think of jazz as having four main periods: the New Orleans period (the name is a useful one; it is *not*, however, a geographical distinction), which starts about 1900 and ends about 1926; the Pre-Swing period, which continues to about 1934; the Swing period, which continues until about 1945; and the Modern period, extending into the sixties and seventies. The dates are, of course, approximate, and there is always an expected overlap when one is distinguishing periods. The New Orleans period contained the earliest jazz, a music that was to attain its characteristic form and content, its characteristic style and breadth, in the early twenties with the work of King Oliver and his Creole Jazz Band. Before the first World War jazz was embryonic and, while deserving of careful study in its own right, must not be confused with the music it became. (Some writers have labeled this early jazz "archaic," "primitive," or "pre-classic.") The earliest years are important historically, but artistically the peak of the New Orleans period must be sought in the early twenties. I believe that the jazz of this time characterizes the New Orleans period, and this style is known as New Orleans style. (The so-called Dixieland style and Chicago style are, in the main, other names for New Orleans style; specifically, Dixieland is New Orleans style imitated by white musicians, and Chicago style is New Orleans style as performed by white musicians in Chicago immediately before and after the first World War.)

The Jazz Age—F. Scott Fitzgerald's term—saw, in its second half, a flowering of jazz characterized by the solos of Louis Armstrong and such exponents of *le jazz hot* as Duke Ellington and Fletcher Henderson; the most distinctive jazz of 1927 to 1934 is called the pre-swing style, and is the style of a transitional period. The characteristic music of the decade 1935–45, as performed by such jazzmen as Benny Goodman and Count Basie, is called swing style. The characteristic style of the middle forties and fifties must encompass both bop and cool jazz. The men of bop and cool, established historically, will include such names as Charlie Parker, Dizzy Gillespie, Miles Davis, and Thelonious Monk. The styles and movements of the sixties and seventies—called variously third stream, the new thing, new wave, free jazz, jazz-rock—are not all firmly established as yet. There seems little question, however, that the names of John Lewis, John Coltrane, Ornette Coleman, and Charlie Mingus will hold high positions in future evaluations of jazz style.

In any discussion of jazz styles, one is bound to omit the names of some jazzmen and include others; there may be only subjective reasons for these omissions and inclusions. Even Leonard Feather, in the exhaustive biographical section in his *Encyclopedia of Jazz*, and Panassié and Gautier, in their *Guide to Jazz*, were compelled to omit the names of certain jazzmen, besides devoting more space to some than to others. The task of comparing the number of words devoted to various jazzmen would seem to be a futile one, nevertheless one does notice obvious relationships. For example, the *Guide* (English edition published 1956) devotes ten columns to Armstrong (about 200 words to the column), two columns to Goodman, and a half column to Parker; the *Encyclopedia* (1955 edition) devotes three columns to Armstrong (about 1,350 words to the column), two and a half columns to Goodman, and one and a half to Parker. It is plain that the encyclopedists agreed that Armstrong, Goodman, and Parker were significant jazzmen historically and musically, perhaps even in that order. On the other hand, when the *Guide* devotes half a column to Frank "Big Boy" Goodie, who receives no mention in the *Encyclo-*

pedia, it seems reasonable to assume that Big Boy Goodie is a historical figure whose artistic contributions to jazz are either questionable or unknown to Leonard Feather, this last being a surmise not readily acceptable. (Goodie was a member of the original Tuxedo Orchestra who afterward spent most of his life playing in Europe.)

When one sets out to enumerate jazzmen, of whatever caliber, there are likely to be not only omissions but unfortunate comparisons. In any consideration of the jazzmen who were responsible for bringing a style to its peak, there are bound to be those transitional figures who, with their feet in two styles so to speak, never become as famous as those who make an abrupt entry onto the jazz scene. Both types are hard to rate: the transitional figure often spends himself without ever achieving the fame that may rightly be his, while the true value of the jazz star may be lost in the dazzling brightness of his publicity. The most difficult men to rate are those who are considered dyed-in-the-wool jazzmen by some and out-and-out businessmen by others—the men who have sought to reconcile the commercial and artistic sides of jazz. Many of these figures were men with an eye to popular acceptance who came onto the jazz scene in the thirties and forties when, for the first time in the history of jazz, little distinction could be made between what was popular and what was jazz. Stan Kenton is such a figure. The Kenton band at the peak of its popularity produced a sound, a big-band sound, unique for its time, that was the logical outcome of the big-band jazz of the Goodman era. The ultimate weakness in Kenton's position was brought about not because he helped create a sound identifiable as "Kenton," but rather because he did not continue to develop. Early in his career he discovered a formula for big-band jazz that turned out to be commercially successful and, despite numerous financial and artistic setbacks through the years, continued to promote and sponsor a type of big-band jazz that during the sixties and seventies became only curious and unprovocative.

Kenton is considered by some to be the outstanding exponent of what was called progressive jazz; André Hodeir, the distinguished jazz writer, listed Kenton and Brubeck as the leaders of progressive jazz. Unquestionably, Kenton and Brubeck have had considerable influence, but on whom? I believe the answer will have to be recorded in the social history of jazz rather than in the musical history. (See also the discussion of the stage-band phenomenon in our final chapters.) If jazzmen had been as eager to acknowledge the influence of Kenton and Brubeck as the public was to acknowledge their impact, Kenton's and Brubeck's positions in jazz history would be as secure as Goodman's or Tatum's.

In selecting the names of a few jazzmen as representatives of the styles in the chapters to follow, my intent is to hold up to the light those who have made artistically significant contributions to jazz, particularly those who, while perhaps not always the creators of a style, nevertheless brought a style to its peak by molding its characteristics into a unified whole, thereby communicating the meaning of the style in its highest sense.

Style, according to the *American College Dictionary,* is "a particular, distinctive or characteristic mode or form of construction in any art or work." One of our tasks is to isolate the distinctive qualities of each style and to group those qualities which will then characterize or denote this style. This backward-forward-backward practice usually ends when we arrive at what may be considered a logical classification and terminology—in our case, for example, "New Orleans," "preswing," and so forth. The serious seeker after style is not always completely satisfied with this or that classification, and, even after apparently accepting it, continues searching for more logical ways to classify the material, perhaps with the hope of eventually creating, if not simpler classifications, at least self-explanatory ones.

Athanasius Kircher, a seventeenth-century archeologist with an interest in musical styles, believed that styles were best classified in three main orders: individual style, national style, and functional style. A contemporary illustration of Kircher's classification might be: individual style—jazz as played by Gillespie or Armstrong; national (regional) style—jazz as played in Kansas City or Los Angeles; and functional style—jazz as played by big dance bands or small pit bands, or jazz-as-protest groups. In his last order Kircher enumerated nine styles, such as dance, theater, and others. Later, the Italians also classified music according to three styles: church, chamber, and theater. Their criteria, however, were not functional in Kircher's sense, but rather were technical, dealing with such musical aspects as harmony and rhythm. The two views combined make up the modern view of musical style.

Some jazz writers continued to classify all jazz as either solo improvisations or collective improvisations, while others, seeking broader relationships, found reason in "hot" jazz and "sweet" jazz—the hot jazz presumably encompassing the solo and collective improvisations and allowing room for whatever it was the classifier considered "sweet." In the thirties certain enthusiastic if somewhat inept classifiers found a solution in "white" jazz and "Negro" jazz—a distinction some made even more strongly in the sixties and seventies. A system of classification by Aaron Copland, however, deserves wider attention. Concerned with clarifying the confusion, he wrote in the *New York Times* for December 25, 1949:

It might be helpful, therefore, to start by trying to bring some order into the apparent chaos of contemporary composition by dividing its leading exponents according to the relative degree of difficulty in the understanding of their respective idioms:

Very Easy: Shostakovitch and Khatchaturian, Francis Poulenc, Erik Satie, early Schoenberg and Stravinsky, Vaughan Williams, Virgil Thomson.

Quite Approachable: Prokofiev, Roy Harris, Villa-Lobos, Ernest Bloch, William Walton.

Fairly Difficult: late Stravinsky, Béla Bartók, Chavéz, Milhaud, William Schuman, Honegger, Britten, Hindemith, Walter Piston.

Very Tough: middle and late Schoenberg, Alban Berg, Anton Webern, Varèse, Krenek, Charles Ives, Roger Sessions.[1]

It is worth noting that a number of composers in Copland's "very tough" category became for the classical music public in the seventies only "fairly difficult." Compared to certain composers of the seventies —late Cage, Babbitt, Stockhausen, and others—Alban Berg and Charles Ives would have to be considered only "fairly difficult." In any case, studying the categories above, we may properly ask, What makes Milhaud or William Schuman "fairly difficult"? It is necessary at once to make it clear that Milhaud and Schuman have written compositions that range from "very easy" to "very tough"—Milhaud a considerable amount in all categories; however, the music we think of most often as being Milhaud's or Schuman's, the music that is *characteristic* Milhaud and Schuman, is fairly difficult for the layperson to understand. Granted, Copland's distinctions may be considered arbitrary by some; nevertheless, the principle on which they are based has much merit. Returning to the principal question, we may again ask, What makes certain music easy and other music difficult? The answer must be sought in the technical musical aspects of dissonance, texture, structure, and the many others that in their totality make up the form and content of style.

Barry Ulanov, in his *History of Jazz in America,* sets out to analyze three general standards of evaluation—freshness, profundity, and skill —in short, a plea for an analysis of the qualities that make up a style.[2] Once the spotlight is turned on notes and chords and rhythms and the entire method of developing musical materials, we can then proceed logically to weld the technical style criteria to the functional. When this is accomplished, the style of a jazzman will be based first on what he plays, not on what he would like to play or where he plays or with whom he travels. Properly speaking, it is only after an analysis of the jazzman's characteristic handling of musical materials that other, functional, style points may be studied; characterizing the musician as a player of ballads or jump tunes, or as hailing from Copenhagen, has no immediate bearing on the question of his style, while his use of the appoggiatura or his avoidance of diminished seventh chords does.

In 1911 Guido Adler, the founder of the modern system of style criticism and analysis, presented the basic principles of style criticism in his book *Style in Music.* "What determines style?" he asked. And his answer includes melody, tonality, harmony, polyphony, thematic material, timbre, rhythm, and analysis of form and content. "By considering the reciprocation and correlation of the analyses of form and content," he continued, "we arrive at authentic style-criticism of a higher order. . . ."[3]

Much jazz criticism of the past seems to have been more concerned with individual style traits than with general characteristics. This has been particularly true among writers who, week after week, were compelled to analyze subjectively, for the edification of the jazz fan, the playing of individuals. Even so, occasional notices implied, correctly, that an individual's particular style traits were the property of others as well. No creative jazzman likes to think he is consciously borrowing or imitating another jazzman's style; nevertheless, at any given time there is a common cache of chords, chord progressions, ornaments, and a host of other musical properties available to all, and it is the frequency with which these materials are used by all that identifies them as general characteristics; but it is the manner in which they are used by the individual that identifies his individual style.

The real error arises when a writer's view of the general characteristics of a group is obstructed by the height of one great jazzman. The writer's intention is commendable; he wishes everyone had the genius of the genius. The fact is, however, that a genius is unique: there is only one Armstrong, one Tatum, one Parker, one Coltrane. The genius is ahead of his time, and it is unfair—incorrect, in fact— to compare his style traits with those of jazzmen playing characteristically for their time. However, the history of jazz shows that imaginative jazzmen eventually do catch up to the genius—that is, they begin to understand what he had in mind, what he was trying to do, and they set about achieving the same end, and from this moment starts the development of the characteristic jazz of the period. Sometimes the genius goes on to greater accomplishments, and the growth of a characteristic jazz is halted; sometimes he is cut off by sickness or death, and the jazz he originated seems to shoot up as if a great pressure had been removed, and for a time jazzmen seem to be clambering over each other to complete the structure that is to be a characteristic jazz until another jazzman, a genius, perhaps, breaks loose and the whole process is again set in motion.

The complete story of jazz style is to be found not only by analyzing the individual styles of such jazzmen as Count Basie, Sidney Bechet, Cootie Williams, Dizzy Gillespie, and Ornette Coleman, but by analyzing and isolating those characteristics of their individual styles that eventually passed into the jazz mainstream. Aside from the pleasure the individual may give to listeners, his eventual position is usually determined by his influence on his less gifted colleagues. The combined influences of the people at the top help determine the general characteristics of a style. Certain ones, like Armstrong, may be the fountainhead in their time; others, like Basie or Gillespie, may contribute a rhythmic idea or a melodic idea that swirls around the mainstream until it is absorbed by the general flow. So-called mainstream jazz is neither better nor worse than old-time jazz or jazz of the future. It is simply the characteristic jazz of its time, moving along with the current now smoothly, now roughly, occasionally listlessly but always with direction, however imperceptible it may be at the moment. It is the mainstream jazz that must inevitably be the point of departure for new styles, and to understand the evolution of style one must stand in midstream, so to speak, and look both ways.

Style criticism or analysis, as we know, must begin with the individual. Analysis with respect to the individual can be criticism in its highest form provided the investigator's study does not degenerate into a recounting of the subject's love life, what he thinks of Raquel Welch, of the Dallas Cowboys, of pizza. This is not to say that biographical studies are something less than style studies; on the contrary, they can be wonderfully illuminating in the hands of writers who seek to present their subjects as human being and artist. But we are a little ahead of ourselves here.

The immediate problem is one of selecting individuals for style study, and here we have a choice of two types: the innovator or the representative. In instances in which the innovator is also an outstanding representative of the style, the choice may be a simple one; on the other hand, a strong representative of a given style can be a satisfactory subject for style analysis even if style innovation is not his forte. It is not necessary for a jazzman to help originate a style in order to be highly creative within it. Charlie Mingus and Bill Evans illustrate this. Restricting oneself to study the work of Armstrong, Ellington, Parker, Davis, and a few other innovators can lead to valuable individual style criticisms. However, such studies must then be used as a basis for wider studies of the characteristic jazz styles.

Furthermore, it is likely that an innovator's reputation may be based not on any sustained creativity, but on only one invention. This is not to disparage such an invention, but merely to point out that perhaps more emphasis should be placed on the invention and less on the inventor. Certainly this has been the case in classical music where, in the early days of twelve-tone composing, Schoenberg dominated the entire genre. His influence was so great and his utterances seemed so profound that studies, writings, and analyses of and about Schoenberg became required reading for all conscientious composers. As time went on, however, it became apparent that many were to surpass Schoenberg in the handling of his own technique—Berg and Webern, for example—and today Schoenberg's name is identified not so much with the personality that was his as with the style he initiated.

In one sense, what is true of Schoenberg is true of Armstrong. There are many who believe that Armstrong's rise and influence ended in the early thirties, after which he went into a decline, except for rare flashes of the qualities that made him the best-known name in jazz. At his peak he was an outstanding representative of New Orleans style and a major pre-swing innovator; in addition to his musical talents, he was endowed with an unusually robust personality. Armstrong's personality remained as radiant in the sixties and seventies as it ever was, and it was this quality that kept him in the public eye until his death.

In the days before mass-communication facilities and voyages into space, there was a school of thought that believed that there was a proper time for discovery and invention, and that when this time was at hand different inventors would be found at work on the same invention in different places, each unaware of the others. This theory probably had a measure of truth. The fact is, there are few innovations that are the sole property of one person. This is particularly true in jazz: no one man was responsible for New Orleans jazz—despite Jelly Roll Morton's exaggerated, good-natured claims—or for swing, or bop, or cool jazz, or jazz-rock. There are, of course, those to whom writers have attributed the discovery of these styles, and there is a measure of truth in this also. As we know, a style evolves; it may receive impetus from the contributions of an individual or, as is more likely, from a number of individuals, each aware of the others' work, reacting to the others' intention, and, in turn, being reacted upon. Those jazzmen who received their early musical training in the marching bands of the 1890s and early 1900s—Buddy Bolden, Freddie Keppard, and Joe Oliver, for example—learned something from the straightforward rhythmic and harmonic style of the march as utilized by the men to whom the march and marching band were the culmination of musical training and thought. Bolden (1878–1907), to use one example, picked up whatever musical influence there was in New Orleans, and apparently influenced many of the next generation of jazzmen who heard him. The evidence of his influence offered by those who heard him play around the turn of the century is conflicting and unreliable, to say the least; however, the reports seem to agree that he played an exceptionally "loud" horn for his time.

Later in the century, evidence of the influence individual jazzmen may have had on their colleagues is easier to find. The earliest jazz recordings, while incapable of faithfully reproducing the quality of a jazzman's tone either in a solo or in ensemble, nevertheless were able to establish, reliably and as never before, who were the innovators and who were the imitators. And from this point on the contributions of Armstrong and the subsequent emergence of the solo improvisation as the first real break with the past are available for all to follow. The part played by Fletcher Henderson in the evolution of swing, for example, and by Duke Ellington in the evolution of jazz orchestration, may also be followed. Goodman, whose discipline and dedication brought a style to its peak; Basie, who managed to remain distinctive while those about him were being nudged into commonplaces; Tatum, Coleman Hawkins, Gillespie, Parker, Miles Davis, John Coltrane, Ornette Coleman, and many more jazzmen whose influence is solidly established—the work of all of these is available for everyone to follow and study.

Valuable deductions and contributions in the study of jazz may come as a result of comparing individual styles: the harmonic style of Tatum, say, compared to the harmonic style of Thelonious Monk; the use of the saxophone section in Ellington's band compared to its use in Lunceford's; the degree of contrapuntal independence in Gerry Mulligan's duet performances compared to that in the Modern Jazz Quartet. These and similar comparisons can provide wide areas for study and exploration, and by exposing the strengths and weaknesses in individual styles such investigations can become the foundation for broader, more comprehensive studies of entire periods and their characteristic styles.

There are, of course, other kinds of studies, nonmusical or, rather, nontechnical studies—what we may call jazz studies, studies that grow out of a writer's desire to explain what Adler called "the flowering of artistic accomplishment." Style criticism with respect to place comes under this category. The state of jazz in a nation, a state, a city, a district may be studied in the light of the people and the language peculiar to the region. The relationship of the jazzman to the general citizen may be investigated where the similarities and differences in physical and intellectual environment bear on the creation of jazz. Political events may also be studied for their influence on jazz. What, we might ask, were the consequences of the opening of the Storyville district, of its closing? What influence did the Pendergast regime have on jazz in Kansas City? What was the state of jazz before and after World War I, World War II, the Korean war, the Vietnamese war? How was jazz affected by Prohibition, the Depression? The necessities of local demand may prove upon study and synthesis to be not unique, but part of a larger scheme. What historical events may have had a peculiar influence on one jazz style and perhaps not on another? What general educational facilities are available to the jazzman in some regions and not in others? To what extent is jazz self-taught? What have been the influences of private jazz schools, jazz courses, and even jazz degrees in higher education?

In what way has the course of jazz been affected by music publishers, instrument manufacturers, and public school administrators? To what extent has jazz been influenced by one-night stands, the death of vaudeville, the Carnegie Hall concerts, the summer festivals, Jazz at the Philharmonic, the jazz repertory companies? To what extent does the jazzman's economic condition affect the quality of his playing? What has been the influence of the musicians' union on jazz? Certainly any explanation of "the flowering of artistic accomplishment" will include studies of the position and influence of radio, the movies, television, the popular press, and the jazz fan magazines. The influence of the recording industry on jazz has been approached gingerly by a few, but much more needs to be done. There is no doubt, too, that the form of much jazz has been influenced by the time restrictions and limitations of the various sizes and speeds of records—a subject we will return to in a later chapter.

But, in the end, unless we are to be sociologists, we must realize that the kind of studies we have been speaking of cannot be considered as terminal studies; we must use these studies as a frame of reference for understanding the evolution of musical style. The leader in this, our guide so to speak, is the jazz theorist, and if we are to be led to a greater understanding of all jazz, it may be useful to look closely at the special requirements of what we might call our ideal theorist. What is his function, what does he do, how can he help us to understand?

If the critic points out that there are differences in periods, in styles, the theorist analyzes and catalogues the differences and sets up the criteria for style. The astute critic will refer to the theorist's work and use it as a basis for making critical evaluations. The imaginative theorist, it is hoped, will realize the use to which his work will be put and understand that his studies, like those of the nontechnical writers, are not intended to be terminal. He will recognize that it is proper and desirable for his work to be the point of departure for esthetic analysis, and he will hope that his work can eventually dispel the ambiguity in much critical writing. The theorist will understand that subjective writing and evaluation are necessities if jazz is to continue to flourish, and that his work can be an aid to those writers and critics who guide and mold public opinion. He can stress constantly the difference between objective and subjective evaluation, the difference between what may be artistically significant and what may be historically significant.

In the past jazzmen and certain critics have tended to confuse a jazz player's style with his excellence according to their personal taste and preference. This is a natural and understandable error that, unfortunately, leads only to misunderstanding and puzzlement. The theorist will emphasize that a statement such as Ellington's "Jelly Roll played piano like one of those high school teachers in Washington; as a matter of fact, high school teachers played better jazz" [4] is a personal and subjective evaluation that may have little to do with whether Jelly Roll actually played that way or not.

The jazz of any period needs critical comment and evaluation, but criticism must be based on something more than personal preference or personal opinion. The jazz fan who prefers jazz-rock to the third stream need not justify his (or her) taste; it is a choice for which he need not apologize. The professional jazz writer who prefers jazz-rock to the third stream is, however, in a different position. While he has as much right to his opinion as the jazz fan, he has the responsibility of justifying his taste if he is going to impose it on impressionable, susceptible readers whose taste is perhaps in the formative stage. It is obvious that Ellington's opinion of Jelly Roll Morton's playing would have had considerable weight with many who were faithful fans of Ellington's music, and it is likely they would have accepted his view without question. However, it must be remembered that it is not Ellington's point of view that is in question, nor his influence on others; what is in question is the method by which he arrived at his conclusion and the method by which his followers may have arrived at the same conclusion. The function of a critic—and when a man of Ellington's position makes a public statement on jazz he is a critic —ought to be to teach, to persuade, and to encourage the jazz public, lay and professional alike, to study jazz, to explore it, to become acquainted with its rich history, its various styles, and the contributions of individual jazzmen old and new. In order to make pertinent critical judgments one must listen not only to the words of those who have the public's ear, but above all to the music under discussion, for it is only by listening that one may arrive at sound reasons for one's preferences. This is what Schoenberg meant in his *Style and Idea*, when he said: "Yes, the role of memory in music evaluation is more important than most people realize. It is perhaps true that one starts to understand a piece only when one can remember it at least partially." [5]

It is the responsibility of the theorist—and, by extension, of the critic—to impress upon the world of jazz that the quality of jazz does not depend on its chronological position in jazz history. "Art is not a question of precedence," George Antheil wrote, "but of excellence." Swing is not in itself "better" jazz than New Orleans jazz or modern jazz. (It was not too long ago that swing, itself, was "modern" jazz.) The fact is that the quality of jazz may vary within a given period and even within a given style. The history of jazz consists of countless examples of good jazz and bad jazz, and discussion and debate over the relative merits of different kinds of jazz can be healthy and rewarding provided they are based not merely on opinion but on significant analysis and interpretation.

The theorist will seek ways to define and illustrate those aspects of jazz which in the past have seemed not to be demonstrable; he will attempt to clarify problems even when they seem insoluble; he will attempt to express clearly in prose what the jazzman finds it difficult to say but nonetheless "digs." He will try gradually to bring scholarship and the general level of jazz information and communication closer together, and at the same time avoid the dangers of both intellectual and anti-intellectual snobbery, but he will be prepared to receive the rebuffs of both sides. Finally, he will be as convinced of his position and the importance of his work as the jazz connoisseurs are of theirs, and he will proceed with his work according to his disposition—nimbly or cautiously, hopefully or apprehensively, humbly or arrogantly, conservatively or radically. As serious students of jazz, perhaps the foregoing is not within the reach of most of us, but it is surely something we can all aspire to, if not always successfully, at least with style.

6

New Orleans
style

(Overleaf) *Louis Armstrong*

THERE IS SUFFICIENT EVIDENCE TO INDICATE THAT THE STYLE WE KNOW as New Orleans is more directly connected with military band music of the late nineteenth century than with any other single source. From shortly after the Civil War to the end of the century the United States stood in the front rank of military music, and there was scarcely a village or a town whose musicians did not come under its influence. In the 1890s the band of John Philip Sousa, for example, played Fayetteville, North Carolina, the St. Louis Exposition, and the Cotton States Exposition. "In 1899," Sousa wrote in his autobiography, *Marching Along*, "our tour stretched from coast to coast and from the St. Lawrence to the Gulf." [1]

Sousa's band was the most popular military-style American band in history, but Patrick Gilmore's band set an early precedent. Gilmore, born in Dublin in 1829, went to Canada with an English band, and organized his own band in Massachusetts in 1859. During the Civil War he and his band served in a Massachusetts regiment. In 1864 he was bandmaster in the federal army in New Orleans. Richard Franko Goldman, in *The Concert Band*, tells us, "His first immense festival took place in New Orleans in 1864, where he celebrated the inauguration of Governor Hahn with a chorus of 5,000 adults and children, a band of 500, a huge trumpet and drum corps, and lots of artillery." [2] In the 1870s Gilmore and his men traveled throughout the United States, often playing "When Johnny Comes Marching Home Again," his best-known march.

An incident that took place in 1861, shortly after the Civil War began, illuminates certain aspects of military band practice and its probable influence on the pioneers of jazz. The story, recounted by Louis C. Elson in *The History of American Music*, concerns the origin of the Civil War march we know as "Glory Hallelujah":

["Glory Hallelujah"] was begun as a hymn-tune in Charleston, South Carolina. . . . The song was used at many a Southern camp-meeting before the war, and was also employed in many of the colored congregations. It even made its way into the Methodist hymnals at the North.

. . . We therefore find "Glory Hallelujah" closely entwined with the history of the Twelfth Massachusetts Regiment, as the following (gathered by the author from Captain Henry J. Hallgreen and other officers of the regiment) will clearly show.

One day, while the regiment was still at Fort Warren, Captain Hallgreen heard two new recruits from Maine, in the throes of homesickness, most mournfully singing the hymn, "Say, Brothers, will you meet us?" He was struck by the melody, and taught it to some of the "Tigers." It spread like wild-fire, and at once became a camp tune. As there was no rhyme or complex construction to the words, the men soon found they could add their own improvisations to the tune, a fact which made it all the more popular. Meanwhile Gilmore, who frequently came to the fort with his band, caused his men to "vamp" the tune (that is, to improvise harmonies to it), and often accompanied the singing of it.[3]

This example of the practice of improvising harmonies with band instruments precedes by twenty years, at least, the work of such famous New Orleans pioneer groups as the Olympia Band, the Eagle Band, the Imperial Band, and the Superior Band, not only in spirit but in instrumentation as well. There is little doubt that the standard New Orleans instrumentation and its function have their foundation in the last strain of band marches where characteristically the melody is carried by the cornets or trumpets against a countermelody in the low brasses and a florid embellishment in the high woodwinds. The most famous of the New Orleans marches is Porter Steele's "High Society," in Alphonse Picou's treatment, while Sousa's "The Stars and Stripes Forever" is the most famous of the standard marches; it is not difficult to hear the relationship between the treatment of the last strain in these two examples, and many other similar ones. Picou's clarinet solo in "High Society," however, must not be considered typical of the technical ability of early jazzmen. Picou was a trained musician. In Alan Lomax's *Mister Jelly Roll,* Picou tells us, ". . . my father did not know *I* had taken lessons from a flute player at the French Opera House. I did not explain him nothing, but one time I just sat down and played *Cavalleria Rusticana.*" [4] As a descendant of early French settlers, a so-called "Creole," Picou had certain advantages not available to the freedmen who flocked to the cities and river towns after the war, for Creoles had many of the privileges of the whites. Alan Lomax tells us that "cheap instruments left behind by the Confederate Army bands, filled the pawnshops. Creole freedmen could afford to buy instruments and pay for music lessons as few other Southern Negroes could. Almost any Creole oldtimer can recall his childhood musical instruction—given in the strictest style of the French Academy." [5]

It is interesting to compare Picou's conception of "High Society" with the "Gettysburg March" as performed by Kid Rena's Jazz Band in a recording made in New Orleans in 1940, in which Picou plays clarinet in this characteristic Civil War march. The impression one has on listening to the "Gettysburg March" is of its authenticity—the small-town-band spirit that can only be manifested by exuberant amateurs. One can see the parade of half a dozen players, inspired by the jaunty beat of the snare, stepping along the cobbled street. Picou's fluffed notes, Ed Robinson's stylish trombone, the straight trumpet of Kid Rena, the rousing forte of the last strain, and the delightful innocence of the last two bars all seem to give off the light of truth.

But their playing is not the source of New Orleans style; it is more likely once removed from the source. It is the second step; the first is the performances of marching bands and performers that inspired imitation. Kid Rena's performance is an imitation that has become, for some people, the real thing. It is possible that these people are correct; in the process of jazz evolution who is to say, once imitation has set in, what is being imitated? We know that many Creole musicians received sound musical training; we know, too—if Picou may be used as an example—that imitation by trained musicians is often difficult to distinguish from its source; we also know that, at a certain time after the war, Creole musicians played with relatively untrained black musicians who must certainly have been influenced by the Creole technique and knowledge of instruments. It would seem, therefore, that the pioneers derived much of their manner of playing and the major part of their instrumentation from military bands.

The immediate response of many blacks to freedom was to leave the rural areas and head for the cities and river towns. In 1865 many were intent on being footloose. As they moved around the countryside they neither sought nor were interested in permanent employment, and life away from the farm held a strong attraction. Once they had reached a city they found occupation in domestic service, or frequently just loafed, seeking only those jobs that required a minimum of responsibility. The work sought was, of necessity, in keeping with an almost total lack of education; nonetheless, a number of the more persevering did manage eventually to support themselves in small business enterprises. Since they were now free, many blacks saw little reason for working six days a week when they could support themselves in the style to which they had earlier been accustomed on what they could earn in two or three days. They ate cheaply, with little variety, and usually lived in ramshackle, one-room cabins on the edge of town, or in squalid slum flats, often with six, eight, or a dozen friends and relatives. Their Christianity, as rural blacks had practiced

it, was a code of beliefs, not of morals. Being a Christian meant pray-
ing and singing in church and, when life in this world was over,
traveling to another world; life was grief and sorrow, and death was
a welcome, perhaps happy, relief. Meanwhile, they could console
themselves with recreation, a part of life for which, until emancipation, they had had little time, and to which, after emancipation, many
devoted themselves wholeheartedly. In *The Negro Freedman,* Henderson H. Donald tells us:

> It is highly probable that the great majority of the forms of recreation
> were originated by the Negroes themselves. They seemed generally to
> harmonize with the Negroes' temperament, inclinations, and peculiar
> life conditions. It should be noticed also that the recreation of the
> Negro freedmen for the most part was of the active rather than of the
> passive type. They preferred amusing themselves to being amused by
> others. In time, however, they adopted many of the forms of recreation
> prevailing in the general society.[6]

Music has always been an acceptable form of recreation, and the
postwar South apparently had almost as many bands as there were
towns—the number of bands in New Orleans alone invites special
study. The freedmen of the South—as has been pointed out by many
writers—were particularly fond of organizing and joining societies and
were never quite so happy as when they were marching in a parade,
and they could find some joy in any sort of parade. Secret societies and
marching societies (they were often, no doubt, the same) were formed
in Maryland, Virginia, District of Columbia, Florida, South Carolina,
Louisiana—in short, throughout the South. As Donald wrote: "Likewise, the Negroes of middle Georgia were particularly fond of parades,
and were constantly organizing societies. And it seemed that they did
the latter mainly to get an opportunity to march about after a fife

and drum." [7] They followed much more than "a fife and drum" when it was available, and in New Orleans, at least, instruments and subsequently players and bands were plentiful.

New Orleans became a haven for black musicians. At first, the center was the waterfront district that made up the *Vieux Carré*, the old French Quarter—an area of about thirteen blocks along the arc of the Mississippi and about eight blocks that ran uptown. Later, in the 1890s, the river town boomed and jobs along the wharves, docks, levees, and in the warehouses were plentiful, and for legions of black workers the money was good and the livin' was easy in an atmosphere of "anything goes." And now the physical manifestations of the Old Quarter's highlife—the eating, drinking, and recreational establishments—continued to spread uptown far beyond Rampart Street, which marked the boundary of the original French settlement. The growing district, tacked on to the Old Quarter, now competed with the Quarter itself.

At the behest of concerned uptown citizens, Sidney Story, one of the city's governing officials, found a way to stem the tide. In 1897, he helped establish a *legal* red-light district in the United States. By the time Storyville was disestablished in 1917 (America's entry into World War I was around the corner, and sailors from a U.S. Naval Station across the river were becoming heavily infected by the spirit of Lulu White's $40,000 Mahogany Hall, Emma Johnson's Studio, and the special joys of Basin Street), saloonkeeper Tom Anderson's *Blue Book*, a 25-cent guide to the district's sporting life, provided interested readers with a list of the names and addresses of the "Storyville 400." At its peak operation, the district boasted 200 houses of prostitution, and a wide variety of gambling halls, honky-tonks, barrel houses (where wine was sold from barrels), saloons, restaurants, hotels, gin mills, and dance halls. Altogether, an inspiring and provocative backdrop for the creation of a new jazz style, and the formation of new bands.

Even a hasty study of New Orleans bands shows an extraordinary amount of musical activity. Thumbing through jazz histories, newspapers, and volumes of reminiscences brings to light the St. Joseph Brass Band, the Imperial Band, and the Excelsior Band, all of the 1880s. (It is sometimes difficult to establish the names of the leaders in these and subsequent bands, since the bands often met without schedule for funerals and for special celebrations. Usually the leader was the contractor, as is still the case in union "pick-up" bands.) There is reason to believe, however, that Claiborne Williams led the St. Joseph Band and Immanuel Perez the Imperial Band; the Excelsior Band, which continued to flourish through the 1900s, may or may not have been led by the renowned John Robichaux—there is little question that he played in the band, at one time or another, with such pioneers as Louis and Lorenzo Tio, Picou, and Perez. Jelly Roll Morton, who didn't pass out compliments lightly, said, "John Robichaux probably had the best band in New Orleans at the time, a strictly all-reading, legitimate bunch." [8]

The 1890s saw the flourishing of such New Orleans bands as the Peerless, Indian, Columbus, and Diamond Stone; the Onward Brass Band with Perez and Joe Oliver; Adam Olivier's Band with Bunk Johnson; and, continuing through the decade, the already mentioned Excelsior Band. In the 1900s the Olympia Band was led by Freddie Keppard and had Picou and Louis "Big Eye" Nelson; the Eagle Band had Sidney Bechet, "Papa" Carey, Bunk Johnson, and, from 1907 to 1915, Keppard, who also played for a while with Bill Johnson's Original Creole Band. From 1905 to 1912 the Superior Band had Bunk Johnson, and this period also saw the ascendancy of the Magnolia

Band with Joe Oliver. An important white band of the period was "Papa" Laine's Reliance Brass Band, which included Nick LaRocca, later the leader of the Original Dixieland Jazz Band. These men and their various groups worked both in and out of Storyville—uptown, downtown, and nearby resorts.

Before the Storyville district was established in 1897, there was a much clearer distinction between bands than there was afterward. In the eighties and nineties most of the bands were just marching bands that paraded for social functions including funerals and special celebrations, and, when the celebrations called for dancing, the bands were able to provide dance music of a sort. But dance bands, of the kind that had an influence on New Orleans style, were relatively few in this period. Papa Laine is reported to have had a ragtime band in 1888, but the most important was Buddy Bolden's Ragtime Band of 1893. Bolden, who had a brass band before he had his ragtime band, was an untrained musician who played a "powerful" trumpet. He was able to draw on legitimate players for his band because New Orleans Creoles of the 1890s who earlier had practiced music as a matter of culture now needed money as badly as did the rural blacks who had come to the great port of New Orleans to work on the docks and levees. The Creoles came to Bolden, and they played his way. Wallace Collins, a New Orleans musician who claimed to have played in Bolden's Ragtime Band, told Rudi Blesh, in Blesh's *Shining Trumpets,* that Bolden's was the first band to play rags.

> To "rag" a tune, Collins says, "he'd take one note and put two or three to it. He began to teach them—not by the music—just by the head. After he'd get it down right, he'd teach the others their part.
>
> "They had lots of band fellows who could play like that after Bolden gave 'em the idea." [9]

Paul Dominguez, a New Orleans violinist, corroborated Collins' testimony when he told Alan Lomax that "Bolden cause all that. . . . He cause these younger Creoles, men like Bechet and Keppard to have a different style from old heads like Tio and Perez." [10]

While the influence of the marching band was directly responsible for the manner of performing New Orleans style, the players came to the marching band with a wealth of musical background both secular and religious. Starting with a background of West African culture, for about two centuries they had heard and made music at Saturday-night dances, weddings, baptisms, candy stews, corn shuckings, evening gatherings, picnics, parties, and funerals; they knew work songs, love songs, devil songs, jigs, quadrilles, and stomps. They had heard the folk tunes of Scotland, Ireland, and England, the art songs of Italy and Spain, the melodies of French operatic arias, and the bright tunes of minstrel shows. The heat of plantation religion brought them the spirituals based on the simple harmonies and ardent spirit of the evangelical hymn. And, above all, they knew the blues. Add to these ragtime—the notated piano music that originated in the Midwest and flourished throughout the South about the same time Storyville did (1896–1917)—and all the ingredients are gathered in. What the New Orleans bands and their immediate successors played must be sought in the conglomeration of religious, secular, notated, and improvised music.

Joseph "King" Oliver and his Creole Jazz Band brought the New Orleans style to its peak. Why Oliver's band should have been responsible for this is not difficult to understand in retrospect. By 1923, the year of the culmination of the New Orleans style, Oliver and the band members had among them all the qualities and influences of the period from the end of the Civil War to the end of the first World War. The personnel of the band—which included Louis Armstrong on cornet, Honoré Dutrey on trombone, Johnny Dodds on clarinet, Baby Dodds on drums, Bill Johnson on banjo, Lil Hardin Armstrong on piano, and of course Oliver on cornet—had participated in just about every kind of musical organization that had anything to do with the evolution of New Orleans style. The Creole musician, Dutrey, had played with Oliver's band in New Orleans. Johnny Dodds, a self-taught musician who had played with many New Orleans bands, had been in Chicago twice—once on his own and once with Oliver; both times he went back to New Orleans, and in 1920 he returned once more to Chicago to join Oliver's band. His brother, Warren "Baby" Dodds, a longtime friend and colleague of Armstrong's, had played in marching bands and in ragtime bands and had worked the Mississippi riverboats. Bill Johnson, born in 1872, was an old hand with the "spasm" instruments: harmonica, guitar, and banjo; around 1900 he took up the bass fiddle and created the organization whose name Oliver was to assume in 1920. Lil Hardin Armstong (she married Armstrong in 1924) had studied piano at Fisk University and later was a member of Freddie Keppard's band in Chicago. The history of Louis Armstrong's rise is too well-known to be recounted again here; it is sufficient to say that his experience before he joined Oliver's band included playing with marching bands, dance bands, and riverboat bands. The total experience of the Original Creole Jazz Band, in short, encompasses the history of New Orleans style specifically and early jazz in general; and it took a man of Oliver's wide experience and theretofore untapped organizational ability to weld the 1923 organization into the most important exponent of New Orleans style.

King Oliver was born in New Orleans in 1885. Little is known about his youth except that by the time he was in his early teens he was already involved in a brass band. While he may have received spasmodic instruction from any one of a dozen oldtimers, chances are that his musical education was picked up on the run or, perhaps more correctly, on the march. Soon he was sharing solo cornet honors with Perez in the Onward Brass Band. Like most of his contemporaries Oliver played music for extra money; he was regularly employed as a butler. But his outstanding work with the Eagle Band and later with the Magnolia, Olympia, and Kid Ory bands made his playing a full-time job.

By the time Storyville was closed down in 1917, King Oliver was reputed to be the best cornet player in New Orleans. Although he was playing with Kid Ory's band along with Johnny Dodds, and enjoying a reputation envied even by Louis Armstrong, the idea of leaving New Orleans and going to Chicago was in his mind. By 1918 there were two good reasons: Storyville had been closed down; and Chicago's war industries, which had absorbed tens of thousands of black workers from all over the South, seemed to have room for many more. (Between 1910 and 1920, fifty thousand blacks came to Chicago.) Long before the Storyville days, Chicago had had a reputation for bigness, wickedness, and violence. When the war in Europe began, the citizens of Chicago, tired of depression and repeated vice crusades, elected "Big Bill" Thompson, an uncommonly exuberant Republican, as their mayor. Thompson promised them a big city, and by 1922 he had given it to them. Chicago had always enjoyed the reputation of being a wide-open town with a sporting tradition, and to those who worked the shadowy side of the street Chicago had always been a sanctuary. "The sporting spirit," Lincoln Steffens said, "is the spirit of Chicago." King Oliver was obviously a man who had the sporting spirit; besides, 1918 seemed like a very good time to go to Chicago.

Once he was in Chicago, Oliver's ability enabled him to work in shifts between Lawrence Duhé's New Orleans Jazz Band and Bill Johnson's Original Creole Band, and in 1920 he took over Bill Johnson's band. About a year later he apparently found Chicago less taken with his new band than he had hoped, and off he went to California, where during the next year he played in various dance halls and night spots in San Francisco and Los Angeles. In 1922 he returned to Chicago and persuaded Armstrong to leave New Orleans to join his band, and it was at the Lincoln Gardens Cafe that the band finally hit its stride. After Oliver and Armstrong had played together for a year, there was not a jazzman in Chicago, black or white, who was not aware of the transformation that had taken place in what was now "the best band in the land," Alexander's Ragtime Band notwithstanding. The Lincoln Gardens could accommodate between six and seven hundred dancers, and the band played regularly to a capacity house. Frederick Ramsey, Jr., in *Jazzmen*, describes a typical evening at the Lincoln Gardens:

> . . . Joe tooted a few notes down low to the orchestra, stomped his feet to give the beat, turned around, and they were off on a new piece. . . . Lil Hardin bit hard on her four beats to a measure, while the deep beat of Bill Johnson's string bass and the clearly defined foundation of Baby Dodds' drum and high-toned, biting cymbal filled out the "bounce" and kept the others sweeping forward. . . . Then Joe and Louis stepped out, and one of their "breaks" came rolling out of the two short horns, fiercely and flawlessly.[11]

There has been much conjecture on the reason for the band's success in 1923. Some writers have attributed it to the social atmosphere in Chicago and have suggested that the band's music reflected the spirit of the times; others have suggested that the arrival of Armstrong provided the band with the spark it needed. There is, of course, some truth in both these conjectures. Certainly the social atmosphere of the period was friendly and encouraging, and there is little doubt that Armstrong lent a certain solidity to the ensemble. Sidney Finkelstein, in *Jazz: A People's Music,* however, points out still another aspect of the question:

> The Negro community for whom Oliver played in Chicago was different from the Negro community in New Orleans. The music that Oliver played was still New Orleans in its march tempo, its rag, blues and stomp content, its collective music making and self-absorption in the music on the part of the players; but it also reflected the new Chicago audience. The opportunity to make records, as well, induced a greater attention to technical detail and formal organization, making the music a rounded out unity with beginning, middle and end.[12]

The main clue to the truth may be in the words "formal organization." Probably of the highest significance is the fact that the band had stayed together long enough for its individual members to know each other's minds, musically speaking, and in a band where the emphasis was on playing collectively, this knowledge was all-important. Baby Dodds told Larry Gara in *Jazz Journal,* May 1955, "Those of us who worked with the King Oliver Band had known each other so long we felt that we were almost related. That outfit had more harmony and feeling of brotherly love than any I ever worked with. And playing music is just like having a home." [13]

In the postwar period Chicago was well on its way to becoming the national headquarters for jazz and aspiring jazzmen. Oliver was king, but his position was not unchallenged. Nor had he, in 1918, come into virgin territory. Perez had come to Chicago two years earlier and had operated out of the Deluxe Cafe with a band that included Sidney Bechet. And even before that, in 1915, Tom Brown, a white New Orleans trombone player who had played with Papa Laine's band, came up to Chicago with a band to take a job at the Lambs' Cafe where they had the distinction of being advertised as "Brown's Dixieland Jass Band." The following year, 1916, Alcide "Yellow" Nunez, a white New Orleans clarinet player, came up to Chicago with a band that later, after some shifting of personnel, became the Original Dixieland Jazz Band with Nick LaRocca on cornet, Larry Shields on clarinet, Eddie Edwards on trombone, Henry Ragas on piano, and Tony Sbarbaro on drums. In 1921, while Oliver was trying to impress Californians with his band, a group led by Paul Mares came up from New Orleans and opened as the Friars Society Orchestra; they later called themselves the New Orleans Rhythm Kings. While groups like these were very popular with the general public, Oliver probably worried little about them. In fact, the members of these groups after playing on their own jobs, would gather at the Lincoln Gardens to listen to the Oliver band. It is likely that the only band that caused Oliver concern—if any band in 1923 did—was "Doc" Cook's Dreamland Orchestra, mainly because Cook was using Freddie Keppard on cornet. In New Orleans Keppard had carved himself an important reputation, and some thought him far superior to both Oliver and Armstrong.

At any rate, King Oliver ruled a musical domain that included the most significant jazz players of the period. Chicago had taken up where New Orleans ended, and in 1923 the Creole Jazz Band was the royal representative of New Orleans style. Before we move on to the technical aspects and characteristics of New Orleans style, it seems proper to point out that the early Dixielanders—Tom Brown, Nick LaRocca, Larry Shields, and others—receive little attention here because, properly speaking, they helped neither to formulate nor to fix New Orleans style. Dixieland, as we have already stated, is an imitation of New Orleans style by men who, because of their race, lack the economic, social, musical, and religious background to do anything more than copy the superficial aspects of the style. These men did, however, have some small weight in the development of style during the pre-swing era, and they will be treated in more detail in the next chapter.

New Orleans style is characteristically an instrumental style performed on three or four wind instruments: one or two cornets or trumpets, a clarinet, and a trombone; and a combination of various other instruments carrying out a rhythmic function: piano, bass, drums, guitar, banjo, and tuba. Ernest Borneman, in *Harper's,* March 1947, outlines the New Orleans instrumentation and the function of the individual instruments:

> Since the elementary laws of harmony require a minimum of three notes to form a chord, the essential jazz orchestra should have three wind instruments—no less and no more; and since jazz is essentially rhythmic music, a rhythm section made up of drums, bass, and guitar or banjo should be added. The piano is optional, and the sole function of the rhythm section should be to mark the beat and the basic chords. The modern tendency of the piano, the bass, the guitar, and the tuned drums to act as solo instruments and play whole melodies on their own is abhorred by the Fundamentalists as an essentially unorganic use of jazz instrumentation. The organic use of the basic instruments calls for the cornet or trumpet to play the melodic lead, the clarinet to play a syncopated obbligato, and the trombone to fill in the harmony with propulsive glissandi.[14]

The cornet stays close to the melodic line even on those infrequent occasions when it has a solo. Although the ensemble characteristically plays collectively, and each of the three wind instruments is thought by many to have equal independence, the fact is that the clarinet and trombone play "around" the cornet. For this reason, the cornet may not stray very far; in practice New Orleans clarinetists adjust their "syncopated obbligato" according to the degree of floridness the cornetist bestows on the melody, and the trombonist also varies his bass line accordingly. The success of collective improvisation, therefore, is the responsibility of the cornetist because, in his way, he initiates the musical texture. The function of the rhythm section is to maintain a steady, unaccented 4/4 meter and occasionally to emphasize the harmonic rhythm while varying the rhythm between bar lines.

To understand the various musical textures characteristic of New Orleans style it is essential to understand the difference between polyphony and heterophony. Heterophony is a singularly rudimentary form of polyphony and not, as some writers have implied, a somehow advanced form of polyphony; it is the result of combining two instrumental parts, one of which is not a truly independent part but rather a slightly altered version of the other part. Polyphony, on the other hand, is the result of combining two or more parts of *equal* independence. Rudi Blesh, in *Shining Trumpets,* writes of "the development of polyphony into heterophony"; later on, while discussing the qualities of New Orleans style, he writes, "The three voices together create a polyphony, fervent, eloquent, and logical, in which the harmony, while felt, is never in the focus of consciousness; this polyphony veers continuously into heterophony." [15] The implication one is forced to draw from these statements is that Blesh believes heterophony is properly a higher form of polyphony—which it is not.

Heterophony—one of the principal characteristics of New Orleans style—is no better or worse than polyphony, just as New Orleans jazz is no better or worse than bop, or a major chord is no better or worse than an augmented eleventh chord. Heterophony is a primitive form of polyphony; it is a technique that has been used successfully by such sophisticated composers as Brahms and Stravinsky, and it should need no apologists. When used properly, heterophony can provide interesting textural contrasts to both homophony and polyphony. In a proper context heterophony can be an extremely useful compositional device; often it can provide a much-needed tensional transition from the accompanied solo to the polyphonic collective improvisation. The secret of its successful use lies in the dependence of one part on another. Grossman and Farrell, in their *Heart of Jazz,* seem to think that having voices with dependent parts, or in imitation of each other, would in some way diminish the New Orleans style. They write: "In New Orleans jazz, voices (instruments) rarely imitate each other, and the melodic lines are noted for their mutual contrast and independence. Thus there is greater emphasis on diversity than in most polyphony." [16] What, we may ask, is the criterion of diversity? The answer, of course, would have to be *unlikeness*—in short, the greatest possible independence between parts, the greatest possible disagreement between parts.

Certain writers have said that it requires as much musical training and intellect to listen with understanding to a New Orleans ensemble improvising collectively as it does to listen to a Bach fugue. One has only to listen to a great deal of both kinds of counterpoint to know that these writers have understated their case. It is easier to follow and understand a Bach three-part fugue (or, for that matter, any premeditated, composed fugue) than a collective improvisation because the trained composer is concerned with keeping the various strands independent of each other; he knows that comprehension comes from the listener's being able to distinguish each part from the others. Since rhythm impresses itself on most listeners before pitch, the simplest music to understand is homophonic or chordal, where, despite the use of three or more individual voices, there is really only one part, one rhythm to follow. Even in polyphonic music, in which the parts are truly independent, the listener is able to separate the parts in his mind

135

because the composer has worked to distinguish them from each other, to give each part independent melodic and rhythmic activity, direction, climax, and so forth. With concentration and experience, the strands of a composed fugue can therefore be followed with relative ease, especially if the fugue is performed by a group of instruments, each with its own tone color.

Despite the advantages of having three distinctive tone colors to distinguish its lines, New Orleans heterophony is more difficult to follow and comprehend than a Bach fugue. The reasons are not difficult to understand when we consider three individuals trying to achieve on the spur of the moment, often publicly, what the composer is able to calculate privately and at his own pace. It is no wonder, then, that much of what is created by the New Orleans ensemble, when they are improvising collectively, is, so to speak, heavy, dense, not easily penetrated, and often without apparent direction. If one is to understand the structure and design of New Orleans jazz—and there is a design—one must hear it as a chiaroscuro: as a pattern of light and dark sections, what Italians call "clear dark."

The characteristic New Orleans forms are blues, stomps, rags, and marches; these forms, however, are not structurally fixed. The blues chorus, for example, while it is twelve bars long, may be preceded or followed by interludes or transitions in four-, eight-, or sixteen-bar sections; and, when the melodic and harmonic materials in these latter sections are similar to the chorus material, it is often difficult to determine exactly where one section begins and another ends unless one is able to see a notated outline of the work. Perhaps it is proper here to point out that, while New Orleans jazzmen may on occasion have improvised on the traditional harmonies of the blues, they more often worked with specific blues pieces such as "Jelly Roll Blues," "West

End Blues," "Buddy Bolden's Blues," "Dippermouth Blues" (also known as "Sugarfoot Stomp"), or such pieces with twelve-bar choruses as "Snag It" and "No Easy Rider." Many of these blues included—in the printed version or traditionally—eight-, twelve-, or sixteen-bar verses that, in performance, were not only often repeated but sometimes returned to after a number of repetitions of the chorus, giving the impression of a modified ternary structure or a long bridge propped up on either end by two short pillars.

Stomp pieces, except for a characteristic stomp section, are cast in a great variety of forms. Not counting introductions and endings, and such transitional material as interludes and episodes, it may be said that stomp pieces are constructed in sections of eight and sixteen bars, with individual sections occasionally repeated with variations. Occasionally there is a return to the beginning—a *da capo*—that arbitrarily goes on to the end of any of the sections. Rags, like stomp pieces, are sectional forms with each section having its own tune. New Orleans style marches may be just a sixteen-bar strain repeated over and over, as in Kid Rena's version of "Gettysburg March," or they may be given the full treatment of introduction, repeated first strain, repeated second strain, transition, and trio, with everyone having a go at it, as in Kid Ory's version of "Panama" in a Good-Time Jazz recording, "Tailgate!" Furthermore, it is more than likely that the length of a piece and even its structure were subject to the time and place of its performance. Everyone has heard of the legendary one- and two-hour sessions of blues improvisation in honky-tonks and dance halls. But the fact is that a great many recorded New Orleans style, medium-tempo blues have the same format: a four-bar introduction, nine choruses of blues, and a two-bar tag, and the reason for this is the three-minute recording. In spite of the limitations of recording, however, the New Orleans jazzmen were little concerned with questions of formal structure. They were too busy learning how to finger and blow their instruments; they were still much taken with the curious musical sounds and noises their horns could, on occasion, produce—and they were learning to control them. They were too busy exploring the melodic possibilities of the basic chords to think about formal structure. They did, however, have a feeling for design, for the light and shadow, the chiaroscuro we have already mentioned.

The New Orleans ensemble was able to provide a number of musical textures of varying weight and density, the heaviest texture coming as a result of the polyphonic *tutti*—everyone blowing at the same time —and the lightest as a result of the unaccompanied solo "break"; in between we may list the heterophonic *tutti;* the concerted, chordal, or homophonic *tutti;* the solo against the polyphonic, heterophonic, or homophonic *tutti;* and the solo against only the rhythm section. Without attempting to set up a system of measures and color intensities, it appears reasonable to divide the New Orleans sound patterns into dark, medium, and light. Working mostly by feel and head arrangements, the ensemble leaders often managed to achieve logical and sometimes even interesting designs. While they may have known little of structure, they knew the value of contrast. When one considers how often these contrasts were initiated on the spot, so to speak, the balance is quite good, and—in the work of Oliver's Creole Jazz Band—remarkably deft. With the possible exception of the four-bar homophonic introduction and the two-bar tag, New Orleans jazzmen followed no established formula; it was usual to begin with the polyphonic ensemble, but a piece could just as easily start with a clarinet solo. The number and placement of solos depended to a degree on the color and weight of the ensemble preceding it, the color and weight to be intensified and multiplied by consecutive choruses of the same type. When the chorus itself was divided into multiples of two or four, the rapidly alternating, contrasting short phrases seemed to come in an arrangement of black and white squares.

In constructing melodies, the New Orleans jazzman is characteristically short-winded; he seldom thinks more than four measures ahead, more often only two. This method of constructing melodies usually results in aimlessness in the melody as a whole—that is, there is apparently no direction, no flow, no melodic curve. In its place, however, one finds an abundance of perfectly structured two- and four-bar phrases; the best work of the period may occasionally encompass eight bars, but seldom more. Characteristic melodic curves may be shown as follows: (a) generally upward, with climax at the end; (b) starting high and moving generally downward; (c) generally upward, with climax at roughly three-fourths of the way, followed by a short descent; (d) more or less static, depending on rhythm for interest.

Throughout New Orleans style melodies, the tonality is firmly maintained; it is not uncommon to hear the tonic note ten or twelve times in as many measures of a blues chorus. On occasion there will be a single modulatory passage to a next related key, but in general pieces begin, continue, and end in the same key.

The principal mode of New Orleans jazz is major, but with frequent interchange of the major and minor third scale degrees—the so-called blue notes. A good example of the interchange of the major and minor third is found in the beginning of a characteristic blues solo by Armstrong, as follows (x shows the third):

The harmonies of the New Orleans style are the harmonies of the marching band. The standard blues progression, however, remains predominant. The harmonies and harmonic progressions used by solo pianists of the period are another matter. Jelly Roll Morton, for example, was quite capable of constructing rather complex chords, as can be plainly heard in "Kansas City Stomp." Ragtime, however, while it had an influence on New Orleans style—rhythmic mostly—is essentially a notated music that grew up separately from, but alongside, the New Orleans style; it is basically keyboard music, and its harmonies are thus naturally more sophisticated than those implied in New Orleans solo instrumental music.

Perhaps the most frequent rhythms of the New Orleans style are the dotted eighth note followed by

The sixteenth (♩. ♫)

And the syncopated quarter note (♪♩ ♩ ♩ 𝄾)

one-beat triplets are fairly common, and two-beat triplets are rare. The rhythms of the collective improvisation, between bar lines, usually add up to a straightforward combination of eighth and sixteenth notes, and except for unaccented upbeats the rhythms are fairly square—that is, they agree for the most part with the meter. There is very little significant rhythmic activity across the bar line because, as has already been pointed out, melodies are generally conceived in two-bar phrases. For this reason, the rhythmic effect of melodic improvisation is stop-and-go rather than a rhythmically flowing motion; this is particularly true in solo work. The flow, however, is provided by the steady, unaccented beat of the rhythm section.

In the New Orleans ensemble, as we know, the cornet provides the melodic lead, the clarinet embroiders the cornet lead, and the trombone underlines the harmonic basis. The variations supplied by the trio depend, of course, on how "straight" the cornet plays his lead. In the main, variations consist of arpeggiolike figures, scale figures both diatonic and chromatic, the rhythmic variation of a tone or two, as well as variations of tone quality, and the use of such special instrumental effects as the growl, produced by simultaneously blowing and humming into the instrument; the shake, produced either by an exaggerated hand vibrato or by jaw vibrato; lipping, controlling the pitch by stiffening or slackening the lip muscles; and fluttering, produced by vibrating the tongue against the roof of the mouth. The glissando, produced by sliding from one tone to the next

—more properly called portamento—is the favorite effect of the trombonist and, to a lesser degree, the clarinetist.

Between March and November of 1923 the Oliver band made thirty-nine known recordings, according to Charles Delaunay's *New Hot Discography*.[17] Except for occasional changes in personnel (Charlie Johnson, bass saxophone, replaces Bill Johnson, banjo; Jimmie Noone replaces Dodds on clarinet; and so forth) the band's personnel, as listed earlier in the chapter, remained the same. The thirty-nine recordings include what many consider to be the outstanding examples of New Orleans style: "Mabel's Dream," "Riverside Blues," "Froggie Moore," "Canal Street Blues," "Workin' Man's Blues" (with its two-bar tag that foreshadows the Ellington of the thirties), "Dippermouth Blues" (with Oliver's swinging muted cornet solo), and perhaps the finest of all, "Chimes Blues" (with Armstrong's first recorded solo). Practically every one of Oliver's recordings of 1923 is noteworthy, and all deserve to be better known (Riverside's *Louis Armstrong: 1923*, which contains eleven reissues of the Oliver recordings, and the Smithsonian's Collection *King Oliver's Jazz Band, 1923*, reissued in 1976, and including twenty-nine pieces, should help give them a wider audience). "Chimes Blues," on the Riverside album, has been singled out for special attention here, not because it is the best jazz of the period—although this position may well be defended—but rather because it manages to encompass during its three minutes of playing time a great many of the characterstic New Orleans features as they were handled by the outstanding exponents of the style at the culminating point in its history.

While there are important melodic and rhythmic devices that help create an impression of unity and purpose in Oliver's "Chimes Blues," the total direction of the arrangement is mainly dependent on contrasts of sound. The introduction consists of two bars played by Oliver and Armstrong, followed by two bars of full ensemble in a figure that has long since become a cliché but that nonetheless kicks off the ensemble in an authoritative fashion. The ensemble is heard first in rich but lucid polyphony lightened somewhat by the clickety-click of Baby Dodds' wood block; the clarinet is brought to the fore while the rest melt into a heterophony that creates a warm background for Johnny Dodds' pushing arpeggios. And underneath it all, firmly but without dominating, are Lil Hardin's "chimes" in an adumbration of things to come. The chimes of choruses 5 and 6 are played in even quarter notes in descending arpeggios ending with a characteristic stomp rhythm; and while the ensemble drives the solo piano forward with concerted staccato chords on each downbeat, Oliver's muted triplet filigree is imposed on the stomp rhythm, and Armstrong's open horn for the next two choruses is a strong contrast to the quarter-note flow of the chimes; angular, frenetic, pointedly coarse, his twenty-four-bar solo seems the inevitable result of the six choruses preceding it. The repetition of chorus 3 by the ensemble—this time with Johnny Dodds' clarinet above the lead—is a proper coda, and Dutrey's two-bar solo tag is a good-natured imitation of the two bars preceding it.

In the foregoing I have tried to summarize those qualities of Oliver's Creole Jazz Band that, in 1923, enabled it to bring the New Orleans style to its highest peak. Performances like those of "Chimes Blues," "Dippermouth Blues," and others were the culmination of a quarter-century of sorting out what were to be the essential ingredients of jazz. The brief description of "Chimes Blues" is intended as a guide to the melodic, rhythmic, and harmonic riches inherent in the best New Orleans jazz, and although we have barely touched upon the problem of rhythmic development, for example, it is hoped that students of New Orleans jazz will continue to study Oliver's complete works, where the essentials of the style are available for all who wish to understand New Orleans style. A version of "Jelly Roll Blues" performed by Sidney Bechet and his New Orleans Feet-warmers on a Jazztone Society recording is especially curious in the degree to which it follows the publisher's sheet music version; it is as if each player had been provided with a copy of the music, notified what parts were his, what cuts were to be made, and who was to take which chorus. It is only fair to say that the performance was none-theless first-rate, and as stylistically consistent as it is possible to be thirty years after the culmination of a style. In addition to Bechet, the performers are Wild Bill Davison on cornet, Wilbur deParis on trombone, Ralph Sutton on piano, George Wettling on drums, and Jack Lesberg on bass.

After 1923 the Creole Jazz Band disbanded, and Oliver, having breathed the heady air on the summit, started the long, dreary descent. By the end of 1924 the Dodds brothers and Dutrey were playing with a new group, Armstrong and Lil Hardin were married and Armstrong was playing lead cornet with a new group, and Oliver was playing lead cornet with a new group—Dave Peyton's Symphonic Syncopators. The descent was slow but steady: Oliver went from one group to another, tried the publishing business, one-night stands, New York, New Jersey, Pennsylvania, and West Virginia; in April 1938, after fifteen years of disappointment, confusion, and poor health, he died in Savannah, Georgia. It is not likely that he was aware of his contribution to jazz. A simple man, he thought of himself as an individual, as "the world's greatest jazz cornetist"—a title by which he was often billed. When the band broke up he was certain its members could not go anywhere without his guidance and discipline, and none of them, except Armstrong, did. The Dodds brothers, Dutrey, and the rhythm section were substantial musicians, and Oliver and Armstrong had stood on their shoulders. After the breakup Oliver moved downward, the rest of the band remained on a sort of dead level, and Armstrong, radiantly optimistic, set out to see what it was like on other, perhaps higher, peaks. His new adventures belong more properly to the pre-swing era.

7

pre-swing

THE MEN WHO SHAPED AND INFLUENCED THE COURSE OF JAZZ in the pre-swing era were Louis Armstrong, Fletcher Henderson, Duke Ellington, and a number of other, less substantial figures. The period between 1924 and 1934 is difficult to evaluate. New Orleans style was losing ground and by the mid-twenties had little consequence. Jazzmen, both black and white, moved back and forth between Chicago and New York capriciously, while jazzmen from West Virginia, Tennessee, Georgia, and other southern states congregated in New York and played a notated music as unfamiliar to the musically unlettered New Orleans jazzman as New Orleans style was to the New York jazzman. But, before the decade was over, the direction jazz was to take became clear. It is impossible in a work of this size to treat at length the accomplishments of the period's major figures—those whose work, in the confusion of a transitional period, had direction. However, if we are constrained to treat them briefly, we must nonetheless be aware of their significance. Let us start with Armstrong.

When Armstrong left Chicago and the Creole Jazz Band in 1924, it may have been because Lil Hardin could not tolerate his playing second cornet to anyone—even King Oliver. Armstrong, however, could not have been induced to leave if he did not himself believe in his individuality. The breaking up of the Creole Jazz Band and Armstrong's leaving to play with Fletcher Henderson's band are in many ways symbolic of the crumbling of the New Orleans style, with its emphasis on collective improvisation, and of the rising emphasis on solo improvisation which was to be brought to its highest point more than a decade later. The solo improvisation was, of course, nothing new; but in New Orleans style it had been used primarily as a contrast—an interlude, perhaps—to the polyphonic sections. In a great many performances, however, even in the so-called polyphonic sections, one instrument often dominated the musical texture, and a musician of Armstrong's individuality could not long be kept subordinated to the group. It was therefore more than coincidence—more likely good timing—that, when in 1924 Henderson asked Armstrong to join his band (he had asked Armstrong the same question in New Orleans several years before, and Armstrong had almost accepted the offer), Armstrong felt ready, even anxious, to leave the comparative protection and security of Oliver, who had brought him to Chicago, for the somewhat insecure but more exciting position in New York with Henderson, a man who would allow him to blow his own horn, so to speak.

Before Armstrong joined the Henderson band, it had already enjoyed a modest success as the Club Alabam Orchestra, and when Armstrong was ready to join the group it was moving into its second season at Roseland, New York's immense dance hall. The band consisted mainly of musicians trained in the East, and many of them were to dominate the New York jazz scene for years to come. By the time Armstrong made his first recording with the Henderson band, in the same year he joined it, the band included Elmer Chambers and Howard Scott on trumpet, Charlie Green on trombone, Buster Bailey on clarinet, Don Redman on alto saxophone, Coleman Hawkins on tenor saxophone, Henderson on piano, Charlie Dixon on banjo, Bobbie Escudero on tuba, and Kaiser Marshall on drums. The men in the Henderson band were all in their early twenties (Hawkins, the youngest, had just turned twenty), and Armstrong, who had been the youngest man in the Oliver band, now found himself exceeded in age only by Henderson. But there were further distinctions.

Of the eight members of Oliver's Creole Jazz Band, seven were born in New Orleans and received their musical education there; Lil Hardin was born in Memphis. Of the ten men Armstrong joined in

New York, two, or perhaps three, were born in New Orleans, while the others were born in various southern states. The trombonist, Big Charlie Green, and the tuba player, Bobbie Escudero, knew the New Orleans style for certain. Green was born in New Orleans, and Escudero came to New York with A. J. Piron, the New Orleans clarinetist who led the first black band to play at Roseland. Buster Bailey had played clarinet with a band led by W. C. Handy in 1917, and joined Oliver for a brief spell after Armstrong left; he could play a refined New Orleans style when the occasion demanded it. But primarily Bailey was a "reader"; five years before he joined the Henderson band he had taken clarinet lessons in Chicago with Franz Schoeppe, first clarinetist with the Chicago Symphony. (Some years later Schoeppe also gave lessons to Benny Goodman.) The rest of the Henderson band certainly knew that a New Orleans style existed, but there is little evidence, in the recordings they made at the time, to show that it had influenced them, at least as far as the style of improvisation is concerned.

The Henderson band of 1924 probably had more academically trained musicians on its roster than most of the other black bands combined. Hawkins had studied cello in his youth and later attended Washburn College in Topeka, Kansas; Redman had been a child prodigy who played piano and trumpet at eight and continued with a substantial early training in theoretical subjects that ended, academically speaking, with additional studies at Storer College and schools in Boston and Detroit; Dixon, the banjoist, apparently had sufficient theoretical knowledge to do some orchestration for the band and later some arrangements for Chick Webb; and, finally, there was Henderson himself.

Fletcher Henderson was born in Cuthbert, Georgia, in 1898. From his mother, who was a piano teacher, he learned to read music and play classically; from his father a school principal, he apparently acquired a faint academic air he carried with him everywhere. His early formal training took him through Atlanta University, where he studied chemistry and mathematics. He graduated in 1920 and came to New York ostensibly to further his scientific studies, but a part-time piano-playing job with W. C. Handy's publishing company soon led to a full-time job as staff pianist with Black Swan records, another Handy enterprise. In short order he toured with a group of jazz players as accompanist for Ethel Waters and later played accompaniments for Bessie Smith and most of the important female blues singers of the time. In 1923 Henderson auditioned for and received the job at the Club Alabam. It is apparent that from the start Henderson was a note man; it is no surprise to find him at first attracted to Handy, another note man. However, the tours with Ethel Waters and his subsequent record dates where he came to know many important jazz people certainly added to his growth; he learned much from his relationship with Redman, who did all the early Henderson band arrangements. Not an especially engaging pianist, Henderson spent most of his time gathering potentially good jazz players and giving them the opportunity to express their individuality; he brought them together where they could influence each other and where—most important for Henderson—they could influence him. He listened carefully, and when he was ready he wrote and arranged music that eventually influenced not one jazzman or one jazz band but a whole jazz generation. He surrounded himself with jazz players of the highest caliber and, with his own taste and ability as the focal point, adjusted his view to the jazz era ahead.

Henderson's education, however, might not have been complete without the opportunity of hearing Armstrong during that one important year. And Armstrong's influence was just as important to

Redman and the rest of the band as it was to Henderson. Not only did he bring with him the vitality and exuberance of his solo playing and his personality, but he brought ideas that he had himself learned from Joe Oliver.

To hear some of these ideas, we need only to listen to the similarities between Henderson's 1931 recording of "Sugarfoot Stomp" (with Rex Stewart on trumpet) and the Creole Jazz Band's recording of "Dippermouth Blues," and comparisons become inevitable. It is no wonder that at least one critic, Charles Edward Smith, found reason to say that "the King Oliver style, in fact, formed the basis of swing jazz." [1] However that may be, it is unquestionable that Armstrong influenced the Henderson band. It is also certain that the year he spent with Henderson's group added to his own development. Henderson gave him a chance to sing with the band, and, since Henderson's was a reading band, Armstrong was compelled to improve his reading. The state of his reading ability when he first joined Henderson—and the kind of music the band had to play on occasion—is made clear by an anecdote Henderson told concerning Armstrong's first rehearsal with the band. At one point, during a medley of Irish waltzes(!) the band was required to move down from a triple forte (*fff*) to the barest pianissimo (*pp*), and each player's parts were so marked. Everyone blew softly except Louis, who came on blasting. Henderson stopped the band. "Louis," he said, "how about that *pp*?" Louis's answer was, "I thought that meant 'pound plenty.' " [2]

In the fall of 1925 Armstrong returned to Chicago. Apparently still uncertain where his future lay, for the next several years he alternated between New Orleans groups such as his Hot Five and Hot Seven and Johnny Dodds' Black Bottom Stompers, and groups in which he was permitted the freedom of the soloist, such as the bands of Erskine Tate and Carroll Dickerson (who had Earl Hines on piano). The

Dickerson band was the one Armstrong kept intact in 1927 when he opened at the Sunset Cafe. By 1929 Armstrong was back in New York where he played at the Savoy Ballroom and then at Connie's Inn; after a trip to California he returned to New York and then went on triumphantly to Europe, leaving his mark wherever he played. By the end of the decade he had made his choice for Armstrong the individualist.

The year Armstrong returned to Chicago, 1925, saw the dissolution of Nick LaRocca's Original Dixieland Jazz Band and the end of Paul Mares' New Orleans Rhythm Kings. Dixieland, or Chicago style as some call it, had by the end of the decade little force. An imitation of New Orleans style to begin with, it was destined to remain on a dead level until it reached its apogee in the much-publicized revival after the second World War. The group of young musicians known as the Austin High School Gang—Bud Freeman, Jim Lannigan, Jimmy and Dick McPartland, and Frank Teschemacher—who set out in 1922 to imitate the New Orleans Rhythm Kings and later the Wolverines (white bands that themselves were imitating black bands), went their separate ways and by the end of the decade had lost whatever New Orleans characteristics they may have picked up even at two removes. Their main distinction in this period seems to lie in the enthusiasm for jazz they generated among many of those they associated with, such jazzmen as Goodman, Dave Tough, Joe Sullivan, George Wettling, Pee Wee Russell, and Eddie Condon. Like the Austin High boys, the Wolverines and the almost legendary Bix Beiderbecke spent much of their time trying to sound like the New Orleans Rhythm Kings.

Beiderbecke was, even until the mid-seventies, one of the most talked about and least known of the Dixieland boys of the Jazz Age. Born Leon Bix Beiderbecke in March 1903, in Davenport, Iowa, he died at the age of twenty-eight of pneumonia, alcohol, or both, and nearly immediately became a jazz name to conjure with. Not until 1974, with the publication of Ralph Berton's *Remembering Bix,* and Sudhalter and Evans' *Bix: Man and Legend,* was the full story told, and oldtimers whose admiration of Beiderbecke appeared to be without limits, and who used to say, "You had to *be* there," were discovered to have been telling the truth. In his time Beiderbecke became a cult hero. Eddie Condon, the guitar player who himself had been something of a cult hero, said Beiderbecke could make his cornet sound "like a girl saying yes." In 1975, the New York Jazz Repertory Company presented the second of two Bix Beiderbecke concerts, recreating the jazz atmosphere in which Beiderbecke worked. Characteristic Beiderbecke may be heard on *Bix and His Gang* and *Bix and Tram,* both on Columbia.

The years of the middle and late twenties were a curious time for jazz—a period of transition when jazzmen were divesting themselves of the jazz they thought they knew and were struggling to replace it with a music more restrictive. As if the search for a new jazz style were not enough of a problem in itself, there arose in the middle and late twenties the added difficulty of choosing between jazz, with its minimum financial security, and the lush, full-blown, popular sounds being promoted and dispensed by such solvent groups as those led by Vincent Lopez and Paul Whiteman. The choice for many was a simple one. The names of those who played with the Whiteman band of the twenties, for example, reads like a list of the most important white jazz players of the swing era. (Whiteman bought twenty arrangements from Don Redman for two thousand dollars, but it seemed more like a gesture to justify his self-bestowed title "King of Jazz" than evidence of a true desire to play mainstream jazz.) Despite the money problem, which plagued most jazzmen, there was nonetheless a continuous movement toward the new jazz style. The recording industry was at its peak, and if the prices paid for recording were not precisely munificent there was still something for anyone who wished to preserve his sound on wax. Apparently all the jazzmen who could read—and many who could not—found their way to recording studios in New York, Chicago, St. Louis, and Richmond, Indiana. In 1926, Americans were reported to have bought 100 million records, and Red Nichols, a not particularly distinguished trumpet player, did his share toward supplying those recordings.

Nichols started recording in 1925, but in 1926 he went at it in earnest, recording as Red Nichols and His Five Pennies. Between 1925 and 1932 he recorded about 250 sides—half by the Five Pennies and half by assorted groups known as the Louisiana Rhythm Kings, the Wabash Dance Orchestra, the Six Hottentots, the Midnight Airdales, and others. The original Five Pennies were Jimmy Dorsey on clarinet and alto saxophone, Arthur Schutt on piano, Eddie Lang on guitar, and Vic Burton on drums. As time went on the Five Pennies were inflated in number from six to ten, for Nichols added and subtracted personnel so often that playing with Red Nichols often meant little more than a day's work. Those who managed to play with Nichols frequently enough at the start to be considered associates included, besides those mentioned, Miff Mole, Joe Venuti, Adrian Rollini, Fud Livingston, and several others. In 1929 a typical Red Nichols ensemble might include Nichols and Manny Klein on trumpet, Jack Teagarden and Glenn Miller or Tommy Dorsey on trombone, Benny Goodman on clarinet, Fud Livingston on tenor saxophone, and Gene Krupa or Dave Tough on drums. It is obvious that Red Nichols brought a lot of jazzmen together and for this must be considered at least a minor influence on the development of a jazz style. He gave potentially important jazzmen an opportunity not only to hear one another's individual style, but to perform together and, no doubt, influence one another. The value of the kind of training and performing center Red Nichols conducted was in the long run inestimable.

In Detroit in 1921 William McKinney, a drummer, organized the Cotton Pickers, a band that was taken over by Redman in 1927 and later drew sidemen of the caliber of Rex Stewart, Fats Waller, Joe Smith, and Bennie Carter. The same year, 1927, was the year for wide-open Kansas City, where the Pendergast machine created an atmosphere not unlike that of Storyville, and in 1929 Bennie Moten had his Kansas City Orchestra there—this was a band whose main influence was to come when its piano player, Count Basie, took over in 1935.

During Boss Pendergast's regime, local black bands from Texas, Oklahoma, and Colorado moved regularly in and out of Kansas City. The bands, though generally run of the mill, included individual jazzmen who would distinguish themselves in the swing era ahead—Jimmie Lunceford, for example, and Ben Webster. In the late twenties, the great tenor saxophone player, Lester Young, worked with Walter Page and his Blue Devils, and, afterward, so did Basie. And a swinging group Andy Kirk called his Clouds of Joy were out in the open.

Back East, Fletcher Henderson was about to enter the most productive phase of his band-leading career. After Armstrong had left the Henderson band and Redman had shaped the big-band arrangement that would show off soloists—both vocal and instrumental—to their best advantage, Henderson proceeded to staff his band with the best available jazzmen, and they in turn sought to play with Henderson. By the time Redman was ready to move on to the Cotton Pickers, Coleman Hawkins' drive was helping to carry the Henderson band to its highest point. (Henderson's 1926–28 band is considered by many to have been his best, but others believe his band of 1932–33 was superior.) In December of 1928 Henderson's band included Russell

Smith, Bobby Stark, and Rex Stewart on trumpet; Jimmy Harrison and Benny Morton on trombone; Buster Bailey on clarinet; Hawkins on tenor and Bennie Carter on alto saxophone; June Coles on bass; and Kaiser Marshall on drums. Carter, who had replaced Redman's successor, Don Pasquall, was also a first-rate arranger who had attended Wilberforce University in Ohio and later became one of the outstanding alto jazzmen in the swing era. By the time the Henderson band had run its course, it could boast alumni that included J. C. Higgenbotham, Dickie Wells, Edgar Sampson, Ben Webster, John Kirby, Chu Berry, Russell Procope, and Roy Eldridge. The best were drawn to Henderson because they knew him as a gentle, easygoing leader who was happiest when his musicians were expressing their individuality.

It was not until 1933 that Henderson started arranging in earnest, but it was soon obvious to all that Henderson had mastered the technique of big-band jazz. Here, then, were the main qualities of Henderson's big-band writing: He left plenty of space for soloists to improvise and to engage each other in competition. He scored the ensemble music for the sections of the band in short, provocative explosions. Behind his soloists, he provided the riff—an engaging melodic or rhythmic figure repeated over and over with slight changes, the whole pushing the soloists and band to bring about the rhythmic power and force that would become a characteristic of swing. Much of Henderson's work may be heard on the Columbia 1962 release, *The Fletcher Henderson Story: A Study in Frustration.*

For many the most important figure in this period—perhaps in all jazz history—is Edward Kennedy "Duke" Ellington. Born in 1899 in Washington, D.C., Ellington started piano lessons at seven and played piano for money at seventeen. In high school he became interested in commercial art, and his parents, who were reasonably well off, gave the young man the freedom of choosing his profession. At eighteen he played in dance groups that included Sonny Greer, Elmer Snowden, Arthur Whetsel, and Toby Hardwick. By the time Ellington was twenty-four he had gone off to New York with these musicians, had been rebuffed by the big city, and returned home. But once more, at the behest of Fats Waller, he returned to New York to try his luck. In September 1923, after lucklessly working Harlem nightclubs, Ellington opened on Broadway at the Hollywood Cafe, later called the Kentucky Club, where his band played for almost five years. The big break came in December 1927, when, with the help of Irving Mills, he opened at the Cotton Club with a band that was to remain there, on and off, until 1932. During this period the band acquired many of the men whose names were always to be associated with Ellington. In 1930, for example, one of Ellington's best works of the time, "Rockin' in Rhythm," was recorded by Cootie Williams, Arthur Whetsel, and Freddie Jenkins on trumpet (Williams had replaced the growl trumpet of Bubber Miley only a year earlier); Tricky Sam Nanton and Juan Tizol on trombone; Barney Bigard on clarinet; Johnny Hodges on alto saxophone and Harry Carney on baritone saxophone; Freddy Guy on banjo; Wellman Braud on bass; Sonny Greer on drums; and Ellington on piano.

Whetsel and Greer had, of course, grown up musically with Ellington. Braud and Bigard, however, were both New Orleans men—Bigard was born there—and most certainly must have had a small influence on the band. Bigard had studied with Lorenzo Tio and before joining Ellington had played with many New Orleans–style groups including King Oliver's and, later, Luis Russell's; Braud, at this time, was almost forty years old, and his experience had been mainly with New Orleans–style groups. At the opposite extreme were Hodges, who, except for a short spell with Chick Webb, had had little experience; Jenkins, whose experience was with Fletcher Henderson's brother Horace at Wilberforce University; and Carney, who had joined Ellington's band at sixteen and had had no significant experience. Tizol had come up from Puerto Rico, and his experience had been with a concert orchestra in San Juan and with legitimate reading groups in the States; Williams, too, had had legitimate playing experience in school and a later stint with Fletcher Henderson; Nanton and Guy had taken their training in Harlem's night spots. It was this seemingly awkward and curious combination of talents that Ellington molded into an instrument for jazz that in its time was incomparable.

Ellington's working method has been commented upon in many places. After Billy Strayhorn joined him in 1939, Ellington himself described it briefly in *Hear Me Talkin' to Ya:*

> The music's mostly written down, because it saves time. It's written down if it's only a basis for a change. There's no set system. Most times I write it and arrange it. Sometimes I write it and the band and I collaborate on the arrangement. Sometimes Billy Strayhorn, my staff arranger, does the arrangement. When we're all working together, a guy may have an idea and he plays it on his horn. Another guy may add to it and make something out of it. Someone may play a riff and ask, "How do you like this?" The trumpets may try something together and say, "Listen to this." There may be a difference of opinion on what kind of mute to use. Someone may advocate extending a note or cutting it off. The sax section may want to put an additional smear on it. . . .[3]

This kind of composing-arranging worked for Ellington and his men. Certain writers believe that Ellington's work is unique in that he created music apart from the usual jazz of the period. This may be true in part; however his influence on others is unquestionable.

Ellington-oriented arrangements, backgrounds, rhythms, and tunes can be heard in the work of countless jazzmen, from the thirties to the seventies. Among the best-known performers and leaders we would have to include Charlie Barnet, Woody Herman, Artie Shaw, Charlie Mingus, and Gerry Mulligan, among others.

Ellington, who once said, "I'm not worried about creating music for posterity, I just want it to sound good right now!" [4] deservedly received in his lifetime more effusive and unqualified critical praise than any other jazzman in the history of jazz, with the possible exception of Louis Armstrong. When Dave Dexter put his *History of Jazz* on four recordings for Capitol Records, few thought there was anything unusual in the fact that Ellington or his men appeared on three of them.

Ellington died May 24, 1974, in New York. Earlier, in 1971, Count Basie had said of Ellington, "Edward, he thinks beautiful." The quality of his mind, his inventiveness, his sensitivity, is clearly and abundantly evident in his autobiography, *Music Is My Mistress,* published by Doubleday in 1973. His life in jazz, his contributions to American music, the richness of his music, remain the standard against which all others must be measured.

Before we take a closer look at some specific Ellington contributions, it may be worthwhile to consider the general characteristics of the pre-swing era. In New Orleans style, with its emphasis on individual melodies and counterpoint, it was natural for the musicians to seek to create their jazz on such diverse instruments as the cornet, clarinet, and trombone—instruments capable of remaining tonally independent of each other. With the decline of New Orleans style and the move toward the swing era, with its emphasis on a collective harmonic style, musicians like Redman and Ellington set about composing jazz for groups of like instruments rather than for individual instruments.

(Even when, as in Ellington's case, he continued to score for trumpet, clarinet, and trombone, he arranged them homophonically—that is, in three parts rhythmically identical in effect.)

As bands continued to play in dance halls that grew larger and larger, and in nightclubs with increasingly complicated floor shows, the need for more volume, more variety of sound, more "bigness," became a musical necessity. The result was a division of the band into three units: the brass section, consisting of trumpets and trombones; the reed section, consisting of saxophones and including the clarinet; and the rhythm section, including piano, bass or tuba, banjo or guitar, and drums.

Keepnews and Grauer, in *A Pictorial History of Jazz*, discuss one of the differences between a pre-swing band and a New Orleans style band:

> . . . Henderson . . . opened at the Club Alabam in 1922 [1923] with a ten-man group, which isn't much more than the eight with whom King Oliver was playing in a strictly traditional vein in Chicago at the same time. But those two added men were both saxophone players; the total of three, instead of a single clarinettist, made a "section." That of course is one of the key words, one of the fundamentals of big-band music. Soon enough there were also at least three trumpets and two trombones. Added to the four rhythm instruments, this means a dozen or more men working in unison.[5]

Of the individual instruments to come into their own during the twenties, the most significant are the saxophone and the piano. By the end of the twenties the use of the saxophone was so widespread that it became for many a symbol of the Jazz Age along with F. Scott Fitzgerald's novels, John Held, Jr's, bobbed-haired flappers, the shimmy, the Charleston, and the black bottom. The saxophone, an instrument of jazz practically unknown in New Orleans style, became in the late twenties an instrument capable of producing important and expressive jazz in the hands of such players as Don Redman, Coleman Hawkins, and Harry Carney. The piano, whose function in New Orleans style ensembles had been mainly to thump out four-to-the-bar rhythm, became in the hands of Earl Hines a solo instrument capable of producing jazz melody in an instrumental as well as a keyboard style. Using his right hand to play melodies in single notes and, when he felt it necessary, in octaves, Hines produced a so-called "trumpet" style of playing solos that subsequently influenced many pianists of the swing era.

For the composer-arranger of the period, the combination of brasses, reeds, rhythm, and solo instruments eventually provided a wide variety of sound and texture from which he could fashion his music. In the first half of the decade he moved slowly, feeling his way, seeking to combine brasses and reeds first for themselves and second for the impetus they offered soloists. The earliest arrangements in which these effects were attempted and occasionally brought off were by Don Redman. Before the end of the decade, Redman and others had learned to manipulate the big-band components in a manner that was to remain unchanged until the end of the swing era. A brief look at the development of numbers in big-band sections may help to indicate the direction composer-arrangers took in moving away from the New Orleans style and moving toward swing.

As we have already noted, the King Oliver band in 1923, in addition to its rhythm instruments, included two cornets, clarinet, and trombone; and Henderson's Club Alabam orchestra included two trumpets, clarinet, trombone, and two saxophones (alto and tenor). The same year Cook's Dreamland Orchestra, with Freddie Keppard, included two cornets, trombone, clarinet, and three saxophones, or, to put it another way, three brass and four reeds. When, a year later, Henderson brought in Armstrong, his band included three trumpets, trombone, clarinet, and two saxophones, or four brass and three reeds; by 1930 another trombone had been added, and by 1936 another tenor saxophone, and, since the clarinet was expected to double on alto, the reed section was basically two altos and two tenors opposing a brass section of three trumpets and two trombones. When Redman left Henderson for the Cotton Pickers, he recorded in 1928 with a band that included two trumpets, trombone, and four reeds; three years later his band included three trumpets, three trombones, and four reeds.

The increase in instruments is also clearly pronounced in the bands of Duke Ellington. His Washingtonians in 1926 included two trumpets, two trombones, and four reeds; during the same year he dropped a trombone and a tenor to give his Kentucky Club orchestra three brass and three reeds. He was not to replace the reed until 1935; apparently satisfied with an alto, a tenor doubling on clarinet, and a baritone, he spent the pre-swing period seeking what would be for him the proper brass section. Here is the development at a glance:

Year	Trumpets	Trombones	Reeds
1926	2	1	3
1929	3	1	3
1932	3	2	3
1933	4	3	3
1935	3	3	4

Ellington's replacement of the extra reed may seem rather late when we consider that Redman used four reeds in 1928, Charlie Barnet used five reeds in 1933, and Goodman used five reeds in 1934. The Barnet band, however, had no trombones (they played mostly commercial dance tunes), and the Goodman band used only five brass; furthermore, Redman, Barnet, and Goodman were all reed men and functioned as reinforcements rather than additions to the reed section.

Don Redman was certainly among the earliest arrangers to work out the big-band arrangement. His orchestration, and the characteristic orchestration of pre-swing jazz, includes numerous combinations of sound of which the following seem to be a fair sample. The solos are improvised, of course, and each combination endures two, four, eight, twelve, or sixteen measures:

> muted trumpet solo against sustained chords in saxophones and trombones,
>
> trombone solo against sustained chords with solo trumpet fill-ins,
>
> tenor solo against muted trumpet fill-ins and full ensemble rhythmic punctuation,
>
> saxophones in ensemble against brass ensemble punctuation and fill-ins,
>
> muted trombone solo against sustained chords in saxophones,
>
> trumpet ensemble riffs against trombones and saxophones,
>
> saxophones soli in homophonic ensemble,
>
> saxophones soli against brass rhythmic punctuation and riffs,
>
> saxophones soli against muted brass riffs and fill-ins
>
> trombone solo against rhythm section,
>
> trumpet solo against riffs in saxophones soli,
>
> piano solo against rhythm section.

While occasional use is made of combinations of unlike instruments (particularly the clarinet, trumpet, and trombone), the rule is to keep the sections intact. Trumpets can be used, of course, without trombones, and trombones are often used to reinforce the saxophone section. All instruments can solo; however, solos on rhythm instruments, except the piano, are infrequent and usually restricted to two- or four-bar breaks. Backgrounds are essentially rhythmic chords or sustained chords and—when the top voice of sustained chords has direction—

melodic chords or harmonized countermelody. Although backgrounds are usually in chordal style, infrequently one may hear sections or parts of sections in unison or octaves, but seldom for more than a few measures. The riff background is effected by having one section of the ensemble play slightly modified repetitions of an initial figure or phrase against a "lead" in a solo instrument or in another section; riffs may also be used to oppose each other, as in the call-and-response, where each section may have riffs based on different initial figures. While the riff is sufficiently prominent in this period to warrant making it a part of the period's characteristics, it was not to reach the peak of its use until the swing era. For the purpose of clarification (and for nonmusicians, as a worthwhile *graphic* illustration), here are examples of the most common types of background in this period and the next, and their terminology. It is to be understood, of course, that these are heard in conjunction with a soloist or another section.

Pre-swing forms are not substantially different from those of New Orleans style, with the exception of the increase in the use of the thirty-two-bar AABA popular song form, which during this period started a rise that together with the blues was to dominate jazz to the fifties. The forms of the pre-swing period include those of the earlier New Orleans style: blues, stomps, marches, and rags. The blues continued to be a favorite with jazzmen; stomps began to lose ground; and marches and rags, except perennials like "High Society" and "Tiger Rag," were played mostly by those Dixieland musicians intent on keeping their hands in old-time jazz while they promoted what has happily been called the "vo-de-o-do" style. In general, the Dixieland bands played more commercial song hits than the black bands because their appeal was primarily to white listeners and dancers who regarded these tunes, along with the saxophone and Paul Whiteman, as representatives of jazz.

The popular tunes themselves were to remain in the repertoire, and many of them became standards as more and more their simple structure and harmonies were found to serve well as a basis for jazz improvisation. As early as the first World War the Original Dixieland Jazz Band was playing "Indiana" and "Darktown Strutters Ball"; in 1920 they worked on "Margie" and "Palesteena," and in 1922 they made a good thing of Sophie Tucker's favorite, "Some of These Days." Many black bands, apparently hoping to attract solvent dancers, tried hopping on the commercial bandwagon, and so we discover Cook's Dreamland Orchestra in 1923—when Freddie Keppard played lead cornet and King Oliver considered the band his greatest competition—playing tunes like "So This Is Venice" and "The One I Love." At the same time in New York the Henderson band recorded "Somebody Stole My Gal" and, after Armstrong joined it, "How Come You Do Me Like

You Do," "I'll See You in My Dreams," "Sleepytime Gal," and "Who?" In the next few years such significant jazzmen and bands as Armstrong and the Hot Five, Jimmie Noone and his Apex Club Orchestra, Redman and McKinney's Cotton Pickers, and Ellington recorded tunes like "You Made Me Love You," "Once in a While," "I Can't Give You Anything but Love," "Sweet Sue," "Sweet Lorraine," "She's Funny That Way," "Supposin'," "Ain't Misbehavin'," "Cryin' for the Carolines," "There's a Rainbow Round My Shoulder," and "Stardust." The height was probably reached in 1930 when the Ellington orchestra accompanied Bing Crosby and the Rhythm Boys in "Three Little Words."

The desire for commercial success notwithstanding, the main body of black big-band jazz in the pre-swing period was not altogether based on the thirty-two-bar commercial dance tune. Its jazz was constructed sectionally on two, three, or more strains consisting of four- and eight-bar phrases that occasionally appeared on either side of standard twelve-bar blues phrases. It was characteristic throughout the period, however, for big-band jazz to seek the balance of ternary form, and unifying devices such as the repetition of introductions and the repetition of orchestrational techniques were quite common. Ellington's work of this period is by far the most advanced structurally and shows his special concern for musical form. In the twenties not only was he concerned with the overall semblance of ternary form, as were others, but the separate sections of his compositions are also internally well-balanced. His recording of "Mood Indigo," for example, shows a classic handling of the small form. In "The Mooch," as another example, he places a series of eight-bar phrases on either side of four twelve-bar blues choruses for an exceptionally well-balanced form. For further study of early Ellington, the interested reader may wish to see

Gunther Schuller's book, *Early Jazz.* (New York: Oxford University Press, 1968).

Tonality remained as firmly established in the pre-swing era as it had been in New Orleans style, and again, as in the previous period, the prevailing mode remained major, although reference to the minor mode becomes more frequent as we approach the end of the period. And here again Ellington seems to lead the way with such pieces as the just-mentioned "The Mooch," where minor material appears on either side of the major blues, and once more in his "Black and Tan Fantasy," where the minor mode, while used sparingly, has an integrating influence nonetheless.

Others, of course, made occasional use of the minor mode—Redman, Henderson, and Armstrong, to name the best known—but Ellington seemed to consider the minor mode a primary source of composition, perhaps not equal to the major mode, but important nonetheless. It may be that his early concern with "jungle" effects brought forth a rather nebulous association between "jungle" and "minor." At any rate, he has used the minor mode frequently and successfully, while others have used it only infrequently.

The melodies of this period are either arranged or improvised, and melodic ideas tend to be longer than those of the previous period. The tunes are nevertheless constructed in short phrases, particularly the arranged ideas; the improvised solos, however, often extend over the normal phrase line, giving the impression that the soloist intends to play perhaps sixteen bars instead of the two or four of the earlier period. Pre-swing jazz lines show quite good direction and, in the hands of first-rate jazz players, melodic curves that are impressively worked out. Almost all of Armstrong's solos from 1927 on show an overall direction that somehow does not seem proper in presumably improvised solos, and yet they manage to create an air of free swinging. Particularly noteworthy for this quality is his "Struttin' with Some Barbecue" with the Hot Five, where he starts the piece with a little run up to the E-flat in the top space of the staff; twelve bars later he has worked his way up to G, and twenty-four bars later up to A-flat, where he is interrupted by sixteen bars each of clarinet and trombone solos, but only momentarily. Starting where he had stopped, he moves down and up the scale again, embroidering and spinning until at last he shoots forth two climactic high C's; thirty-two bars later he has gracefully descended to the tone with which he opened the piece. The creation of such melodic direction and tension is not, of course, an everyday occurrence; a great many jazzmen who heard Armstrong during the period, however, were influenced by his style, and, after he was once established as a soloist, length of line and overall conception of a solo must certainly be considered part of his individual style.

The harmonic foundation of pre-swing is considerably more sophisticated than harmonies of the earlier period, and jazzmen began, in this period, to draw heavily on the traditional European system of harmony, including all the harmonies up to nineteenth-century impressionism. In fact, Ellington in this period already dips lightly into the impressionistic well. The harmonic stockpile of most jazz players, however, was not as varied as Ellington's; nevertheless there is, if not a greater variety of chords than New Orleans jazzmen employed, at least a wider use of those chords which earlier had been used less frequently. (For the reader of music, the sheet music of Ellington's "Black and Tan Fantasy," generally available wherever sheet music is sold, provides a succinct illustration of the chords in vogue in jazz at the time.) The most significant harmonic change in the blues of the period is the increase in the use of the minor blues. The standard blues progression remains the most characteristic, of course, although small variations and alterations become increasingly more frequent as the period progresses.

Jazz rhythm in the pre-swing era was directed in part by the necessity of controlling the instrumental section; therefore, while one generally finds more rhythmic freedom and complexity in the improvised solos, the arranged rhythms for the ensemble are relatively square. Because of rhythmic restrictions in writing for jazzmen with little or no tradition of a collective harmonic style, and certainly with little experience until late in the period, arrangers during the twenties drew up a body of rhythmic and melodic formulas that served the average jazzman rather well. (Many of these clichés, with slight variation, were still current in high school and college stage-band arrangements in the sixties and seventies.) An engaging improvised phrase from Armstrong's trumpet or Hawkins' tenor was sure to find its way eventually to the score paper where the figure, break, or rhythmic pattern soon after became part of the public domain, so to speak. The borrowing of such material by lesser jazzmen is not, of course, to be disparaged —borrowing musical material has an honorable tradition.

While the rhythms of this period remain relatively uncomplicated, one has to listen to Armstrong's work, say, "Tight Like This," to hear examples of the type of rhythmic freedom and complexity to be found in the best improvised solos of the period. The entire composition is worth further study as an example of a masterful variation on only two chords—the tonic and dominant.

Similar rhythmic treatment of material may be found in Armstrong's "I'm Not Rough," "Gully Low Blues" ("S.O.L. Blues"), and "West End Blues." As a means of observing the wide use of characteristic melodic and rhythmic figures, compare the following phrases extracted from Armstrong's "Cornet Chop Suey," first recorded in

1926, Ellington's "Down in Your Alley Blues" of 1927, and John Kirby's "Opus 5" of 1939. In its original key the phrase is an essential part of each of these pieces.

One of the high points in the jazz of the pre-swing era is Ellington's arrangement of "Rockin' in Rhythm," a tune composed by his baritone saxophonist Harry Carney and originally used as an accompaniment for Snakehips Tucker, a vaudeville dancer. For this 1931 recording the band included Cootie Williams, Arthur Whetsel, and Freddie Jenkins on trumpet, Tricky Sam Nanton and Juan Tizol on trombone, Barney Bigard on clarinet, Johnny Hodges on alto saxophone, Harry Carney on baritone saxophone, Fred Guy on banjo, Wellman Braud on bass, Sonny Greer on drums, and Ellington on piano. The form is a characteristic three-part form, but with some interesting deviations. The sectional work bounces, there are rollicking rhythms, and the solos of Cootie Williams, Barney Bigard, and Tricky Sam Nanton show the debt other soloists of the swing era owe them. Ellington's melodic inventiveness was at a peak, and he and his men have created in "Rockin' in Rhythm" a significant jazz structure that stands as a landmark in the pre-swing era.

While Ellington's work continued to develop and expand throughout his long career, the same cannot be said of other important pre-swing figures. Armstrong, as has already been pointed out, reached a self-imposed impasse somewhere in the thirties. His occasional appearances on television or as an American representative abroad too often produced euphuistic interpretations of jazz unbecoming to one of America's significant jazzmen. At any rate, Armstrong and Ellington both reaped the financial rewards of successful pioneers, and in this respect they were more fortunate than Fletcher Henderson, who received popular acclaim and less fortune. Henderson's decline somewhat resembles King Oliver's. After innumerable attempts at band leading, in 1939 he finally turned to full-time arranging for Benny Goodman, whose Henderson arrangements had a large part in his early successes. But this brought Henderson no further toward his goal. In 1950 he suffered a stroke and died two years later. His wife, Leora, tries to tell in a few sentences what Henderson apparently endured for a great many years. She says: "The last job that Fletcher had before the stroke was in the *Jazz Train* show that played in that place on Broadway, Bop City. He worked so hard on that. He was really trying to make a comeback—workin' days and nights on arrangements and rehearsals, but all of it was for nothing." [6]

On October 24, 1934, Hugues Panassié completed his book *Le Jazz Hot,* the first attempt at an extensive, serious jazz study.[7] The date of completion may well have marked the end of an era. It is also significant that in the spring of the same year Benny Goodman organized his first big band.

swing

(Overleaf) *Benny Goodman*

"TOWARD THE END OF SEPTEMBER, 1934," Benny Goodman says in *The Kingdom of Swing,* the word got around that the National Biscuit Company was planning to put on a big program at NBC, starting around December. They were going to have three bands playing alternate sets from about eleven o'clock until two in the morning, every Saturday night. The set-up called for a rumba band, a sweet orchestra, and a hot band." [1] In December the Xavier Cugat rumba band, the Kel Murray orchestra, and the Benny Goodman orchestra became the representatives of Ritz crackers, a product sufficiently important to the National Biscuit Company and the National Broadcasting Company to cause them to impose a three-hour program, "Let's Dance"—the longest sponsored radio program up to that time—upon fifty-three stations, coast to coast. Goodman had the last hour to himself, and it is likely that the "Let's Dance" program contributed as much as anything else to the unprecedented success the Goodman band enjoyed until the sound of swing was overwhelmed by the portentous explosion at Pearl Harbor.

Why, after so many years of being relegated to the fringes of social acceptance, jazz should have achieved the wide popularity it did is not easy to say. New York, Kansas City, Chicago, and other jazz centers, like the rest of the country, were in the midst of a great depression. Banking and finance had sunk to a low level, industry was being bolstered by government intercession, and bread lines were a common sight in the big cities. The year before Goodman made his NBC debut, Prohibition was repealed, an event that made public drinking as easy as public dining and dancing. Hotels and nightclubs providing public eating, drinking, and dancing were assured almost instantaneous success, and following close on the heels of these establishments were the public dance halls, which were now able to install bars to keep the thirsty crowds wetted down, and bouncers to keep the soaks off the floor. Furthermore, musicians came cheap (several months before the "Let's Dance" program Goodman and an orchestra worked at Billy Rose's Music Hall for less than the union wage scale), and any club, hotel, or ballroom worthy of the name was able to afford a big band. Working almost as if by plan, the national broadcasters piped hotel music to hundreds of thousands of people who would then flock to dance halls and theaters to hear these same bands on tour, after which the broadcasters could sell the bands to sponsors who wished their products to be associated with these by now "name bands."

The combined efforts of the national broadcasters, the hotel industry with its allied service industries, the recording industry, the advertising business, and the entertainment industries in general made band leaders as well known as major-league baseball players and Hollywood movie stars. The end result was an endless multiplication of big bands. As Goodman told Gilbert Millstein, in a *New York Times* interview in 1953: "The thing got to be an industry. I never considered it one. Others did. I considered it an individual enterprise with each orchestra based upon the qualities of its men. Our band happened to be a pretty good loud band. They never had that kind of music in hotels before. We made good and then the industry came in and said, 'We'll have a band like this, too. It doesn't have to be good, just so long as it's loud.'" [2]

There were undoubtedly enough "loud bands" to satisfy everyone, for by 1938 swing was the country's popular music. On May 29, 1938, a "Carnival of Swing" was held at Randall's Island Stadium in New York, where Artie Shaw, Count Basie, Jimmie Lunceford, and at least twenty other swing groups played for more than twenty-three thousand dancers. In the same stadium three months later, seven thousand so-called jitterbugs and alligators turned up for the first of four swing benefits conducted by Larry Clinton, Richard Himber, George Olsen, and a number of others, who obviously must have been a large segment of the "industry" mentioned above by Goodman.

In earlier times the difference between popular music—that is, *music that was popular*—and jazz was quite distinct even in the mind of the general public; in the swing era, however, there was little distinction because the best swing of the time was popular not only with jitterbugs and hip kids but among the educated and moneyed people as well. In *Eddie Condon's Treasury of Jazz,* Goodman told Richard Gehman:

> . . . the literary set took us up. Clifton Fadiman, the distinguished book critic, did two scripts for our 'Caravan' radio show. He was succeeded by Robert Paul Smith, the novelist. Robert Benchley appeared with us on the program, and he introduced the band to a group of writers for *The New Yorker,* including S. J. Perelman and E. B. White. They used to show up at the Madhattan Room of the Hotel Pennsylvania in New York every Saturday night.[3]

And readers of a *New York Times* item of October 30, 1938, about the fall opening of Goodman's band at the Empire Room of the Waldorf Astoria learned that "Goodman's welcome at the swank hostelry is being closely gauged by the trend-watchers, and if early indications mean anything, one might say that the jitterbug mania is now assured of the blessing of the more polite folk." In short, men, women, and children at all levels of society accepted and, in some instances, embraced swing as the popular music of their time. We have passed lightly over the forces responsible for the promotion and dissemination of swing; let us now look briefly at the people directly responsible for making the music.

Never before had there been as much jazz activity or as many jazz-men as there were in the swing era. Besides the hundreds of dance bands and the hundreds of white and black musicians who sought easy fame and fortune in the swing surge, there were those pre-swing bands and musicians who had laid the foundations of swing and continued to work through most of the period. Of the pre-swing bands that played consequential roles during this time, some of the most important were those of Duke Ellington, Fletcher Henderson, Don Redman, Earl Hines, Chick Webb, Andy Kirk, and Jimmie Lunceford. While there was much activity among Dixieland and sweet bands in the pre-swing era, only a handful contributed to the formulation of swing, and these only through individual jazzmen who gave up the Dixieland and sweet music and went on to become significant swing figures—men from the bands of Ben Pollack, Isham Jones, and Paul Whiteman, to mention a few. The most noteworthy of the white pre-swing bands were the Dorsey Brothers orchestra and the Casa Loma orchestra. Because of the uniqueness of the Casa Loma's early position, it is interesting to compare its qualities with those that later brought success to the swing band "industry." Wilder Hobson tells us, in *American Jazz Music:*

> The band was young and physically attractive. . . . Also, a good deal more than it played jazz, it played the sentimental melodies of the day, orchestrated simply and with finish, featuring the sentimental singing of a handsome young saxophonist, Kenny Sargent. And when jazz was played, it was presented in a way in which it might be easily received. . . . The band's guitarist and arranger, Gene Gifford, wrote scores which allowed for solo improvising in a setting of very simple rhythmic phrases, often with repetitions of the same phrase; and the band played these scores with clean precision. . . . Here was a form in which certain elements of the jazz language, at least the urgency of its

rhythms, reached a huge public, and other musicians began to get the idea. The "swing" fad shortly followed.⁴

It may be worth noting that in the late fifties, after twenty years of little activity, Glen Gray formed another Casa Loma orchestra to record the arrangements played by his original group in the thirties, presumably in the belief that there were still many people who would remember them. And a great many people undoubtedly did; however, their remembrances are more likely to have been tinged with nostalgia for the time than with any feeling that here was jazz. (A vogue for recreating the sounds of the big-band era became current in the seventies, and is discussed in that chapter.) The fact is that, while the period between 1934 and 1945 abounded in good jazz performers, the real success—that is, the popular and financial success—went to the comparative few who were handled properly by the music business interests. For every Goodman, Shaw, Dorsey, Miller, James, and Ellington, to name only the most famous, there were thousands of mediocre bands and musicians whose names came before the public only slightly less frequently than those just mentioned. Toward the end of the swing era, Paul Bowles wrote in *Modern Music:* "The cascade of hyperbolical praise in the form of ecstatic magazine articles and books which appeared about the time commercial 'swing' took the public's fancy, was certainly not designed to keep jazz pure and humble. On the contrary, every performer whose talent ranged from mediocre up was encouraged to think of himself as possessed of a truly personal style." ⁵

Close study shows that with few exceptions the character and individuality of the best swing bands depended more on their arrangers than on their soloists. It was the work of the section men that gave a band its quality; soloists provided bravura and dash. This becomes evident when one studies the seeming itinerancy of any number of first-rate soloists during this period. The impression is that of a circulatory system in which from time to time objects (that is, soloists) swirl around and pass each other, and then go on to the next point (or band). The function of the band leader seems to have been to watch the circulation closely and to capture the proper combination of soloists as they passed through his group. A few examples should make the point clear. Between 1935 and 1939, in addition to a continual round of journeyman saxophone players, these reedmen passed through the Bunny Berigan band: Eddie Miller, Hymie Schertzer, Edgar Sampson, Georgie Auld, Bud Freeman, Artie Shaw, Toots Mondello, and Babe Russin, while the drums were manned by Ray Bauduc, Dave Tough, Cozy Cole, George Wettling, and Buddy Rich. Between 1936 and 1945 Cab Calloway managed to get hold of reedmen Ben Webster, Chu Berry, Ike Quebec, and Hilton Jefferson—Jefferson being the only standby. But the Goodman band holds some sort of hiring and firing record: during the band's eight successful years, over 150 musicians could claim connections with the band.

The Goodman band of 1937 is the band Goodman liked best, and included Gordon (Chris) Griffin, Harry James, and Ziggy Elman, trumpets; Murray McEachern (or Vernon Brown) and Red Ballard, trombones; Hymie Schertzer, Vido Musso (or Dick Clark), Toots Mondello, George Koenig (or Bill DePew), and Art Rollini, saxophones; Jess Stacy, piano; Harry Goodman, bass; Allan Reuss, guitar; Gene Krupa, drums; Helen Ward (later, Martha Tilton), vocals. This was the band that alternated between the Madhattan Room of the Hotel Pennsylvania and the Paramount Theater where, during the first week of March, it smashed all box-office records (first day's attendance: 21,000) and then went on to their important "Camel Caravan" radio show and afterward to Hollywood. Goodman's special feeling of warmth for this group is therefore understandable. In the dazzle of their overwhelming success, however, it is easy to lose sight of their generally undistinguished backgrounds. As for Red Ballard, Dick Clark, Bill DePew, Hymie Schertzer, and Harry Goodman, little is known of their work before they joined Goodman. Vernon Brown came to the band with a Dixieland background, having played with Frankie Trumbauer in 1925 and with Goldkette in 1928, but his primary quality, like that of Chris Griffin, seems to have been that he was capable and steady. Ziggy Elman's principal experience was gained with local bands in Atlantic City, where from 1930 to 1936 he played mostly trombone. Toots Mondello's experience was mainly with sweet bands, and Allan Reuss had apparently had almost no dance-band experience. Murray McEachern, before joining Goodman, did a one-man band act, and Art Rollini had played with the Whiteman band. (As a possible insight into the essential quality of the men so far named, it may be worth while to point out that, once the swing era had begun to wane, Elman, Mondello, Reuss, McEachern, and Rollini avoided the competition and relative insecurity of jazz by entering the more stable field of commercial music: Elman, McEachern, and Reuss became Hollywood studio musicians; Mondello went into commercial radio work; and Rollini became a staff musician for the American Broadcasting Company.)

Of the remaining members—Vido Musso, Harry James, Gene Krupa, and Jess Stacy—Krupa and Stacy had by far the most experience. Stacy had worked the Mississippi riverboats in 1925 and had played with Dixieland bands in Chicago and later with commercial dance bands before joining Goodman in 1935. Krupa's training had been with such Dixieland and sweet groups as the McKenzie–Condon Chicagoans, Red Nichols, Irving Aaronson, and Buddy Rogers. James's early training was legitimate; he had played with Ben Pollack and commercial groups for about a year before joining Goodman in 1936. Musso had little experience, but is bracketed with the others because the members of this quartet showed a degree of individuality by indicating a desire to go it alone. Musso attempted band leading several times but was never quite successful and finally gave it up to freelance in California. Stacy, too, tried his hand at it in 1944. The most successful were the bands of Krupa, started in 1938, and of James, started in 1939. The total experience of Goodman's important 1937 band is not particularly distinguished, as we have seen. What, then, accounts for the acknowledged success of the band? In order to answer this question we must first know something about the band's principal soloist and featured attraction.

Goodman was born in Chicago in 1909, the eighth of twelve children. At the age of ten he was already able to play some clarinet, and at twelve he was alternating professional imitations of Ted Lewis, the then-current popular success, with the scales and arpeggios forced upon him by his teacher, Franz Schoeppe, clarinetist with the Chicago Symphony. Between the ages of fourteen and eighteen he played with local Chicago bands, where he was undoubtedly influenced by the Dixieland music all about him. During this period he was particularly influenced by Leon Rapollo, a New Orleans jazzman then working with the New Orleans Rhythm Kings. By 1927 Goodman was well known to local musicians, and during the next few years he worked with Ben Pollack, Isham Jones, and various small recording groups.

In 1929 Goodman left Pollack, with whom he had come to New York, to become a freelance. The desire to be a leader was upon him, however, and in 1931 he led a pit band in a revue called *Fun for All*. That enterprise was unfortunately shortlived; after fifteen performances the revue closed and Goodman was once more—literally—out in the street. In 1933 he met John Hammond, an enthusiastic jazz fan and entrepreneur, who asked him to organize a group for the purpose of making eight records for two English recording companies, and it was this substantial offer plus the unabating encouragement of Hammond that resulted in Goodman's first important band. Hammond was eventually to become involved in the careers of Billie Holiday, Teddy Wilson, Charlie Christian, and others; and in the sixties and seventies, with Bob Dylan and Aretha Franklin. In 1976 the Public Broadcasting Service presented a three-hour television program honoring the work of Hammond, called "The World of John Hammond." In 1934, however, Hammond and Goodman had radio in mind, and that year the "Let's Dance" radio show materialized; the success that followed has already been recounted many times.

Goodman's method of combining his legitimate playing technique with jazz ideas proved so successful that even legitimate music interests found reason to jump on the Goodman bandwagon. As a final note to understanding Goodman's seemingly universal appeal, here are two items from the *New York Times* music page of August 14, 1938:

> The Budapest String Quartet will present a series of five late afternoon concerts next season at Town Hall under the auspices of the League of Music Lovers, to take place on Nov. 5, 12, 19, Dec. 26 and Jan. 2. Benny Goodman, the swingmaster, will assist at two of these concerts. In the first he will make his public debut in classical music by playing the Mozart clarinet quintet. On Jan. 2 he will play the Brahms quintet.

> And now we hear that Béla Bartók, the Hungarian composer, is at work on a new concerto for violin, clarinet and orchestra. Joseph Szigeti is the violinist who has suggested the project to Bartók, and he would naturally be the string soloist. His colleague would be Mr. Goodman. [On September 26, 1938, Béla Bartók completed this work, *Three Contrasts* for violin, clarinet, and piano, in Budapest.]

In addition to his faultless musicianship, Goodman's dress was impeccable and the general impression he gave was one of wholesomeness and studious respectability, and to the public mind these were no small matter; it is certainly more than coincidence that the popular leaders of the swing era—Goodman, Tommy Dorsey, Artie Shaw, Glenn Miller, and others—all publicly emanated a distinctive, salubrious air. At a time when jazz was fighting to come up out of the cellar, so to speak, and into the open, Goodman's healthy appearance unquestionably worked to his advantage. This sort of advantage belongs, of course, in a category of intangibles. More concretely, the success of the Goodman entourage can be traced to his organizational and disciplinary ability, the work of his arrangers, and the featuring of his small ensembles—not losing sight for one moment of the influence and direction of John Hammond and Goodman's business representative, Willard Alexander.

Goodman had a firm idea of what he wanted from his bandmen, and, unlike so many other leaders—Fletcher Henderson, for example, or Bunny Berigan—he was more concerned with getting what he wanted from them than with being considered a good fellow. Popsie Randolph, once Goodman's bandboy, remarked that "Benny wanted what he wanted, that's all. If a guy worked for him, he had to do the job right. Sure, he was changeable, all right, like the weather—a little fickle you might say. But man, he was a perfectionist. A guy would come into the band one day and two days later Benny'd say he was no good—and out he'd go." [6] In 1937 the Goodman band earned $350,000, with each player receiving about $10,000. For that kind of money Goodman could have had a merry-go-round of the biggest names in jazz, yet he continued to choose his men for their steadiness, reliability and ability to assume an unassuming position; exuberance was permissible, but a boyish diffidence was more likely to bring a steady paycheck. Goodman has said: ". . . there was the collective feeling we had. We knew we were doing something nobody else had done. We were all bound and determined to show the public that jazz was a healthy form of expression, not just a passing fancy on the part of some kids. We were dedicated; that's the only word for it." [7]

In the swing era big bands achieved distinction by owning distinctive arrangements, and few band leaders knew this fact as well as Goodman. For the public, arrangements and the ensuing Goodman sound were taken for granted; Goodman, however, realized quite early that his band would go nowhere without the best arrangers, and the arrangers he employed included the best available: Horace Henderson ("Big John Special"), Edgar Sampson ("Stompin' at the Savoy"), Fud Livingston ("Alexander's Ragtime Band"), Spud Murphy ("Get Happy"), Gordon Jenkins (Goodman's closing theme, "Goodbye"), Dean Kincaide, Bennie Carter, Jimmy Mundy, and the redoubtable Fletcher Henderson.

One of Goodman's problems in initiating the "Let's Dance" program was the lack of arrangements—that is, the size of the band's library. Fletcher Henderson, whose band had broken up a year earlier, and who had a stockpile of his arrangements, sold many of them to Goodman for $37.50 each. Later, Henderson contributed many arrangements of popular songs along with what were called "specials," or what the band called "killer-dillers." Goodman said:

> It was then that we made one of the most important discoveries of all —that Fletcher Henderson, in addition to writing big arrangements such as the ones I have mentioned, could also do a wonderful job on melodic tunes such as "Can't We Be Friends," "Sleepy Time Down South," "Blue Skies," "I Can't Give You Anything But Love," and above all "Sometimes I'm Happy." He had to be convinced of it himself, but once he started he did marvelous work. These were the things, with

their wonderful easy style and great background figures, that really set the style of the band.[8]

By the end of the program's twenty-six-week run, Henderson had contributed thirty-six arrangements to the band's book, and, despite the fact that the National Biscuit Company did not pick up its option to renew, the band's style was established. Henderson continued, on and off, to do arrangements for Goodman until the end of the swing period, and together with Jimmy Mundy, who turned out about four hundred arrangements for Goodman between 1936 and 1939, created the Goodman big-band sound. As Marshall Stearns put it, "The Negro supplied the fire and feeling, the white supplied the polish and packaging." [9]

In 1935 Goodman initiated the Benny Goodman Trio, the first of his several small groups. With Teddy Wilson on piano and Krupa on drums, Goodman was able to attract the favorable attention of jazz enthusiasts who had had reservations about big-band jazz, and, while their opinions of big-band jazz were not altered to any great degree, their opinion of Goodman was. Furthermore, the addition of a black jazzman to his unit further strengthened Goodman's connection with jazz, for some jazz fundamentalists at least. The following year the trio was expanded to include Lionel Hampton on vibraphone, and still later various other jazzmen, including the important guitarist Charlie Christian. The jazz treatment of such tunes as "Moonglow," "I Know That You Know," "Rose Room," and "Flying Home," helping to make up sets of such big-band arrangements as "Is That the Way to Treat a Sweetheart," "A Little Kiss at Twilight," "Bob White," and "You're a Sweet Little Headache," spiced by "Don't Be that Way" and "Jam Session," or "Down South Camp Meeting," was calculated to appeal to just about everyone, and the record shows it did.

For some time the Goodman band had the field to itself, but not for long. The success of the Goodman band and the ready acceptance of swing by the public engendered hundreds of big bands, each seeking its share of popularity. Although most of the big bands that achieved success in the swing era came after Goodman's initial success and were undoubtedly on the scene at the right time, a number of bands that had been organized before the Goodman band, and were doing only moderately well, could now reach the spotlight far more easily than they would have otherwise. Notable among these, for example, was the band of Tommy Dorsey, who with his brother Jimmy led the Dorsey Brothers orchestra in 1933; in 1935 Tommy began on his own the climb that eventually made him as popular as Goodman. Charlie Barnet was another who had started early; after having inched along since 1932, he finally vaulted into popularity in 1939 with his recording of "Cherokee."

Woody Herman tried leading a band in 1933 with no success; he finally got under way in 1936 and by 1939 had established himself. Artie Shaw made several unsuccessful starts, but in 1937, after the engaging truculence of "Chant" and other numbers, it became apparent that he was a palpable threat to Goodman's position. Glenn Miller, who had been playing and arranging for many groups, made a number of false starts but by 1939 was also to be reckoned among the most popular leaders. Two years later his recording for RCA Victor, "Chattanooga Choo-Choo," according to George Simon, Miller's biographer, sold over a million copies—the first record to do so since the 1926 Gene Austin hit, "My Blue Heaven." [10] (As an interesting sidelight, we note that the first jazz recording in 1917, by the original Dixieland Jazz Band, made for Victor, also sold a million copies.) Bob Crosby and a Dixieland group from the Ben Pollack band caught the public fancy shortly after Goodman's initial success and continued to promote Dixieland music through the entire period. Of the men from Goodman's original band who formed bands of their own, Gene Krupa and his 1938 band, and Harry James and his 1939 band have already been mentioned. Teddy Wilson organized a band in 1939, and a year later Lionel Hampton tried his hand with considerably more success than Wilson.

The white big bands became prominent and successful early; the black bands—not all, of course—became prominent later. The bands of Chick Webb, Erskine Hawkins, Cab Calloway, and Andy Kirk are several that come to mind. Two that did not reach the popular heights of Ellington or Basie, but that are nevertheless worth mentioning, were directed by Bennie Carter and Jimmie Lunceford. Bennie Carter, who played alto saxophone and arranged for Fletcher Henderson in 1930, started a band of his own in 1933, and after spending some time performing in Europe (from 1936 to 1938), returned to the United States to continue, if not with great commercial success, at least to provide first-rate jazz. Jimmie Lunceford, a Fisk University graduate, joined the list of important swing band leaders in 1935 and during the next few years recorded such swing classics as Sy Oliver's "For Dancers Only" and "White Heat." Leonard Feather writes in his *Encyclopedia of Jazz:* "By 1939 the market was flooded with swing bands. Many of them, like Harry James', came to rely more on insipid commercial performances than on real swinging jazz for their success. Even a second-rate band could by now give a passable imitation of the Goodman or Lunceford ensembles. The only unique sounds and the only completely inimitable orchestral units in jazz seemed to be those of Duke Ellington and Count Basie. Jazz, to some extent, had reached a stalemate as the 1930s drew to a close." [11]

The Ellington band needs no further discussion here, since it simply rolled along the same original and inventive track it started out upon in the pre-swing era. We shall, however, briefly survey the Basie band of 1938–42, which, if not as popular as the Goodman band, was actually more responsible for the musical character of swing. It is significant that Goodman, at the pinnacle of his success, found it necessary to adopt many of Basie's numbers, including "One O'Clock Jump."

William "Count" Basie was born in Red Bank, New Jersey, August 21, 1904, and received his early influence from the jazzmen of New York. In the late twenties, while playing piano with a road show, he was stranded in Kansas City, Missouri, where in 1929 he joined Walter Page's Blue Devils which included Dan Minor on trombone, Walter Page on bass, and Jimmy Rushing on vocals—these were men who, together with Jo Jones, the drummer, were to be his close associates until well after the end of the swing era. About a year later Bennie Moten became the nominal leader of the Blue Devils, and when he died in 1935 the band broke up. Shortly after, Basie and a band that included several members of the Moten band were heard over the radio by Goodman and John Hammond, and in 1936—after Goodman and Hammond had persuaded Willard Alexander, of the Music Corporation of America, to handle Basie's bookings—Basie left Kansas City under a contract to record twenty-four sides for Decca for $750 and no royalties. ("One O'Clock Jump" and "Jumpin' at the Woodside" were included.)

Unlike numerous bands of the swing era, the Basie band remained fairly stable. The band's personnel included, at various times, Ed Lewis, Harry Edison, Buck Clayton, Shad Collins, and Al Killian on trumpet; Dan Minor, Bennie Morton, Dickie Wells, and Ed Cuffey on trombone; Herschel Evans, Earl Warren, Jack Washington, Chu Berry, Lester Young, Buddy Tate, Tab Smith, and Don Byas on saxophones; and the solidly steadfast rhythm of Walter Page on bass, Freddie Green on guitar, Jo Jones on drums, and Basie on piano.

With Goodman's and Hammond's encouragement and numerous arrangements lent him by Fletcher Henderson (Basie has often acknowledged that Henderson was largely responsible for his success), Basie opened at the Grand Terrace in Chicago and shortly after in New York's Roseland Ballroom. "When we first started out," said Buck Clayton, who was with Basie in 1936, "we didn't have good arrangers writing just for the band. We used heads we made up on the job for the first four years or so, and then we began to get arrangements, too." [12] The "heads" were conceived to a large extent in rehearsal; the band had three three-hour rehearsals each week, and during these sessions they worked out many riffs that were afterward picked up and passed around by other bands as common currency. Sidney Finkelstein summed it up when he said, "The riffs of 'One O'Clock Jump,' 'Jump for Me,' 'Swinging the Blues,' have become part of the folk lore of swing music." [13]

In its early period the Basie band exhibited all the best qualities of the small swinging group: first-rate improvisation against provocative riffs, and a vibrant, pulsating, rhythmic background. In the hands of Lester Young, Herschel Evans, and Buddy Tate, the tenor saxophone became the prince of solo instruments. Because of Basie's self-imposed subordinate role—he thought of himself primarily as a member of the rhythm section—his piano solo work has not yet been given its proper study. His practice of playing isolated chords for the purpose of pushing his soloists is too well-known to need recounting here. Freddie Green, who played guitar with Basie, said, "Count is also just about the best piano player I know for pushing a band and for comping soloists. I mean the way he makes different preparations for each soloist and the way, at the end of one of *his* solos, he prepares an entrance for the next man. He leaves the way open." [14] Another Basie veteran, less articulate perhaps but as much to the point, once said, "I don't know what it is. Count don't play nothing but it sure sounds good." [15]

The principal characteristics of swing were already well established in the pre-swing era. The instrumentation of the big band included five to seven brasses, four or five reeds, and three or four rhythm instruments. The combinations of sound remained much the same except for more frequent use of section unisons and octaves. Arrangements included a minimum of one solo, but most big-band jazz included several solos. Preference in solos was usually given to the tenor saxophone, clarinet, trumpet, piano, trombone, alto saxophone, bass, and drums, approximately in that order; the order and frequency were of course affected by the leader's solo instrument.

The most usual combinations of instruments and the various types of background against which solos were heard have been discussed in the chapter on pre-swing. While the types of backgrounds were substantially the same for both periods, swing made more frequent use of a combination of two independent, rifflike lines played against each other simultaneously.

The forms of swing show a marked increase in the use of the thirty-two-bar AABA popular song form; the twelve-bar blues continued to be an important small form; and by the end of the period, stomps, marches, and rags became increasingly rare. Standard tunes such as "Once in a While" and "Avalon" continued to provide the jazzman's thematic material, along with a seemingly never-ending supply of tunes based on two-bar instrumental riffs. Tonality remained firmly established.

In the swing era there is a greater impression of melodic organization simply because the riff repetition lends a more coherent, if somewhat simplified, arrangement to the tones. The riff serves as a motive which, in many works, may be repeated as many as twenty or thirty times, and it is truly an insensitive listener who is not able to understand what the jazzmen are driving at. Riffs at their best are driving, pushing, rocking forces that move the soloist to exceed his limitations; too often, however, the riff becomes an end in itself and the arrangement degenerates into a monotonous repetition of a figure something less than stimulating to either the soloist or the listener. The difficulty is the result of the jazzman's overdependence, in the swing period, on harmony. This is not to say that the problem did not exist in the pre-swing era. It did. In the swing period, however, chords with added notes and chord progressions themselves (what were called the "changes") dominated the jazzman's thought. One could no longer "feel" every progression, so to speak, the way one "felt" the blues progression; one had to learn the progressions of a hundred or more standards, and the jazzman did. The chords that were fresh for Ellington in the earlier period were, by the end of the thirties, the property of the least jazzman. Although there were countless blues played on slightly modified traditional progressions, many "substitute" chords—bigger, fuller, lusher—were also used, particularly in big-band arrangements.

The rhythms of swing are much the same as those of the pre-swing era, and in the late thirties these rhythms could be heard from the sixteen-piece band on the stage of the New York Paramount Theater or from the four-piece band in a St. Louis cellar club. Brass rhythms were frequently effected by placing a metal derbylike hat, or plunger, over the bell of the trumpet or trombone and then quickly removing it. The resulting sound is described by jazzmen as "du-wah"—the "du" being the closed or muted sound, and "wah" the open sound.

In 1942, at a time when the swing era had nearly run its course, the Basie band recorded "It's Sand, Man," a jump tune that is not only characteristic of the period but also shows what arranger Buck Clayton was able to do with a minimum of material. The thematic material was provided by Ed Lewis, and the band's personnel included Lewis, Clayton, Al Killian, and Harry Edison on trumpet; Dickie Wells, Robert Scott, and Eli Robinson on trombone; Earl Warren, Jack Washington, Buddy Tate, Don Byas, and Caughey Roberts on saxophones; and, of course, the Basie rhythm section. The work is essentially in three large sections, with the full ensemble enclosing the solo improvisations of the tenor saxophone and the piano. The piece is full of wonderfully effective melodic and rhythmic devices, plus the driving, pushing, hard and lean Basie piano.

"It's Sand, Man" is a fair example of the kind of jazz that kept Basie popular toward the end of the swing era. Swing, however, could not cope with the tribulations of the second World War, and sometime during the early forties its popularity gave way to other, more important things. Although a good many swing musicians entered the armed forces, many were above the military age limit and, with most of the top jazz groups disbanded, were forced to take musical potluck, so to speak. *Esquire's 1945 Jazz Book* had the following to say about the activities of Benny Goodman:

> This past year Benny Goodman disbanded his orchestra, appeared with a quartet at a jazz concert in New Orleans, made numerous radio guest appearances and formed a quintet including Red Norvo, Teddy Wilson and Sid Weiss, which is featured in the Billy Rose musical, The Seven Lively Arts. Now in his eleventh year as a national jazz figure he again received a strong majority approval (16 experts out of 22) from Esquire's Board as the greatest clarinetist, maintaining the wide margin he held in 1944.[16]

Despite the awards Goodman has received for his matchless musicianship, his influence on jazzmen has been small. Refusing to become interested in the various jazz styles that began to manifest themselves in the forties and fifties, he went into a semiretirement that seemed permanent until the spring of 1958, when the Westinghouse Broadcasting Company undertook to promote and sponsor a band led by Goodman as part of the United States cultural program at the Brussels World's Fair. During the sixties and seventies, Goodman made occasional solo appearances with symphony orchestras, and with small jazz groups on television shows. In 1976 Goodman played to a packed Carnegie Hall, celebrating the thirty-eighth anniversary of his historic 1938 concert. RCA reissued three albums in *The Complete Benny Goodman* series, which will in the end include about two hundred selections he made for them originally. Columbia has reissued a number of 1940–42 selections under the title *Benny Goodman: Solid Gold Instrumental Hits.*

Count Basie, on the other hand, kept a band going all through the forties and, except for a brief period in the early fifties, has managed to continue playing the music he knows best through the middle seventies. In 1954 he made a successful European tour, and in 1958 he recorded two albums—*Basie,* for Roulette, and *The Sound of Jazz,* for Columbia. The *Basie Jam at Montreux,* for Pablo, released in 1975, shows the old jazz master at his roaring best. At this writing, it would appear that Basie will provide first-rate jazz for some time to come.

9

the
modern era

(Overleaf) *Charlie Parker*

BY 1945 MANY FACTORS OPERATED TOGETHER TO BRING THE SWING ERA and its big-band jazz to an end. The strongest was, without doubt, the second World War with its effect on big-band personnel. Although many of the name bands were forced to dissolve, a good many managed to hang on in one way or another; Tommy Dorsey and Harry James, for example, added strings to their bands, while Gene Krupa, Sonny Dunham, Les Brown, and innumerable others turned to out-and-out commercial arrangements of commercial music. Even the redoubtable Earl Hines found reason to outfit himself with a vocal quartet, a string quartet, and a harpist. Almost as strong a factor as the war in bringing the period to a close, however, was the slow rise of a new jazz style variously called rebop, bebop, and, eventually, simply bop. This was the invention of a group of black jazzmen in revolt against commercialism and Jim Crowism in jazz as well as discrimination in general. In July 1948 Richard Boyer wrote in *The New Yorker:*

> Bebop, according to its pioneer practitioners, is a manifestation of revolt. Eight or ten years ago, many Negro jazz musicians, particularly the younger ones, who were sometimes graduates of music conservatories, began to feel, rightly or wrongly, that the white world wanted them to keep to the old-time jazz. They held the opinion that the old jazz, which they called "Uncle Tom music," was an art form representative of a meeker generation than theirs. They said that it did not express the modern American Negro and they resented the apostrophes of critics who referred to them, with the most complimentary intent, as modern primitives playing an almost instinctive music.[1]

The musicians were not involved in the new movement in a formal way, of course. Their problem was primarily one of self-expression, and, while in the beginning there may not have been an organized movement with banners and slogans, the goal was nonetheless clear, at any rate to those who helped create the new style. The musicians were particularly grieved with what they considered to be the defection of such jazzmen as Louis Armstrong. As late as 1949 Dizzy Gillespie, who may be considered a spokesman for many of his colleagues, told a reporter that "Louis is the plantation character that so many of us . . . younger men . . . resent." [2] To a *Time* magazine reporter he said: "Nowadays we try to work out different rhythms and things that they didn't think about when Louis Armstrong blew. In his day all he did was play strictly from the soul—just strictly from his heart. You got to go forward and progress. We study." [3] Nat Hentoff sums up this important aspect of the problem in *Time*, February 21, 1949:

> Jazz, after all, is a medium for urgent self-expression, and the young insurgents of the 1940's could no longer feel—let alone speak—in the language of Armstrong. Aside from musical needs, the young Negro jazzmen, who at first formed the majority of the modernists, felt more assertively combative about many issues apart from music than did Armstrong and most other Negro jazzmen of earlier generations; and this change in attitude to their social context came out in their music. [4]

Ross Russell stated another aspect of the problem in the November 1948 *Record Changer* when he said, "Bebop is music of revolt: revolt against big bands, arrangers, vertical harmonies, soggy rhythms, non-playing orchestra leaders, Tin Pan Alley—against commercialized music in general." [5] It may be of interest to observe specifically the kind of commercial music the early bop musicians were in revolt against. On October 1, 1942—about ten months after Pearl Harbor—the ten most-played records on the nation's jukeboxes, according to the Chicago Automatic Hostess Co., were: (1) Bing Crosby's "Be

Careful, It's My Heart," (2) Kay Kyser's "Jingle, Jangle, Jingle," (3) Glenn Miller's "Gal in Kalamazoo," (4) Kay Kyser's "He Wears a Pair of Silver Wings," (5) Benny Goodman's "Take Me," (6) Harry James's "Strictly Instrumental," (7) Woody Herman's "Amen," (8) Charlie Spivak's "Stage Door Canteen," (9) Benny Goodman's "Idaho," (10) Charlie Spivak's "My Devotion."

Even more significant was the "Victory Parade of Spotlight Bands," a coast-to-coast radio program sponsored by Coca-Cola and featuring a band a night, six nights a week. In the fall of 1942, while a handful of jazzmen in New York's Harlem were probing, among other technical devices, the use of the augmented fourth, the rest of the nation could have their choice of listening to Jan Savitt, Ted Lewis, Dick Jurgens, Jan Garber, and Sammy Kaye, from October 1 to 7; and Herbie Kay, Russ Morgan, Harry James, Lionel Hampton, Sammy Kaye, Charlie Spivak, and Horace Heidt, from October 7 to 16. It is plain that the "Victory Parade" was mainly concerned with bands that played dance music, groups that for various reasons preferred to provide the open, steady, two-, three-, or four-four beat necessary to dancers who grew up in the swing and pre-swing eras. This beat became, in fact, the *bête noire* of the bopsters. As John Mehegan tells us in a 1956 piece in *Saturday Review,* called "The ABC of the New Jazz,"

> The revolution centered about the very core of jazz—the beat. The musicians associated with this movement felt that the time-honored "dance beat" of jazz with the accented second and fourth beats which gave a dancer a "lift" was too restrictive; it prevented the free-flowing expression of melodic ideas. . . . In other words, the musician declared his freedom from the dancer and at this point jazz ceased to be folk music and became a struggling art form.[6]

The seeds of the "struggling art form" had been planted in the middle and late thirties, but it was not until the opening of Minton's Playhouse in New York's Harlem that the seeds could make the most of the cultivated ground, the warm encouraging air, so necessary to their later flowering. Around October 1940, Henry Minton, a former band leader and the first Harlem delegate to Local 802 of the Musicians' Union, opened a room next door to the Hotel Cecil on West 118th Street and installed Teddy Hill, another former band leader, as manager. Hill hired a quartet that included Thelonious Monk on piano, Kenny Clarke on drums, Nick Fenton on bass, and Joe Guy on trumpet. Before long, Minton's policy of allowing jazzmen to spend their free time there eating, drinking, and sitting in with the house band made his place a haven for all the early bop innovators. Minton's principal attraction was what might be called freedom of the bandstand, and it was here that the bop principals gathered nightly to work out the plans for their revolution. Monk and Clarke were soon in association with such early experimentalists as Charlie Christian, Dizzy Gillespie, Charlie Parker, Tadd Dameron, Bud Powell, and dozens of less talented well-wishers, all unknowingly working toward a common goal. Minton's, it should be recognized, was unique only in that it happened to be the place where, at the time, jazzmen were able to focus their attention on each other's experiments; the probing and experimenting had been going on for some time before Minton's opened.

Minton's was a vortex that drew jazzmen who had previously found some encouragement in such places as Monroe's Uptown House and other less-known rooms and clubs. Pianist Thelonious Monk said,

> Nobody was sitting there trying to make up something new on purpose. The job at Minton's was a job we were playing, that's all.[7]

At the outset almost all jazzmen, of whatever school, could mount the Minton bandstand and be accommodated, but as time went on it became obvious that those whose roots were too firmly set in swing would receive little notice. For one thing, not many jazzmen could improvise on the chord changes being punched out by the pianist Monk. It was not that the chords themselves were particularly unusual, although there was certainly a greater frequency of augmented chords; the strangeness to swing jazzmen grew rather out of the fact that the chord progressions of such traditional jamming tunes as "Rose Room" and "Ain't Misbehavin' " were being passed over in favor of such newcomers as "All the Things You Are" and "Lover Come Back to Me." And almost all the old standards yielded to "How High the Moon," a popular song written by Morgan Lewis in 1939 for the musical *Two for the Show* and later fashioned into a bop standard by Dizzy Gillespie. Furthermore, the chord progressions of such standards as "I Got Rhythm" and "Just You, Just Me" were treated in much the same manner as the traditional twelve-bar blues progression—that is, as a series of chords not identified with a particular melody. For swing musicians, an improvisation on "I Got Rhythm" meant a creation based on the melodic outline as well as the harmonic foundation; when a bop musician said "Rhythm"—an abbreviation—he spoke only of the harmonic foundation, a foundation that could serve for any number of original compositions. In Charlie Parker's recordings of "Bird Lore" and "Ornithology," for example, both numbers have their harmonic basis in "How High the Moon"; Monk's "Evidence" is based on "Just You, Just Me," and Dameron's "Hot House" is based on "What Is This Thing Called Love." (Leonard Feather's *Inside Be-bop* [New York: J. J. Robbins & Sons, Inc., 1949], reissued in 1955 as *Inside Jazz* [New York: Consolidated Music

Publishers, Inc.], lists a full page of bop compositions based on the chord progressions in standard tunes.)

Kenny Clarke, nicknamed "Klook" and one of the earliest bop drummers, recalled how the early bopmen rid themselves of unwanted jazzmen—players who wished to sit in at the late-night Minton jam sessions. Early in the day Clarke and his co-conspirators would agree on a set of chord progressions to be used that night. "As for those sitters-in that we didn't want," Clarke said, "when we started playing these different changes we'd made up, they'd become discouraged after the first chorus and they'd slowly walk away and leave the professional musicians on the stand." [8]

There is little question that the intellectual leader of the early bop musicians was Thelonious Monk, born in New York in 1920; it is also likely that, despite the public relations work done in behalf of Dizzy Gillespie, he and other members of the group were not persuaded by it to overlook Monk's position. In a group of eccentrics, Monk was the arch-eccentric. Largely self-taught, he played with a curious combination of classical and jazz styles calculated to estrange him from the middling performers in each of these classifications. Most of his colleagues—and no doubt Monk himself—realized that his technical proficiency at the keyboard could hardly keep pace with his harmonic, melodic, and rhythmic ruminations. His playing is perhaps best described, in a word, as undisciplined. It is likely that the difficulty he encountered in relating his musical thoughts to his technique kept him, for the most part, off the big-band scene. Except for a brief stint with the Lucky Millinder band in 1942—Gillespie was with the band that year and may have been indirectly responsible for Monk's being there—Monk continued to perform with small groups. In 1944 he worked with the Coleman Hawkins Quartet, and in 1958 he recorded for Riverside with a septet that performed five original Monk compositions. While Monk's improvising is dark and scraggy, his notated music generally has been flowing and sometimes, as in his ballad " 'Round About Midnight," even moving. Samples of Monk at his best may be heard on *Thelonious Himself, Monk's Music, Brilliant Corners, Thelonious Monk Plays Duke Ellington,* and others, all on Riverside. During the sixties his position in jazz continued to expand, and his work on twenty-some albums released during the sixties (his *Greatest Hits* on Columbia makes a good introductory album) indicates he will remain one of the acknowledged leaders of modern jazz.

The strength of Charlie Christian's influence and direction during the short time he reigned at Minton's Playhouse strongly implies that, had he lived, he, too, would have been among the jazz leaders of the future. In 1939, when Mary Lou Williams suggested to John Hammond that he go hear a guitar player she had heard in Oklahoma City, Charlie Christian was twenty and untried; on the strength of a brief audition, Hammond arranged for Christian to join the Goodman band. Upon his arrival in New York the young jazzman was introduced to the group at Minton's Playhouse by Mel Powell, the Goodman pianist. The Mintonites, impressed by the freshness of Christian's amplified single-string style and the uniqueness of his invention, quickly gave him a place of honor and enjoined all other guitarists from sitting in. Jerry Newman, a jazz fan, recorded some of the 1941 Minton sessions, which were released in a Vox album in 1947 and later on two records for Esoteric. These records, made by a quintet that included the Minton quartet mentioned above, consisted of a long treatment of "Stompin' at the Savoy" and an original composition known variously as "Swing to Bop" and "Charlie's Choice." With the Goodman band Christian is heard to good advantage in "Honeysuckle Rose," recorded at the end of 1939, and "Solo Flight," recorded early in 1941 by Columbia. He may also be heard in nine selections—some with Goodman, some with Basie—in "Spirituals to Swing," John Hammond's records of 1938–39 Carnegie Hall concerts released by Vanguard in 1959.

Christian may have been influenced by the French guitarist Django Reinhardt (there are similarities in their styles) but he must certainly also have been strongly influenced by the bounteous jazz harvest reaped around Oklahoma City in the early and middle thirties. Ralph Ellison, who knew Christian as a boy, tells us in *Saturday Review*, May 17, 1958,

> . . . perhaps the most stimulating influence upon Christian, and one with whom he was later to be identified, was that of a tall, intense young musician who arrived in Oklahoma City sometime in 1929 and who, with his heavy white sweater, blue stocking cap, and up-and-out-thrust silver saxophone, left absolutely no reed player and few young players of any instrument unstirred by the wild, exciting original flights of his imagination. Who else but Lester Young, who with his battered horn upset the entire Negro section of the town.[9]

When Lester Young arrived in Oklahoma City, Christian was ten years old, and, while he may have been stimulated by Young's presence, it does not seem likely that there could have been, at that time, much transference of technique. However, Young, as we shall see further on, influenced an entire generation of young jazzmen, and perhaps his presence in Oklahoma City was itself sufficient to create a desire in young Christian for the technical perfection that was later his.

Christian helped free the guitar from its traditional confining position as a rhythm instrument. He combined the sound of his single-string work with wind instruments as if he were part of the wind section, and he inspired the rest of the rhythm section to do likewise. In short, he was responsible for the emergence of the rhythm section as a group able to think and play as individuals. In the spring of 1941, after two years of New York's excitement—some of it artificially stimulated—Christian was taken to a sanitarium for tubercular patients where, the following winter, he died.

John Birks "Dizzy" Gillespie, while contributing as much technically to the new jazz movement as Monk and Christian did, has had the additional distinction of being a personality to bring bop to the attention of the critics and the public. The antics of Gillespie in the early forties were recorded by the press with a fervor and delight they had previously shown only toward the most idiosyncratic Hollywood stars. Gillespie has matured considerably since those early days and therefore no longer inspires the press he once had; however, his musical contributions to modern jazz have remained, along with Charlie Parker's, a dominating influence.

Gillespie was born in Cheraw, South Carolina, in 1917. By the time he was fifteen he was studying trombone and trumpet and, at the Laurinburg Institute, an industrial school in North Carolina, the elements of harmony. Three years later he moved to Philadelphia, where, when he was not studying and imitating the florid trumpet style of Roy Eldridge, he was playing with local bands. In 1937, when Eldridge left Teddy Hill's band, Gillespie was asked to join the trumpet section his idol had dominated, and in May of that year he participated in the recording of six sides for Bluebird, including an Eldridge-like solo in "King Porter Stomp." Between 1939 and 1941 Gillespie worked with the Cab Calloway band; then he tried his hand at arranging, placing arrangements with Woody Herman, Earl Hines, and Jimmy Dorsey, occasionally working into his arrangements those musical ideas he had heard passed around at Minton's.

Between 1941 and the time he organized his own big band in 1945,

Gillespie played with the bands of Benny Carter, Charlie Barnet, Earl Hines, Lucky Millinder, Duke Ellington, and Billy Eckstine, to mention some of the best known. Then there were, of course, the nights at Minton's, where he continued to work out with his colleagues the melodic, rhythmic, and harmonic ideas that were to become the characteristics of bop, the musical ideas that he was even then using freely in his solos with the big bands. These were the years of experimenting, analyzing, editing, and codifying, the years that saw the death of Charlie Christian and the fading of the Minton sessions, the years when Gillespie learned of Charlie Parker's ability (when Parker played in Jay McShann's band and Gillespie and Parker played in Earl Hines' 1943 band), the years of the rise and decline of Parker. Leonard Feather, in his piece on Gillespie in *The Jazz Makers*, wrote:

> . . . it is a fact that even in 1943 he was the subject of much excited conversation among fellow musicians and was well on the way to becoming a cult.
> The year 1945, though, was the most significant in that it brought to records the first evidence of bop's most fruitful partnership, that of Gillespie with the alto saxophonist Charlie Parker, who was to Dizzy what Wilbur Wright was to Orville.[10]

In 1945 Gillespie and Parker, with various small groups, made a number of first-rate sides for Musicraft (originally Guild) including "Dizzy Atmosphere," "All the Things You Are," "Lover Man," "Salt Peanuts," and "Hot House." The growing popularity of Gillespie with modern jazz fans led to the formation of his first big band, which, after one unsuccessful tour in combination with a revue called *Hep-Sations of 1945*, was disbanded. He tried another band the following year, and this, after a slow start, achieved sufficient success to be featured in a concert at Carnegie Hall. A European tour followed in 1948, again with varying degrees of success (Gillespie had to wire his agent for money to bring the band back to the United States), and in 1950 the group was once more disbanded. Shortly before this, Aaron Copland wrote, in the *New York Times,*

> It is interesting to note in this connection that bebop, the latest jazz manifestation, has been introducing more and more dissonant harmonic textures into popular music. thereby arousing some of the same resistance from the mass public as was encountered by the serious composers in their field.[11]

For Gillespie and the bop musicians, however, the problem was an old one: where to put the explicit beat. For the paying customers, the dancers, that is, the answer was of course a simple one. In the fall of 1950 Gillespie told a *Newsweek* reporter his side of the story. "It really broke my heart to break up that band," Gillespie said. "But there wasn't any work for us. Right now it's rough. Everybody wants you to play what they call dance music. What they mean is that ticky-ticky-tick stuff. Man, that ain't dance music!" [12] During the late fifties Gillespie emerged as a serious jazz musician with serious intentions. Representing the United States on State Department tours to the Middle East and South America, he proved that it is not always necessary for a jazzman to be a tragic figure in order to be significant.

Perhaps the most tragic figure in modern jazz is Charlie Parker. In a business where superlatives are a commonplace, few are able to express what Parker was about. His unbelievable technique and improvisational ability, like much of his disorganized, hapless existence, seemed rootless and, for the most part, inexplicable. Listening to certain of Parker's improvisations, one has the impression that he finds little to approve of even in his own work. His dominant attitude seems to be one of chill, corrosive bitterness and intentional cruelty; his playing, the outraged cry of a man at the end of his endurance. There are many lyrical passages in his work, and buoyant ones, too, and, on occasion, tender ones, but inevitably he returns to the anguish, the violent convulsion. It is plain that in the thirty-five years of his life Parker had little to be tender about.

He was born in 1920 in Kansas City, Kansas. His father was a some-time singer and dancer, and later a gambler and pimp. Parker entered high school in Kansas City, Missouri, where he played baritone horn, unhappily; later, his mother bought him a saxophone, an instrument more to his liking. The Kansas City young Parker knew enjoyed the easy money and high life that symbolized the Pendergast regime. The sounds of jazz came through open windows and doorways, from dance halls and juke joints, and Parker flourished in that ambiance. The city was a center of saxophone activity, and Parker listened to Ben Webster, Herschel Evans, and—above all—to his idol and greatest single influence, Lester Young.

At fifteen he was through with school and tried to jam his way into the jazz business by sitting in with any outfit that would have him. And, when it seemed that few would have him, he found comfort in the cocaine some of his more or less convivial friends taught him how to use. He found further comfort in incessant practicing. Essentially self-taught—although he had had formal instruction—he discovered the value of knowing his saxophone intimately, and he explored its every potentiality. At the age of seventeen, with the help of a stack of Lester Young's recordings, he memorized all of Young's solos note for note.

The following year, 1938, Parker found his way to New York, where he tried out his newly acquired stuff at Monroe's Uptown House. In this period, he ran across the flashing elegance of Art Tatum's piano playing and absorbed this, too. By 1939 he evidently played well enough to join the Jay McShann band, a rough and ready group with roots in Kansas City, specializing in the blues. After several years with McShann's band, Parker left the group to seek his own way. Between 1941 and 1942—the period of his first prolonged contact with Harlem and its jazzmen—he apparently found himself, musically speaking, particularly at the Minton sessions. And now the use of morphine and heroin became, for him, a way of life.

Between this time and 1946, the year he had a breakdown and was taken to Camarillo State Hospital, his technical proficiency and his musicianship expanded despite the self-imposed hardships he endured playing with the Noble Sissle band ("Sissle hated me") and the Earl Hines band, where he had to play tenor. He played irregularly with bands led by Cootie Williams, Andy Kirk, and Billy Eckstine, as well as in numerous small groups. By 1945, when he recorded for Savoy (with Miles Davis on trumpet, Curley Russell on bass, Max Roach on drums, and Dizzy Gillespie on piano) a group of engaging compositions—"Billie's Bounce," "Now's the Time," "Thriving from a Riff," and "Ko-Ko" with a muted trumpet solo by Gillespie—his manner of playing was well established. Whitney Balliett, writing in *Saturday Review* in 1956, said:

> The heart of Parker's style was its unceasing and uncanny projection of surprise. It was composed, principally, of long and short melodic lines, legato and staccato phrases, simple one-two-three rhythms and intense Stravinsky-like rhythms, a sometimes whiney tone and a rich, full-blooded sound, as well as that rare thing among jazz musicians, an acute grasp of dynamics.[13]

To illustrate the point one need only listen to Parker's twelve-bar chorus in "Slam Slam Blues," made with Red Norvo in 1945 for Comet and later reissued by the Jazztone Society, with Norvo on vibraphone, Flip Phillips on tenor, Teddy Wilson on piano, Slam Stewart on bass, and either J. C. Heard or Specs Powell on drums, in which first-Parker and then Gillespie show the wide contrast between their modern styles and the solid, on-the-beat style of the others. After Wilson's four-bar introduction, and coming hard on Stewart's dark, slogging bowed-bass solo, Parker's searing alto splits the darkness with a savage forward thrust, moving ineluctably into a fluid, undulating exhortation exceeded in invention only by the stunning fantasy of the last six bars. The impression is not of a twelve-bar chorus, but rather of an ingeniously worked out composition—short, but superbly complete.

After his release from Camarillo State Hospital, Parker enjoyed a period of comparative well-being and success. He worked with many small groups, including those of Norman Granz's Jazz at the Philharmonic; he went to Europe in 1949 and again in 1950, and his playing, when he was not fighting his affliction, became singularly distinguished and celebrated among his contemporaries.

Before he died in March 1955, Parker left an abundance of music on records, not all of it first-rate, but enough of it to show the power of his work when he was in control of his remarkable faculties. An album recorded for Verve, in which Parker is accompanied by strings, shows him ill at ease with the pretentiousness of the backgrounds for "April in Paris," "I'm in the Mood for Love," and others; he nevertheless manages to take the measure of "Just Friends." He overcomes the pomposity of Machito's bongo rumba group to bring off "Mango Mangue" and "Okie-doke," and, pitted against a cloying vocal group, he manages to overpower them with "Old Folks." These last were, of course, attempts by the music business to capitalize on Parker's growing reputation. His best recorded work continued to be done in small groups, some of the most noteworthy being the sides he made for

Verve with Al Haig on piano, Percy Heath on bass, and Max Roach on drums, released under the title *Now's the Time*. (An exhaustive Parker discography may be seen in Ross Russell's biography, *Bird Lives!*, published by Charterhouse, N.Y., 1973. In 1976, Arista Records reissued *Charles Christopher Parker, Jr.: Bird/The Savoy Recordings*, including, in thirty sides Parker made for Savoy in 1944–48, many of Parker's best efforts.)

Yet in spite of his remarkable powers, he was not accepted or even understood by certain jazzmen and the general public. Many jazzmen were more widely known to the public in the late forties and fifties, and certainly many enjoyed greater personal satisfaction and financial success, but no one, excepting perhaps Louis Armstrong and Duke Ellington, had as much influence on jazz as Parker did. The reasons for his bitter disappointment, which led to frustration, outrage, and, finally, torment and defeat, were set forth with great perception by Wilder Hobson in the January 15, 1958, issue of *Saturday Review:*

> The fact is that any genuinely creative artist—one who is breaking esthetic ground in an inevitably uncomprehending world—must carry a certain baggage of bewilderment as part of his standard gear. And his unease and his experiment, his imbalance as he works toward balance, his disorder as he works toward order, are apt, if they are not definitely bound, to result in a more or less chaotic personal life. This is in the nature of the contract. And if this be true of major creative figures think of the confusions and complexes of the second and third rate and of the pathetic, self-deluded sixth raters who can merely attitudinize on the fringes of the arts. The jazz world, like every other field, is full of these.[14]

In his probing and moving biography of Parker, Ross Russell wrote, "In the monumental disorder of Charlie Parker's life, the one thing that always mattered and for which he lived obsessively was his music.

There he was completely serious and disciplined. His place as a germinal figure in American music is only in the process of being realized." [15]

Of the jazzmen that surrounded Monk, Christian, Gillespie, and Parker, a number have become significant in their own right. The scope of this work forbids any wide-scale effort to include all those who are responsible for the rise and development of modern jazz; we may, however, mention a number of those who gained some special notice. Kenny Clarke was one of the pioneers; a member of the first Minton band, he, along with Christian, helped create the new concept of the rhythm section. "Around 1940," Clarke said, "I was playing with Roy Eldridge and it was chiefly through Roy that I began to play the top cymbal—superimposing rhythms with the left hand—and that helped me develop my ideas all the more." Earlier, when Clarke and Gillespie were in Teddy Hill's band, they were both working toward the new style. Clarke said: "It was the turning point of the whole business, because I could feel Dizzy changing his way—he used to play like Roy —and he dug my way. Later, every drummer who worked with him, Dizzy taught to play like me. He really taught Max Roach and Art Blakey how to play their particular ways." [16] After Kenny Clarke, the most important early modern jazz drummers are Max Roach, Art Blakey, and Stan Levey.

Tadd Dameron, a pianist-arranger and intimate of Monk (in the early forties he was called "The Disciple"), helped move bop out of the small band into the larger ensemble. A swing arranger, Dameron was concerned with adapting the new musical ideas of the Minton improvisers in order to create a new big-band sound. Although he wrote many arrangements and original works for Count Basie, Jimmie Lunceford, Gillespie, and many others, his most personal work can be heard to excellent advantage on the Prestige recording *A Study in*

Dameronia. Bud Powell is one of the early Minton pianists whose technical capacity could at once match the difficulties of the new style. Owner of a facile technique that has been compared to Art Tatum's, Powell has a vigor and lyricism matched by few. What Parker brought to the alto saxophone, Powell brought to the piano. A fine example of his exceptional drive and apparently limitless virtuosity is on Clef's *Bud Powell's Moods,* and, for a show of his lyrical sense, one can turn to his *Bud!* on Blue Note. His later work may be heard on *Bud Powell: 1924–1966,* on ESP. Other significant early bop pianists are Al Haig and George Wallington.

As for the remaining instruments, the bass was represented by such jazzmen as Oscar Pettiford, George Duvivier, Ray Brown, and Percy Heath; the vibraphone by Milt Jackson, and by Terry Gibbs of the Woody Herman band; the clarinet was being transformed by Buddy DeFranco, of the Charlie Barnet band; but the saxophones—alto, tenor, and baritone—like the trombone, were not to come into their own until the later, cool period. While Charlie Parker's sound may have overawed alto saxophonists during the early days of bop, Gillespie's trumpet, on the other hand, had many disciples from the start. Among the best known of these are Benny Harris, Howard McGhee, Fats Navarro, Kenny Dorham, Red Rodney, and Miles Davis; of these, Davis deserves closer attention as one of the founders, in the late forties, of the new cool jazz. But before we discuss this, it is necessary to consider briefly the state of the phenomenon usually referred to as "progressive jazz."

For the general public the bands of Stan Kenton, Woody Herman, Boyd Raeburn, and other so-called progressive jazz groups constituted the logical extension of swing as exemplified by Goodman, Shaw, and the bands that had apparently run their course by the mid-forties. The

Kenton band, which got its start in California in 1940, first came to the special attention of the public in 1946 with a number of recordings arranged mainly by Pete Rugolo, who helped determine the band's principal style.

Despite the protestations of critics who were not much taken with Kenton's heavy reeds and massive brasses, Kenton's big-band style was certainly one of the most popular in the middle forties. Some characteristic Kenton records made between 1945 and 1947, at the peak of his popularity, are "Artistry Jumps," "Artistry in Bolero," "Opus in Pastels," "Machito," and "Theme to the West." From 1950 on he tried without success to recapture his popularity; his attempts have included organizing a forty-piece touring orchestra and other smaller groups in order to produce such expansive works as are included in *City of Glass, Innovations in Modern Music, Contemporary Concepts,* and a number of others, all to be heard on Capitol recordings. Although the Kenton band has included, from time to time, important soloists (Eddie Safranski, Shelly Manne, Kai Winding, Art Pepper, and Lee Konitz), its mainstay was elaborately arranged ensemble work by highly competent jazz arrangers and composers more concerned with orchestration and the creation of sounds per se than with creating backgrounds for improvising soloists. Kenton's arrangers (perhaps arrangers writing for the Kenton band would be more nearly correct) have shown a tendency to give more independence to the sections of the band, and even to instruments within the sections; the simpler rhythms of Stravinsky and Bartók were discovered, and Ravel reigned harmonically.

During the sixties, Kenton created a special band he called the "Neophonic Orchestra," which specialized in a sort of symphonic jazz. In the sixties and seventies he also helped promote and develop the stage-band movement that swept American high schools and colleges.

In 1945 Woody Herman had a band that included trumpeter Neil Hefti and pianist Ralph Burns, both journeyman performers but exceptionally gifted arrangers. Hefti and Burns were cognizant not only of the current jazz scene but also of a large body of contemporary music, and they did not hesitate to draw from both. Herman gave his arrangers complete license, and the results justified his confidence. "Caldonia," "Northwest Passage," "The Good Earth," and "Bijou," all recorded by Columbia in 1945, reflect the spirit of the new jazz as much as a big band could at the time. Characteristic bop treatments of engaging subject matter were much in evidence, and, as in the work of other "progressive" groups, Stravinsky and Ravel received their due; Stravinsky's influence was, in fact, acknowledged in the Herman band's recording of "Igor." The progressives' enthusiasm for contemporary music may have been dashed by Stravinsky's "Ebony Concerto," written for the Herman band and recorded by them in 1946—a composition that produced more publicity than it did jazz. But, like Kenton's band, the Herman band was playing big-band jazz, and, though Herman attempted some pretentious, overblown works, on the whole he concentrated on his imposing soloists. Many of these became leaders in the jazz of the fifties: Billy Bauer, John LaPorta, Shorty Rogers, Bill Harris, Stan Getz, Al Cohn, Jimmy Giuffre, and Milt Jackson.

Of the several progressive big bands in the late forties, Boyd Raeburn's achieved some special distinction. Better known to jazzmen than to the public, he mixed—with the help of his arrangers George Handy and Eddie Finckle—a dash of bop with a touch of Debussy and a large helping of Stravinsky to produce an occasional *pièce de resistance*. Like Herman, Raeburn had many exceptional soloists with whom to work; among the best known are Dizzy Gillespie, Benny Harris, Trummy Young, Johnny Bothwell, Al Cohn, Oscar Pettiford,

Shelly Manne, and Dodo Marmarosa. Dave Dexter, Jr., in what seems now—thirty years after the fact—an imprudent prophecy, wrote in 1946: "Boyd Raeburn's incredibly cubistic, imaginative experiments are most comparable to some of Stravinsky and Milhaud's works. The public is yet to hail Raeburn, a saxophonist, but in all probability his magnificent music will some day be acclaimed by other than musicians." [17] Raeburn's most characteristic sounds may be found on the Guild recordings—also reissued on other labels—"Interlude," "March of the Boyds," "Boyd's Nest"; and on Jewel, "Yerxa," "Boyd Meets Stravinsky," and the overexpansive but nevertheless good-humored "Dalvatore Sali."

As one studies the development of jazz in the forties and fifties, the problems of jazz seem often to be as much semantic as they are musical. The term "progressive jazz" implies that other, unprogressive kinds of jazz were also current; this, of course, is absurd when one studies the work of the Mintonites or Ellington, for example. The "progressives" could not expect to rally strong support among those serious jazzmen who happened to be working in another direction. Furthermore, seeking musical materials in Stravinsky, Debussy, Ravel, Bartók, and Schoenberg is in itself neither progressive nor regressive. What is important is the manner in which such material is used. When devices from classical music are simply superimposed upon a jazz background, the result is at best a clever sham and at worst clumsy and inept. In the past jazzmen of Ellington's caliber, for example, have found a way of assimilating classical techniques without obtruding their progressiveness upon the listener. Despite the favorable connotation of "progressive," the label was doomed to the same limbo as "bop." The terms "rebop," "bebop," and "bop" are not the kind that inspire confidence; their very sounds suggest ephemera. Bop's life was nonetheless a long one as those things go; unnamed at the beginning of the forties, it reached the peak of its popularity about 1947 and by the early fifties had been absorbed by cool jazz—a category not so much substantially different as more felicitously entitled; but in the late fifties a school of "hard" bop appeared as a contender for recognition.

The trumpeter Miles Davis, with the eight-piece ensemble he organized in 1949, is generally considered the founder of cool jazz. The cohesiveness of the early bop jazzmen was at an end. This is not to say that the music itself was at an end; what was finished was the "togetherness" of the early bop musicians, and the exclusion of jazzmen who had not been a part of the Harlem-Minton milieu. The Miles Davis group was formed as a result of Davis' desire to create an ensemble sound that would not only be unique in jazz but would, at the same time, provide stimulating support for soloists. Together with Gerry Mulligan and Gil Evans, arrangers sympathetic to his plan, Davis worked out an instrumentation consisting of a trumpet, trombone, French horn, tuba, alto saxophone, baritone saxophone, piano, bass, and drums. In January 1949, with the additional help of arrangements by John Lewis, the group recorded four compositions for Capitol—"Godchild," "Budo," "Geru," and "Move." The ensemble sound was indeed new to jazz. The scoring for the brass instruments— horn and tuba particularly—lent roundness and depth to the group and provided an admirable richness of texture that was immediately distinctive, and a voicing of the entire ensemble that was imaginative and compelling. After two more recording sessions, in April 1949, and March 1950, the group was disbanded because it showed little promise of commercial success. However, its relaxed sound, the careful scoring of its arrangements, its spirit—in short, its entire approach to jazz—could not be dispelled as easily as its organization. The sound of the Davis group may be heard in *Birth of the Cool,* on Capitol.

The Davis group may have gone unnoticed by the public, but its special quality was not lost on serious jazzmen. In its three sessions the group included, besides Davis on trumpet, J. J. Johnson or Kai Winding on trombone; Sandy Siegelstein, Addison Collins, or Gunther Schuller on French horn; John Barber on tuba; Lee Konitz on alto saxophone; Gerry Mulligan on baritone saxophone; Al Haig or John Lewis on piano; Nelson Boyd, Joe Schulman, or Al McKibbon on bass; and Max Roach or Kenny Clarke on drums. Many of these expert jazzmen eventually went on to become the center of their own little groups. Some, like Konitz and Mulligan, became formidable soloists, while the technical facility of others, Johnson and Winding, for example, remained incomparable. (The Dixielandish trumpeter Ruby Braff, in reviewing a recording made by the two trombonists, wrote, in the *Saturday Review* of January 11, 1957, "J. J. Johnson and Kai Winding are two instrumentalists who have more technical facility than anyone needs in jazz.") Of the group's longtime jazzmen, only Davis lacked the technique to express intelligibly all his musical thoughts; however, continued practice and study have removed many of his earlier technical impediments, and a first-rate representation of his later work may be heard on the 1954 Prestige recording *Bags' Groove: Miles Davis and the Modern Jazz Giants.* The Columbia recording *Kind of Blue* is representative of Davis' work in 1959. We will encounter Davis once again in chapters dealing with the sixties and seventies.

Orrin Keepnews, in his notes to Riverside's *Mulligan Meets Monk,* wrote, "You would be fairly safe, even in so argumentative a field as jazz, in reducing matters to the simplest terms and saying that bop begins with Monk and cool jazz begins with Mulligan." Whether or not one would be "fairly safe" in saying this, the name of Gerry Mulligan ranks high as an advocate and performer of cool jazz. In 1952 he moved from the East to California where he organized a jazz quartet that excluded the piano. Working at various times with a trumpet or trombone against bass and drums, Mulligan soon became an important and highly influential figure on the West Coast jazz scene. His arranging, even though it was sparse and featured much octave doubling as well as simple two-part counterpoint, was extremely effective mainly because of his simple melodic and harmonic sense; rhythmically, his approach to jazz may be briefly summed up as sprightly. With the death of Serge Chaloff in 1957, Mulligan became the most important baritone saxophonist on either coast. The baritone in Mulligan's hands lost its grotesqueness and became an instrument capable of producing a multiplicity of tone qualities at a rate of speed that used to be associated only with the smaller saxophones.

With the rise of cool jazz, saxophonists seemed to have worked their way from under Charlie Parker's green thumb and were found in profusion everywhere. This renaissance was certainly due in part to the reaffirmation of Lester Young's influence. Technically, Young was no Parker, and he contributed nothing to the harmonic and rhythmic style of the fifties; nevertheless he exerted a strong influence in the forties on many young jazzmen, saxophonists particularly. What these young jazzmen admired in Lester Young, in addition to his lyric inventiveness, was his "coolness." For the new jazzmen who felt hampered by swing—by what they perhaps thought of as its sentimentality —Young's soft, flat, relaxed delivery and tone were the welcome antithesis of the driving, dramatic approach affected by most swing tenor players and exemplified by Coleman Hawkins. Of Young's disciples, Stan Getz, Al Cohn, and Zoot Sims merit special notice, and of these

Getz has worked hard to establish himself as an individual stylist. His recording, *Stan Getz and J. J. Johnson at the Opera House* (Verve), illustrates what may well be the foremost examples of cool tenor and trombone playing.

On the other hand, examples of modern-era saxophone playing inspired by Coleman Hawkins—frequently found in the "hard bop" category—are certainly not wanting. Sonny Rollins, who may be the hardest-working practitioner of the hard bop tenor school, illustrates the style to good advantage in *Way Out West* (Contemporary), and *Freedom Suite* (Riverside). In 1958 some critics referred to cool jazz, as exemplified in the work of Miles Davis, Getz, and others, as "soft bop" to distinguish it from "hard bop." We need only remember that the distinction is one of approach rather than of musical materials.

In 1957, Rollins' recording of "Blue 7"—a part of *Saxophone Colossus* (Prestige)—brought him immediate critical success and notice. Gunther Schuller pointed out in *Jazz Review* that "what Sonny Rollins had added conclusively to the scope of jazz improvisation is the idea of developing and varying a main theme, and not just a secondary motive or phrase. . . ." The idea of motive development in jazz was in the air and Rollins was a pioneer here, but his great potentiality remained unfulfilled by his fitfulness, his sporadic moving in and out of the jazz world, and the frustrations in his personal life. In 1976, at the age of forty-six, he gave a concert in Carnegie Hall in which he continued to show flashes of what he might have been.

Of the cool brassmen, trumpeter Shorty Rogers, formerly of the Woody Herman and Stan Kenton bands, came under the influence of Miles Davis. His big-band arrangements included a light touch of what the less commercial jazzmen were experimenting with, and a fair sample of his work can be heard in the Victor recording *Shorty Rogers and His Giants*. In addition to the trombonists already mentioned, Bob Brookmeyer, who specialized in valve trombone, played with the ease and facility of the top trumpeters. His versatility and technical facility are apparent in *Traditionalism Revisited* (World Pacific Jazz), *The Modernity of Bob Brookmeyer* (Verve), and *Storyville Presents Brookmeyer* (Storyville).

On clarinet, Tony Scott came into the cool spotlight in the middle fifties with a bop-oriented style and a technique that pushed all others aside; *The Complete Tony Scott* (Victor) shows him to good advantage. Jimmy Giuffre, with little real technical facility, distinguished himself nonetheless by exploiting the clarinet's chalumeau register and by almost making up in musical idea and content what he lacked in technique. The quality of his playing and composing is clearly evident in *The Jimmy Giuffre Three, The Jimmy Giuffre Clarinet* (Atlantic), and *Tangents in Jazz* (Capitol).

In a 1957 survey of jazz pianists, in *High Fidelity Magazine*, John S. Wilson listed sixty-five as "modern." [18] It is possible, however, to make this formidable number manageable by considering only the fairly well established of these. In addition to Thelonious Monk, John Lewis, Al Haig, and others mentioned earlier, the following have distinguished themselves: Erroll Garner, Hank Jones, Dodo Marmarosa, Phineas Newborn, Bernard Peiffer, Oscar Peterson, George Shearing, Horace Silver, Billy Taylor, and Lennie Tristano. Of these, Tristano certainly made the most significant contribution to the development of jazz harmony and counterpoint, if not to his own popularity. A fair sampling of Tristano's work can be heard in *Lennie Tristano and Lee Konitz* (Prestige), *Tristano* (Mercury), and *Lennie Tristano* (Atlantic).

The pianist John Lewis, whose position at the time matched Tristano's in many respects, is often judged by his work with the Modern Jazz Quartet, certainly among the best known of small jazz units. The group was organized by Lewis in 1952 and included Lewis on piano, Milt Jackson on vibraphone, Percy Heath on bass, and Kenny Clarke on drums; except for Clarke, who was replaced by Connie Kay in February 1955, the personnel remained unchanged until the group dissolved in 1974. With Lewis doing the arranging, the quartet managed to achieve a small-ensemble sound as distinctive as that of the Miles Davis ensemble of 1949. The quartet emphasized a delicate, intimate, *sotto voce* style that, particularly when the performers were not improvising, suggested great cohesion by occasional simple imitative and contrapuntal devices. The faintly baroque feeling of the music was frequently offset by a swinging blues, often modal in quality, which was at once crafty and charming—if one may use these words to describe the blues; "Ralph's New Blues," included in the Prestige recording *Concorde,* is a typical example of the quartet's handling of such material. The work of the quartet has been variously described as "cerebral," "intellectual," and the like. While much of their musical quality was often difficult to discern through the clink of glasses and the buzz of small-talk, their music was in fact quite direct and unassuming, particularly when heard in the quiet of one's study. A broad view of the quartet's contribution to the jazz of this period can be found in *Django* (Prestige), and *Fontessa* and *The Modern Jazz Quartet at Music Inn* (Atlantic).

It is likely that history will eventually show the era of the fifties as the period in which the big band declined and the small ensemble dominated the field. The bop revolution was, among other things, a revolt against the big band, and the revolutionaries had come to equate the idea of freedom with the idea and function of small groups. What had been the brass section became the trumpet; the reed section became the saxophone; and to these was added the three-piece rhythm section. When Charlie Christian was available, the early rhythm section had four pieces; for some time after Christian's death the guitar was not generally considered an essential part of the section.

In the fifties the clarinet and trombone attained recognition as "legitimate" small-group instruments, but by that time, although the instrumentation of the big bands still extant was substantially that of the big swing bands (seven or eight brass, five reeds, and rhythm), the combinations of instruments in the small groups were being multiplied beyond anything the swing jazzman could imagine. Tenor saxophonist Charlie Ventura, for example, had a small group that included a vocalist who sang in unison with his saxophone; Gerry Mulligan often used his baritone saxophone without piano and in combination with trumpet, trombone, or whatever was handy; the Miles Davis group, as mentioned previously, made use of the French horn and tuba; pianist Dave Brubeck teamed up with the alto saxophonist Paul Desmond; and drummer Chico Hamilton organized a group that included guitar, bass, cello, and flute.

Again, while such instruments as the accordion and Hammond organ could in earlier periods be found only in sweet swing salons, they were now to be found in the hands of such serious jazz musicians as Mat Matthews (accordion) and Jimmy Smith (organ). The ten tracks of *Critics' Choice* (Dawn), offer typical examples of the various small instrumental combinations to be found in the middle fifties. Two of the selections are played by piano, bass, and drums; two are played by tenor, trombone, piano, bass, and drums. The others are alto, piano, bass, and drums; clarinet, guitar, bass, and drums; French horn, tenor, harp, soprano voice, piano, bass, and drums; accordion, French horn, guitar, bass, and drums; guitar, accordion, bass; and a band consisting of a tenor and a baritone saxophone, three trumpets, trombone, piano, bass, and drums.

There was little difference between the functions of big-band sections in this period and in the two preceding periods. Backgrounds were essentially of the same type, and riffs were still very much in evidence, as were the saxophone section chorus and the brass ensemble punctuation and reinforcement. It is in the small group that we must look for differences. While the small swing group functioned primarily as a group of soloists against a rhythm background, the modern small group tended to think of itself as a unified whole. The individual members played solos, of course, but, where the swing soloist merely waited his turn, so to speak, the best soloists in this period were concerned with the overall structure of the work; that is, the soloist made an effort to relate his work to that of the entire ensemble.

The so-called solo instruments in the small ensemble were equal in function: all were required to play, usually in unison or octaves, composed lines; all were required to improvise solos; and all were required either to read or to improvise secondary melodic lines against an improvised solo. The greatest change in the function of instruments, however, occurred in the rhythm section.

The pianist, whose function in the thirties was to provide a steady four-four, discovered in this period that the strong, steady beat of the plucked bass made the work he was doing with his left hand redundant. More and more he came to rely on the beat of the bass and to concentrate on the single notes he could play with his right hand. He kept his left free to punch out a chord whenever it seemed necessary to reinforce something his right hand was doing, provide an especially strong up- and downbeat punctuation for the soloist, or occasionally to remind himself and the others of a particular chord progression or cadence—to play what some jazzmen call "feed" chords. A characteristic piano accompaniment for a soloist may be illustrated in brief as follows:

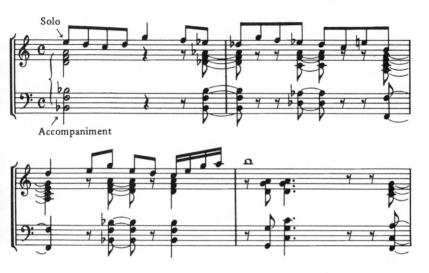

The most revolutionary change, however, came about in the function of the drummer. His aim, like that of the swing pianist, had previously been to maintain a straightforward four-beats-to-the-bar, which he accomplished by tapping his foot on the bass drum pedal; meanwhile he created a variety of rhythms with the sticks in his hands, frequently using the high hat (foot cymbal) for afterbeats and the suspended cymbals for occasional crashes. The modern drummer attempts to create a sustained legato effect by setting the suspended cymbals to vibrating in order to produce a fluid, unaccented four-four beat; the bass drum is used to punctuate or reinforce the rhythm with soft explosions intended to stimulate the soloist. The use of the fingers, sticks, and brushes on various-sized cymbals has opened new and delicate tonal variations to the modern drummer. (A particularly fine display of the use of these devices can be found in any of the Modern Jazz Quartet's recordings.)

Probably in no technical jazz area was there so little progress as in

structure. Whatever formal changes came, generally appeared internally; the mileposts and guidelines of the thirty-two-bar popular song
form and the twelve-bar blues dominated structure as they did in
previous periods. The typical small-ensemble form of the time consisted of an introduction, in which arrangers seemed to extend themselves most; an ensemble unison or octave presentation of the first
sixteen bars; a solo during the eight-bar bridge; and an ensemble
return to the last eight, followed by an agreed number of improvised
solos, after which the original chorus was repeated, sometimes followed
by a short coda. Blues were generally handled much as they had been
since the twenties—that is, by twelve-bar choruses, occasionally broken
by eight- or sixteen-bar episodes. John Lewis, whose work with the
Modern Jazz Quartet showed a rare concern with form, said in a piece
he wrote for the International Music Council: "The audience for jazz
can be widened if we strengthen our work with structure. If there is
more of a reason for what's going on, there'll be more overall sense,
and therefore, more interest for the listener. I do not think, however,
that the sections in this 'structured jazz'—both the improvised and
written sections—should take on too much complexity. The total effect
must be within the mind's ability to appreciate through the ear." [19]

When Lewis said that structured jazz should not "take on too much
complexity," it is apparent that he believed that, in some instances
at least, it had. The complexity however was not, and had not been,
the result of the form, or frame; this had not become more complex.
What had become more complex was the manner in which the musical
material was stretched over the frame, particularly in improvised
music. While notated jazz continued to remain foursquare, improvised
music had developed a technique of what we may call "free phrasing"
that was intended to escape the tyranny of the four- and eight-bar
phrase. Players were then able to stop and go whenever the spirit

moved them, instead of being controlled by traditional melodic or harmonic stopping-places.

The use of classical forms did not appear to satisfy the need of all jazzmen; neither did the "extended form" promulgated by Charlie Mingus in his *Pithecanthropus Erectus* and *Love Chant* (Atlantic). Mingus' use of extended form was by harmonic repetition or augmentation, that is, the soloist "stayed' with a chord until he felt he had explored it sufficiently, after which he moved on to the next chord or measure—a variant of the classical contemporary composer's use of continuous development. In practice the improvised solos of the time frequently fitted a category somewhere between the free phrasing just mentioned and the square phrasing of earlier periods. This combination of both kinds of phrasing may be what Lewis meant when he said, "The total effect must be within the mind's ability to appreciate through the ear." It also seems to be the answer to the problem as summarized by Gunther Schuller in "The Future of Form in Jazz," *Saturday Review,* January 12, 1957: "Experience," he said, "has shown us that the borrowing of a baroque form such as the fugue—the most widely used non-jazz form at the moment—very rarely produces the happiest results. Even when successful, it is certainly not the ultimate solution to the problem of evolving new forms in jazz, mainly because jazz is a player's art, and the old classical and baroque forms are definitely related to the art of composing. (Bach's ability to improvise complete fugues notwithstanding.) Used in jazz these classic forms can, at best, produce only specific and limited results, but cannot open the way to a new musical order. Jazz, it seems to me, is strong and rich enough to find within its own domain forms much more indigenous to its own essential nature."

While avant-garde jazzmen were beginning to explore the use of such classical techniques as modal, twelve-tone, and atonal composition, none of these techniques were actually in the mainstream; modal composition, however, made the greatest headway. Minor blues, for example, while not yet common, appeared with consistently greater frequency, and was only a slight remove from the declared use of the Dorian, Phrygian, Aeolian, and Locrian modes. Since the mainstream jazzman has no more compunction about a pre-established chord progression as a basis for original composition than the classical composer has in borrowing a theme for a set of variations, the basic harmonies of this period must be sought in the progressions of such tunes as "Just You, Just Me," "Cherokee," "Idaho," and a number of similar standards, in addition to variants of the twelve-bar blues. The most popular chord progressions, particularly in the forties, were those of "I Got Rhythm" and "How High the Moon."

In discussing the jazz rhythm of the time, we must distinguish between the notated rhythms of arranged ensemble music and those of improvised music. The arranged rhythms were, to a large extent, swing-oriented. An important aspect of the performance-practice during this time was the slight stress placed on the weak part of the beat in consecutive eighth-note patterns: du-*dah,* du-*dah,* du-*dah,* du-*dah.* As an example of masterful handling of rhythm, and for a study of individual technique, Dizzy Gillespie's extended solo in "Tour de Force," an original work, found in *Dizzy Gillespie, World Statesman* (Verve), is incomparable, and must be heard. The work, arranged by Gillespie in Athens while he was on a tour for the State Department, is quite simple in form and serves mainly as a showcase for Gillespie's brilliantly conceived forty measures of trumpet solo. The thematic material is quite ordinary and rifflike in character; the harmonic foundation, for all its simplicity, is interesting; and during Gillespie's solo the muscal transformation is extraordinary. The structure of the work is plainly perceived on two or three hearings. On the other hand,

Gillespie's treatment of the melody over the harmonic foundation is more complex.

The process of improvising rapidly must, of necessity, lead to the playing of a great many figures and lines that lie in the hand, and mediocre improvisers often rely on these devices even in a slow tempo. However, Gillespie's ingenuity in handling these devices is most remarkable. A study of his work shows that he had learned to organize the ascending and descending diatonic, chromatic, and whole-tone scale patterns, and arpeggio patterns, in such a way as to make them seem at once both calculated and reckless. His solo in this work shows an exceptional concern for the proper balance between tension and release; the impression he creates by contrasting passages of little intervallic motion with rapidly moving jagged lines is not unlike a panoramic view of mountain peaks descending to plains and valleys. Gillespie's most brilliant work in "Tour de Force" is unquestionably the seven-bar phrase that constitutes the bridge of his solo, and is a monument of its time.

the
early sixties

(Overleaf) *Miles Davis*

FOR A TIME IN THE SIXTIES, jazz appeared to be on its way to extinction. The extreme view was that jazz, along with God (and anyone over the age of thirty), was dead. The survival of jazz and its economic health have always depended heavily on the sale of jazz records. The promotion of these records by manufacturers, disc jockeys, booking agencies, and the jazz press constitute the major part of the jazz industry, and without the sale of records to support the promotion, advertising, publicity, entrepreneurs, and jazzmen, the jazz business becomes dangerously ill.

Young people, always critical to the life-support of the record industry, didn't stop buying records in the sixties, they stopped buying *jazz* records. They bought records, of course, but they bought rock records, folk records, folk-rock records, and pop records, and they bought these in the tens of millions. As one could expect, there was little money left for jazz. In the next several chapters we will see how jazz suffered under this adversity, observe its slow recovery, and wonder at its marvelous vigor in the mid-seventies. But in the sixties, jazz, once considered the happiest of all music, apparently could not function as background music to the decade's appalling tragedies, to the assassinations of President John F. Kennedy, Senator Robert F. Kennedy, Malcolm X, Martin Luther King, Jr., and the despair and disillusionment brought on by the war in Vietnam.

Jazz artists watched the rise and fall of rock festivals, black nationalism, jazz as protest, and along with others became frightened of government. Some simply stood by and watched; others tried to speak through their jazz; still others turned away or found refuge in the world of Cage, Stockhausen, Webern, and Babbitt. Jazz changed in the sixties and seventies; it changed slowly, but it changed. Popular figures reached their peak and declined; bop moved to cool, third stream, the new thing; and the sounds of rock became a pounding at the door. A few masters of the past—Armstrong and Ellington, for example—rolled on; old stars began to fade—Brubeck and Monk and the Modern Jazz Quartet. And new heroes rose: Ornette Coleman and John Coltrane and Cecil Taylor and, especially, Miles Davis.

"Well," Quincy Jones asked, "what do you say about him?" In *Down Beat,* July 18, 1974, he offered one answer:

> Wherever [Miles Davis] goes it's a great trip. He's shown all of us the way for a long time now—and he's always been right . . . the lyricism, the cool: it's like he's a stepchild of Lester and Bird, that combination of hot and cool. Duke used to say that Miles is like—and I know you've heard this—Picasso.

Comparing Miles Davis with Pablo Picasso may seem to some ingenuous indeed. Picasso was, after all, a world figure. Davis, on the other hand, although firmly established in the world of jazz, has not yet achieved (at least in the mid-seventies) the position of, say, Armstrong or Ellington. Just the same, what Ellington, Quincy Jones, and others have said—the *meaning* of their comparison—stems from Davis' position as a jazz innovator and creator of the first rank. On more than one occasion in his lifetime he has brought about fundamental changes in both the style-direction and performance of jazz, creating the melodic, harmonic, and rhythmic bases for new jazz styles, touching all those about him, and influencing all those he touched. It may be proper to say that what art meant to Picasso, jazz has meant to Davis. Picasso embraced the nineteenth-century artist's life in its fullest and most romantic sense; and Miles Davis remains, for many, the twentieth century's arch-jazzman.

Miles Davis was born in Alton, Illinois, in 1926, and his father, a dentist, moved the family to East St. Louis soon after. Davis enjoyed the advantages of growing up in a middle-class family; he was given a trumpet for his thirteenth birthday and began lessons with Elwood Buchanan, the local trumpet teacher. By the time he was sixteen, Davis was playing professionally and had come under the influence of Clark Terry, a local trumpeter who later was to spend eight years playing with the Ellington band.

In 1944 Billy Eckstine's band came through town. The band included Dizzy Gillespie and Charlie Parker. Gillespie was much taken with young Davis' playing, and gave him a chance to play with the band during the short time they were there. The following year Davis left for New York to study at Juilliard, but his enthusiasm for the rigors of the conservatory life lasted only one semester. No doubt Gillespie and Parker, both of whom he was now seeing regularly, were distractions. Eventually Davis moved in with Parker. Taking turns at looking after the musical life of their protégé, the men helped Davis find occasional gigs, used him on their own playing dates when they could, and, in general, introduced him to the New York scene and the life of a jazzman.

Davis worked in a variety of night spots, toured across the country and back, and, through Parker, met Charlie Mingus, Lionel Hampton, Art Blakey, and others. He joined Billy Eckstine's band, played several recording dates, and at last played his first important date as a leader, the whole culminating in the seminal *Birth of the Cool,* the 1949 Capitol recording we discussed in Chapter 9. Between 1950 and 1957, Davis led or played in a number of groups (mainly quintets) that at various times included Max Roach, Sonny Rollins, John Lewis, J. J. Johnson, Milt Jackson, Mingus, and Monk. Eventually the right quintet came together, with John Coltrane on tenor saxophone, Red Garland on piano, Paul Chambers on bass, Philly Joe Jones on drums, and Davis as leader. Later, he replaced Garland with Bill Evans, and from time to time used Cannonball Adderley on alto saxophone. In 1957, Davis and the composer-arranger Gil Evans completed the first of their significant collaborations, with the recording of *Miles Ahead* for Columbia. (They had worked together eight years earlier, of course, when Evans contributed his "Boplicity" to *The Birth of the Cool,* of which André Hodeir said, " 'Boplicity' is enough to make Gil Evans qualify as one of jazz's greatest arranger-composers.") Their *Porgy and Bess* collaboration in 1958, followed by *Sketches of Spain* in 1960, both for Columbia, were evidence of a creative synergism rare in the jazz experience.

Shortly after he recorded *Sketches,* Davis set out on a European tour. In Sweden, John Coltrane, who had been part of the Davis quintet on and off for about five years, left the group. Davis was first irritated, then perplexed, then gravely concerned. Coltrane had provided a good deal of the group's electricity, and he would be sorely missed. Davis tried to revitalize the group by hiring Sonny Stitt in Coltrane's place. To no avail. He later gave opportunities to Hank Mobley, Wayne Shorter, George Coleman, and Sam Rivers—all good solid jazzmen— but it became obvious to Davis that the quintet lacked the Coltrane power. He was to learn to go on without Coltrane.

Davis had now served his apprenticeship; he had listened, absorbed what he heard, and, in the language of jazz, paid his dues. The sounds that now came out of his horn came out wonderfully well. Still, some found his technique wanting. What he could not do he wisely—some think unwisely—avoided. His solos were shortwinded, with rhythmic statements far more frequent than melodic ones; he had great difficulty with really fast pieces; and his improvisatory essays were confined nearly entirely to the trumpet's middle and lower registers. (In a jazz joke of the sixties, one jazz musician says to another, "Say, I hear Miles is gonna teach trumpet at the new School of Jazz." His friend, amazed, says, "He is? Hell, who's gonna teach the *high* register?") Although later in his career Davis became technically more proficient, and more comfortable in higher registers, his home base, his first love as it were, was never far from "My Funny Valentine." Given a choice, he preferred ballads with slow-moving, infrequent harmonic changes, and, from the middle fifties on, modal scales and modal harmonies, all of which can be heard on *Kind of Blue* (Columbia). In summarizing Davis' playing in 1963, Whitney Balliett put it this way: "Davis' slow playing is a calculated lisping, an attack of hesitancy and discreet forward rushes; at its best it is striking, at its worst it is messy. The excitements in Davis's work are small and intense and enduring." [1] *Intense* is the appropriate adjective.

By the time he reached thirty-eight, Davis had experienced wide popularity and some financial success. In 1947, at twenty-one, he had been *Esquire's* trumpet star of the year; from 1951 to 1953 he took first place in the *Metronome* polls; and from 1954 on, he won the *Down Beat* Readers Poll almost every year. During his career he had made dozens of successful recordings, but that was past. He was painfully aware that for some time now he had been doing nothing new. The music he was making was business as usual at the same old stand. The spirit and excitement were gone, and a brash young audience was caught up in rock and appeared to be hanging on to it for dear life. Money had also become a problem; Davis' high-flying lifestyle required more and more. In the jazz life, big money comes mostly from tours and record sales, so Davis made his first tour of Japan in 1964 and later in the year went on to Berlin. The tours were unproductive. Tours are intended to promote large record-sales, which in turn assure successful tours, and Davis' latest record-sales were his worst in years. Record buyers were buying records, but not jazz records. In any case, not Davis'.

If his popularity was to revive, change was imperative, and he now thought of change—any change. By 1967, with Wayne Shorter, Herbie Hancock, Ron Carter, and Tony Williams, he began small, tentative explorations. To the quintet he added George Benson on guitar; for Davis the guitar was an innovation. The following year he had Hancock try the electric piano, and suddenly there was a new flavor—a smidgin of rock. In the fall he replaced Hancock with the electric piano of Chick Corea. And now his direction seemed straightforward and clear. By February 1969 he was using Hancock *and* Corea; Joe Zawinul on electric piano and organ; and pop-rock superstar John McLaughlin on electric guitar. The stage was set.

That fall came *Bitches Brew,* with Corea, Zawinul, and Larry Young, all on electric pianos; McLaughlin on electric guitar; Dave Holland on bass; Harvey Brooks on Fender bass; and four drummers whose booming paradiddles on such tracks as "Spanish Key" and "Miles Runs the Voodoo Down" sometimes sounded a lot like Top 40 rock. *Bitches Brew* was recorded for Columbia in August, released the following spring, and by that summer had sold more than 400,000 copies, and Davis must have felt he was finally on his way. There were those, of course, who believed he had compromised his position in jazz by submitting to the pressures of the recording industry. Davis ignored their views. He now electrified his trumpet, explored the uses of the pedal, added echo chambers alongside his electric pianos, and appeared to be committed to using elements of rock not only in his recorded performances but in his public appearances (at least those at which I was present). His ensemble was not yet complete: in 1971 he added Khalil Balakrishna on sitar; in 1972 he added the tabla, the synthesizer, and M'tume on congas.

Davis has been called our most influential contemporary jazz musician. In 1974, Ralph Gleason, at that time the most widely read jazz critic in the English language, said, "Miles Davis' influence is all-pervasive in modern American music. Look at the Billboard chart," he continued, "although Miles is not on it at the moment. In the last year, all sorts of groups who studied at the Davis Conservatory, from Chick Corea to Herbie Hancock, have been. Miles is like Picasso. He has made change into style and wherever you go you bump into little fragments of his music." [2]

Between the time he joined Miles Davis in 1955 and his untimely death in 1967 at the age of forty, John Coltrane became firmly established as a major jazz force, although a controversial one. His slow rise made him seem subordinate to Davis and, later, to Thelonious Monk, particularly during the early years. The truth is he was not so much subordinate to the men around him as he was slow, tentative. His early tenor and soprano saxophone improvisations seem hesitant and, like early Davis, shortwinded. But this was no undisciplined, blind search, and ultimately he would display one of the most formidable and dazzling instrumental techniques in the history of jazz.

He left Davis' group to join Monk, and he left Monk's group to rejoin Davis. Finally, in 1960, confident that he was ready and that his hither-and-thither sideman's apprenticeship was now at an end, he formed his own group. What was Coltrane's playing like at that moment? Ira Gitler, in his record-jacket notes for *Soultrane*, exhorts the reader with, "Ripping, roaring, hotly pulsing, cooking, air-clear-ing." Which is one view. Critic Mimi Clar said it more quickly: "Coltrane's playing," she said, 'is like an electric fan turned on and left on." [3] Both writers were describing Coltrane's "sheets of sound" which, technically, consisted of a long string of consecutive sixteenth-notes played at blinding speed. It was at this time, too, that Coltrane saw an affinity between the soprano saxophone and modal melodies—a subject he would continue to explore.

In his youth Coltrane was interested in a variety of instruments until he settled on the tenor saxophone, in high school. He was born in September 1926, in Hamlet, North Carolina, where his father (who also played a number of instruments) worked as a tailor. After the death of his father, the family moved to Philadelphia, where young Coltrane continued his studies in local music schools. At nineteen, he joined a U.S. Navy band, and upon his release spent the next seven years as a relatively unknown professional jazz musician. After his period with Davis, he continued his slow development until 1960–64, which we may call his middle period.

Coltrane's first group, his quartet, included McCoy Tyner on piano, Elvin Jones on drums, and Jimmy Garrison on bass, and their first Atlantic recording was *Giant Steps* which, in the sense of Coltrane's development and contribution to jazz, was aptly entitled. It was not, however, until Coltrane's version of the popular song "My Favorite Things" (in the Atlantic album of that name), with its pseudo-Eastern qualities and Coltrane's probing of its modal possibilities, that he found himself with his first hit record and a fit subject for the popular jazz press. The following year he became associated with Eric Dolphy, whose specialty was bass clarinet; Dolphy joined Coltrane for some experimental performances, and the controversy over experimental jazz that raged in other quarters (particularly around Ornette Coleman) now came to Coltrane in full cry. John Tynan, an important critic of the time, after hearing a performance by Coltrane and Dolphy in 1961, said: "I listened to a horrifying demonstration of what appears to be a growing anti-jazz trend exemplified by these foremost proponents of what is termed avant garde music. . . . They seem bent on pursuing an anarchistic course in their music that can but be termed anti-jazz." [4] Concerning "Chasin' the Trane," from *Coltrane 'Live' at the Village* (Impulse), recorded at about the same time, Pete Welding, reviewing for *Down Beat*, said, "This piece, with its gaunt, waspish angularities, its ire-ridden intensity, raw, spontaneous passion, and, in the final analysis, its sputtering inconclusiveness, seems more properly a piece of musical exorcism than anything else, a frenzied sort of soul-baring . . . and as such is a remarkable human document." [5] Let us say the performances were adventurous.

During Coltrane's late period, the last several years before his death, his solos became as long as symphonies, alternately pleading and raging, now European, now Asian, now African, and, with the release of *A Love Supreme* (Impulse), deeply religious. The titles of its four parts indicate the spirit in which Coltrane conceived this work: Acknowledgment, Resolution, Pursuance, Psalm—the whole dedicated to the praise of God. *A Love Supreme* is, for its time, a peaceful work, and a work of peace, and readers of *Down Beat* chose this work as Record of the Year, and Coltrane as Jazzman of the Year. His *Transition* (Impulse) came six months later, followed by *Ascension,* the logical and spiritual successor to *A Love Supreme* and recorded with pianist Alice Coltrane, whom he had married in 1963. Upon Coltrane's death, Phyl Garland, in a touching "Requiem for 'Trane" in *Ebony* (November, 1967, p. 67), spoke for the black community when she said, ". . . the importance of John Coltrane exceeds his prominence as a musician. He was known to be a gentle and deeply religious man who had succeeded in finding a path to personal truth while making his way through the dusky evening world." And the jazz world mourned.

"I have listened long and hard to Coleman's music . . ." jazz critic Don DeMicheal wrote in *Down Beat*, May 11, 1961, "I have tried desperately to find something valuable in it, something that could be construed valuable. I have been unsuccessful. . . . Coleman's music, to me, has only two shades: a maudlin, pleading lyricism and a wild ferocity bordering on bedlam. . . . 'Beauty' from the Atlantic recording *This is Our Music* descends into an orgy of squawks from Coleman, squeals from Cherry, and above-the-bridge plinks from Haden. The resulting chaos is an insult to the listening intelligence. It sounds like some horrible joke, and the question here is not whether this is jazz, but whether it is music."

This is a fair sample, in my judgment, of the general reaction to Ornette Coleman's music at nearly every stage of his career in jazz (and I have read and heard hundreds of these opinions—in different styles and language, but all making much the same point). Still, in 1972, 1973, and 1974 he took first place in the Down Beat polls as the readers' choice for favorite alto saxophone player. Is it possible to reconcile these opposite views—this paradox—to everyone's satisfaction? Not likely. Nevertheless, we may attempt to trace Coleman's development, with the hope that in so doing his position in jazz history will be made clear.

Ornette Coleman was born in March 1930 in Fort Worth, Texas. In high school he played in the band; outside school he listened to rhythm and blues bands and whatever was musically current in the hustling after-hours spots in Fort Worth. A local saxophone player and bandleader, Red Connors, taught Coleman the value of ensemble playing, and introduced him to the music of Bud Powell and Charlie

Parker. In 1949, when he was nineteen, he joined a touring minstrel show and eventually arrived in Los Angeles, by way of New Orleans. Los Angeles musicians recall that Coleman played so badly (according to their standards), they avoided playing with him. Most musicians, Coleman said later, "didn't take to me; they said I didn't know the changes and was out of tune." For years Coleman suffered similar rebuffs; as a result, he earned little money and had few friends. Isolated, most of the time living alone, he set out to teach himself theory. Eventually he met trumpeter Don Cherry and several other sympathetic souls, including the drummer Billy Higgins, and a long period of practicing together began. In 1958 Coleman made his first record album: *Something Else! The Music of Ornette Coleman* (Contemporary). The record was not successful.

Later, in happier circumstances, Coleman, who had been playing frenetically in an open jam session in a Los Angeles after-hours club, was heard by an incredulous musician who told a friend about it, who in turn passed the word to several members of the Modern Jazz Quartet, then playing in Los Angeles. They, in turn, brought John Lewis, leader of the Quartet, to hear Coleman. At the time Lewis was heavily involved in the promotion and development of the School of Jazz in Lenox, Massachusetts, and he persuaded both Coleman and Cherry to leave Los Angeles for the annual summer session at Lenox. In the fall, after a rigorous reinforcement of what they had been doing straight along, they returned to Los Angeles just long enough to reconstitute their old quartet; then they went back to New York, with bass player Charlie Haden and drummer Billy Higgins, to open at the Five Spot Cafe on Manhattan's Lower East Side. The audience could not believe what it heard. The impression, as editors Rivelli and Levin said in their *The Black Giants,* was that four musicians were playing "with apoplectic intensity and near-intolerable volume, four simultaneous and very disparate solos which had no perceptible shared references or foundation." [6] The sound was new and the fury intense, and the quartet was taken up heavily by the jazz press, intellectuals, society folk, and Leonard Bernstein, who publicly declared he was in favor of this new thing. Meanwhile, Contemporary released another Coleman album, *Tomorrow is the Question,* and the Five Spot suddenly became a very popular place to be seen.

(In my own experience with Coleman's music, I heard this album, his second, before any of his other music, which I think was fortunate. *Tomorrow is the Question* was, and is, quite approachable; in fact, it was, for me, considerably less unnerving than, say, the first time I heard one of the early Parker *prestissimo* solos. Thus, when the news broke about Coleman's opening at the Five Spot—I was in the Pacific Northwest at the time—I could not understand what the brouhaha was all about. It was not until I heard his 1959 *The Shape of Jazz to Come* and his 1960 *Free Jazz,* both on Atlantic, that I was able to fully understand what Coleman's impact must have been.)

In the three years after the Five Spot opening, Coleman recorded seven albums, and his music was being described and explained endlessly. Balliett wrote about Coleman: "At first hearing, he sounds inflexible, crude, and even brutish. His tone appears thick-thumbed and heavy. He plays insane and seemingly purposeless runs. His intensity is apoplectic." Martin Williams gave a good deal of space to Coleman in the *International Cyclopedia of Music and Musicians;* in brief, he said, "Coleman's improvisations are largely modal, but he occasionally strays into a quasi-atonality. He does not necessarily use regular harmonic changes; he relies on unusual rhythm, accentuation and phrasing; his rhythm section does not always maintain steady time-keeping, and he often plays purposely out of tune." [7] Regarding a first hearing of *Free Jazz,* John Tynan called it "a sprawling, discursive, chaotic jumble of jagged rhythms and pointless cacophonies, among which however are interlarded a number of striking solo segments. . . ." [8]

In December 1962 Coleman presented himself in concert in New York's Town Hall, where in addition to his own group he used a rhythm and blues group and the Fine Arts String Quartet. In his work for the Quartet (a new medium for Coleman), which may be heard on *At Town Hall* (Atlantic), he headed out toward what were for him unexplored territories, and although his composition "Salute to Artists" had some interesting sounds, on the whole it was a poor imitation of Bartók. His work for the combined trio (Coleman, David Izenzon on bass, and Charles Moffett on drums) and the rhythm and blues group, was tonally and rhythmically more accessible. A. B. Spellman, Coleman's foremost biographer, believes this to be one of the two most important works that Coleman ever performed. The other is *Free Jazz*.

Coleman was bitterly disillusioned at the incongruity between his considerable publicity and fame on the one hand and his small financial reward on the other. Further, he was certain he was being exploited by nightclub owners, record companies, publishers, and the music industry as a whole, and he was not averse to broadcasting that message to anyone who would listen. As a result, he found himself unable to work in jazz, and he retired. For the next two years he composed some, played a little, and worked assiduously at teaching himself to play trumpet and violin. At the end of his self-imposed retirement, he opened at the Village Vanguard in New York—an opening covered by *Time, Newsweek, The New Yorker,* and the *New York Times.* The notices were mixed. Late that summer, after receiving a large sum of money for composing a movie background score (it eventually was not used) he was able to take his trio on a European tour. The tour was a *flop d'estime.*

In 1967 *The Empty Foxhole* (Blue Note) was released, with Coleman's teenage son, Ornette Denardo, on drums. Shelly Manne, a fair drummer himself, wrote a review in which he said, "As a drummer that kid will probably turn out to be a good carpenter." [9] In a live performance with his trio and the Philadelphia Woodwind Quintet, Coleman again showed his interest in serious composition with his "Forms and Sounds," in which he played trumpet, and his "A Cappella for Three Wise Men and Sage," in which he played violin. Despite his continuing disenchantment with the financial aspects of the music business, Coleman continued to record albums regularly for the next several years, among them *New York is Now!*, *Love Call* (upon which Bill Cole commented, "On his most recent recordings Coleman has left his violin at home; many of us think that this is good. Should he decide to leave his trumpet at home and concentrate on searching for ways in which to grow as an altoist, still more people would be happier" [10]); and the 1972 release, *Science Fiction* (Columbia), with two quartets, a reciter, a vocalist, and a number of Coleman's songs with words. And 1972, as we pointed out earlier, was the year Coleman won the *Down Beat* poll as favorite alto saxophone player. And Ornette Coleman rolled on.

Late in the 1950s, the phenomenon known as "third stream" occurred; it had significant influence on jazz styles through the sixties and seventies. In its most simplistic sense, it implied that jazz was one stream and classical music another, and that a proper synthesis of these would bring about a third stream. This striving, by jazz players with some serious academic training and classically oriented musicians with some interest in jazz, to combine their major and minor interests is, I believe, a natural development in the history of jazz styles. A musical style, as we know, generally begins with simple materials; it is at first relatively innocent, but grows heavy in sophistication and complexity until it can no longer bear its own weight. At that point someone says, "For heaven's sake, let's go back to the roots!"—he does, and the process starts all over again. In the late fifties, to many with one foot in each stream, the time seemed right. Don Ellis, an early exponent of the Third Stream, responding to criticism, in 1961 said: "It is time for jazz to enlarge its vocabulary. . . . It is time that we all stopped worrying about whether music is jazz or not and simply view each work on its own terms. . . ." [11] Miles Davis, and others, had already made attempts in this direction. Still others were more ambitious.

Some looked upon third stream as music with composed classical backgrounds against which the jazzman improvised—something like a concerto, or, where a jazz ensemble played opposite a classical ensemble, a concerto grosso. There was also much talk of classical forms and baroque spirit, mainly from jazz writers trying to describe for their readers what was happening. The fact is that from the 1920s on (I have in mind Paul Whiteman's and George Gershwin's attempts at "symphonic jazz"), serious composers have regularly found jazz, or what they thought was jazz, fascinating. Jazz, to them, meant the characteristic cliché rhythms and melodic figures and "blue" notes from the stockpile used by jazzmen from Jelly Roll Morton to Bill Evans. From the twenties on we can taste these jazz flavors in Carpenter's *Krazy Kat*—"a jazz pantomime"; in Gershwin's *Rhapsody in Blue* and, later, his *Porgy and Bess;* Honegger's piano concerto; Krenek's *Jonny Spielt Auf,* his so-called jazz opera; Copland's *Music for the Theater* and his piano concerto; Kurt Weill's *Mahagonny;* Antheil's *Jazz Symphony;* and Milhaud's *Creation of the World.* And as many more attempts at injections of pseudo-jazz into serious music are evident in the thirties.

Still, in 1957, Gunther Schuller, the third stream's prime figure, was able to say, concerning a synthesis of jazz and ancient musical traditions, "Speaking for myself, I can only say that the possibilities seem to me both exciting and limitless, and it seems irrelevant to worry about whether this will be jazz or not." [12] Schuller, who coined the term "third stream" as an adjective, wished to have the jazz idea and the classical idea occur simultaneously. (A concert he gave at the University of Chicago was entitled "Simultaneous Music.") Schuller was born in New York in 1925. His father was a violinist in the New York Philharmonic, and Schuller heard music as soon as he could hear. At six he could sing chunks of Wagner; at eleven, as he later put it, he could "sight-read like a whiz." In his teens he transferred from the flute to French horn, joined the Cincinnati Symphony at seventeen, composed a concerto for himself, and heard Ellington for the first time. At twenty he joined the Metropolitan Opera orchestra. By the early sixties he was not only an internationally known composer, but had established himself as one of the most remarkable organizers and administrators (without a commercial interest) in the world of jazz. Equally adept at conducting, managing festivals, writing profoundly on jazz or contemporary serious music, he remained a *wunderkind* far into the seventies.

As Gunther Schuller celebrated his fiftieth birthday, in 1975, he was president of the New England Conservatory, co-director of the Tanglewood music festival, author of the definitive *Early Jazz: Its Roots and Musical Development,* conductor and promoter of Scott Joplin's ragtime opera *Treemonisha,* and he had just completed recreating, for a record album, the Paul Whiteman band of the twenties. In a taped interview with Robert Palmer, for *Down Beat,* Schuller said, "Now, years ago I formulated the Third Stream idea, by which I mean just a lot of musics coming into each other, intersecting in different ways with different strengths and in different combinations. That process is going on right now, and I wouldn't be able to predict where it will be ten years from now. We do that more than any other country in the world, and that, I think, is one of the characteristics of American music making. And it's very exciting." [13]

"Perhaps the most influential catalyst in the rapprochement between jazz and classical music," Schuller wrote for Feather's *Encyclopedia of Jazz*, "has been the Modern Jazz Quartet." [14] John Lewis, its founder and nominal leader from 1952 (the quartet disbanded in 1974) received his master's degree in music from the Manhattan School of Music in 1953, and it is no surprise to learn that his musical views and Schuller's coincided at many points. During the sixties, Lewis' position in the amalgamation of the two musics was second only to Schuller's. They consulted and worked on a number of third-stream projects, including three especially significant ones: Schuller's "Conversation," in the album *Third Stream Music: The Modern Jazz Quartet* (Atlantic), in which the Beaux Arts string quartet joined the Modern Jazz Quartet; Schuller's "Abstraction," for Ornette Coleman, on *Jazz Abstractions* (Atlantic); and the formation of Orchestra U.S.A., a twenty-nine-player cooperative group organized, directed, and conducted by Schuller and Lewis.

There were, of course, others involved in third-stream music, but none so heavily or publicly as Schuller and Lewis. Space forbids a discussion of everyone, but we must include George Russell and what he called his "Lydian Concept of Tonal Organization" (and whose music in 1976 was still available on a number of albums); some early Charlie Mingus, some of Jimmy Giuffre's work; the Davis–Gil Evans *Sketches of Spain* (Columbia); Larry Austin's *Improvisations for Orchestra and Jazz Soloists* (Columbia); and, of course, parts of nearly everything by the Modern Jazz Quartet.

What, then, we may ask, appear to be the principal objections to third-stream music, especially at its inception and during the uncertainties of its early years? John S. Wilson, writing in *Hi Fi* magazine in 1960, said ". . . if this 'third stream' could absorb the concert hall ambitions that some people have for jazz, then jazz—basic, unadulterated jazz—might once more be able to become just jazz, a vital, moving and unique music with a direction of its own, a music which should be accepted for what it is or else left alone." [15] Martin Williams, in an early magazine piece on the third stream reprinted in his book *Jazz Masters in Transition—1957-69,* objected, and properly so, to the use of the expression "third-stream jazz." What was going on, he pointed out, was an alliance between jazz and classical music. "There is, therefore," he said, "no such thing as 'Third Stream jazz,' no matter what liner-note copy says. There can't be; it would be like a male hermaphrodite or a pure-bred mule." [16] Finally, Gene Lees, in *Down Beat* (1964) in "View of the Third Stream," said, "I am objecting to transferring the dead blood of classical music into the live and virile animal that jazz essentially is—and of wastefully transfusing the healthy blood of jazz into senile musical forms that are beyond saving." [17] Which we might call the case for euthanasia.

Just the same, here, from the 1970s, is a healthy and interesting array of third-stream material and sounds in Bill Evans' "Twelve Tone Tune Two," on Fantasy's *The Tokyo Concert* (it may be worthwhile to compare this with a 1962 piece called "The Twelves," by John Benson Brooks, who had his own method for improvising with twelve tones); Cecil Taylor's *Silent Tongues* (Arista), an incredible blending of Bartók, Tatum, and Taylor; and a number of Keith Jarrett pieces, particularly his "Crystal Moment," from *In the Light* (ECM Records), of which he explained in his liner notes that he was experimenting not so much with melody and harmony in their usual meaning, but rather with scale, pitch, range, consistency, and diversity ("Its success surprised me," he ended modestly).

It seems proper to close this section with an attempt at a brief summary of what sorts of things Third Stream composers included in their works from the fifties to the middle seventies (although there is no substitute for hearing the music itself).

All music includes in part—to a greater or lesser degree—melody, harmony, rhythm, counterpoint, form, and what the Germans call *Klangfarbe* or, freely translated, tone-color. Traditional mainstream jazz uses melody that is essentially tonal—that is, in an established key or tonality with frequent use of so-called blue notes; and uses mainly diatonic harmony to accompany the melody—that is, harmonies or chords that are found regularly in that key or tonality. Rhythms are generally constructed to agree with the meter with, however, considerable syncopation, or displaced downbeats; true counterpoint, where two or more parts are of *equal* independence is absent or is held to a minimum; form is generally fixed—regular four- and eight-bar phrases, twelve-bar blues, thirty-two-bar ternary forms, and so forth; tone-color, on the other hand, has been a special concern of all jazzmen throughout the history of jazz, from the development of the New Orleans–style small ensemble to the Neophonic Orchestra of Stan Kenton.

What, then, did the third-streamers contribute that traditional jazz did not already encompass? We must remember that throughout the history of jazz certain individuals or groups made special advances in one or more of these musical techniques. It was not, however, until the early sixties that we find sufficient activity for the third stream to be considered a stylistic trend. Furthermore, parts of what was initiated during this time were still being used by significant jazz figures in the mid-seventies, fifteen years later.

Melodically, there was considerable use of modal scales; some use of the whole-tone scale; tone rows (usually the twelve tones of the chromatic scale arranged in a pattern that does not suggest a traditional key); wide and jagged melodic leaps; and a special manner of playing isolated notes in imitation of a style of painting with dots and tiny brush strokes called "pointillism." Harmonically, of course, modal harmonies would accompany the modal melodies; chords would be constructed with intervals of seconds, fourths, and fifths instead of the traditional third; chords from two established keys would be used simultaneously (try playing a chord on the white keys of the piano and on the black keys *at the same time*); finally, there is the avoidance of any semblance of traditional key, or tonality, called "atonality." (This last eventually resulted, in the mid-seventies, in what has been called "clouds of sound.") Rhythmically, third-stream people sometimes used an implicit beat instead of the regularly heard, recurring beat supplied by members of the traditional rhythm section. Meters, too, could be irregular, mixed, or even free, so that strong and weak beats could not regularly be anticipated by the listener.

Counterpoint was the *sine qua non* of third-stream music, particularly the use of eighteenth-century contrapuntal techniques if not eighteenth-century tonality. Two-part counterpoint was obligatory, and no self-respecting third-stream piece would be without it—the style of the counterpoint, of course, being absorbed into the general style of the piece, that is, modal or bitonal or polytonal, or atonal, or plain dissonant. It must be pointed out, however, that there were occasions in which quite straightforward eighteenth-century counterpoint, in the style of Bach, was used. Any counterpoint was considered better than no counterpoint at all. For this reason, many third-stream pieces imitate eighteenth century musical forms both in title and in structure, with fugues and other variation forms much in evidence.

(One clue to third-stream music in the sixties and seventies is the abstract title, presumably meant to alert the listener to its proper connotation. In past centuries, the titles "fugue," "concerto," "sonata," "symphony," "variations," helped to serve this purpose; in the sixties and seventies, titles including such words as "abstraction," "essay," "tangents," "space," and the modest "Music for . . ." frequently serve the same purpose.) In addition, traditional forms of jazz were frequently modified, extended, and, by the seventies, expanded to correspond to the large forms used by contemporary serious composers.

Charlie Mingus is unclassifiable. One of the most creative jazzmen of his time, he has managed to avoid being pigeonholed, classified, or declared a member of any in-group. While this is in keeping with the creative and independent spirit, it has also made it difficult for the public, the critics, and the historians to place him in his proper position. Historians, particularly, are frustrated when a jazzman like Mingus cannot be securely classified; but let us try.

From the early fifties, when he came to New York from California, he managed to become involved in whatever was going on in jazz without actually becoming part of any movement. In his time, and in his role as one of the great bass players in jazz, he could work equally well with Stan Getz or Charlie Parker, Art Tatum or Jaki Byard, Red Norvo or Roland Kirk, Miles Davis or Duke Ellington. From Ellington, a major influence in Mingus' life, he drew a musical sophistication; from his mother, a fervent Holiness churchgoer with young Charles inevitably in tow, he picked up a down-home Holy Roller spirit, and a musical taste and inclination that would continue to show itself from time to time throughout his career.

Mingus was born in Nogales, Arizona, in 1922, and moved to Watts, California, while he was still quite young. After his aspiring parents had him try trombone to no avail, he was provided with a cello, and from there it was but a step to the bass and study with jazz bassist Red Callender. Once in New York, he formed a number of groups with various personnel including Thad Jones, Jackie McLean, and Bud Powell, and began his five-year studies with H. Rheinschagen, bass player with the New York Philharmonic Orchestra. By the late fifties he had found drummer Dannie Richmond (who would turn out to be his most frequent sideman) and had started on a series of recordings that would include "Haitian Fight Song," in which his bass playing foreshadowed bass techniques of the seventies; and later, the hilarious "Eat That Chicken," and the 1961 "Hog-Callin' Blues" (all on Atlantic's *The Best of Charlie Mingus*); in the latter Mingus does a scat vocal introduction worthy of Armstrong at his best, and Jimmy Knepper plays an earthy trombone solo that would make a statue smile. (Two years later Mingus was to knock out two of Knepper's teeth, but for the present all was well.) He had also organized his Jazz Workshop, where at various times he worked with Roland Kirk, Booker Irvin, John Handy, and others, and his influence on the young jazz bassists of the late fifties and sixties was without peer. Some of Mingus' best work of the early sixties may be heard on *Charles Mingus Presents Charles Mingus* (Candid) and *Tonight at Noon* (Atlantic), which are representative of the sort of creativity Mingus was interested in, and at the same time, in the *Tonight* album, show his homage to Ellington, in the Ellingtonish "Invisible Lady."

By the middle sixties Mingus had attained the position of the bad boy of jazz, the rebel musically and socially. Whether it was all true or not, it was reported that he was irresponsible, fractious, and would just as soon punch you in the nose as not. Some of the reports were, of course, true. He had been in violent fights; he had refused to honor contracts; he had walked away from jobs before they were finished; he

had insulted audiences who paid to hear him play. Mingus believed
he was justified in all instances. Although he managed to become part
of everything new in the world of jazz, he nevertheless found a way to
remain independent. He said, "Man, I'm a single movement."

By the middle seventies Mingus had mellowed—a word he would
like. For twenty-five years he had said his piece and, because of that,
had paid heavy dues. Now he would receive *his* due. He became a
part-time instructor in composition at the State University of New
York in Buffalo; he completed his biography, *Beneath the Underdog:
His World as Composed by Mingus,* and Knopf published it in 1971;
he received a Guggenheim grant in musical composition. And he now
appeared to be as comfortable with lobster and Pouilly-Fuissé as he
once was with ribs and beer. Still and all, he found time in 1974 to
round up John Handy, Rahsaan Roland Kirk, George Adams, Hamiet
Bluiett, Charles McPherson on saxes; Don Pullen on piano; Jon
Faddis on trumpet; and the redoubtable Dannie Richmond on drums,
and bring about the greatest jam session since the expression was
coined. The session includes a wonderfully spirited and inventive
"C Jam Blues" and a joyful "Perdido," and they may be heard on
Atlantic's *Mingus at Carnegie Hall.* Perhaps the classification for
Charlie Mingus is catalyst.

II

toward
the seventies

(Overleaf) *The Modern Jazz Quartet. Milt Jackson on vibraharp; Connie Kay, drums; John Lewis, piano; and Percy Heath, bass*

AT THE BEGINNING OF THE SIXTIES, few could have predicted that Julian "Cannonball" Adderley (born 1928, died 1975), a bop saxophone player whose idol was Charlie Parker, would in the course of the next seven years appear on *Billboard's* "Hot 100" charts with "African Waltz" in 1961; "The Jive Samba" in 1963; and twice in 1967, with "Mercy, Mercy, Mercy" and "Why (am I treated so bad)." Adderley apparently had discovered the secret of at least sporadic popularity, and was therefore eligible to join the company of those moneymaking pop and rock stars on the charts of *Billboard, Variety, Cashbox,* and others who keep score for the trade.

In the decade of the sixties, only twelve jazz figures and groups made the *Billboard* "Hot 100." In addition to Adderley, they are Louis Armstrong, the Dave Brubeck Quartet, the Count Basie band (twice), Stan Getz (twice), Charlie Byrd, Al Hirt (four times in 1964), the Jazz Crusaders, Herbie Mann (five times), Bud Shank, Cal Tjader, and Kai Winding. What do we call these men? The jazz pop stars of the sixties? I think not; that would be misleading. They may have discovered the right song (Louis singing "Hello, Dolly"), or were first with a rhythmic idea that caught on (Getz and "The Girl From Ipanema"). Whatever they did may have had great popularity, but had little impact on the history or development of jazz. Nevertheless, I believe their contribution *in the sixties* gives them a position in what Stanley Dance termed "mainstream jazz." Their category, if we had to have one, would be "popular, but not historically significant." Another category might include those jazzmen who were neither popular nor especially significant. (They are found in nightclubs and jazz clubs in nearly all of the world's major cities.) And we would certainly have to find a place for those lucky few who were both popular and historically significant—the Modern Jazz Quartet, for example. Others, particularly those who seldom or never have achieved popularity but are historically important, would seem clearly not to be in the mainstream, but even here we are sometimes surprised. Finally, we must remember that jazzmen, like all creative artists, have periods in their lives during which they may be more or less popular, and more or less historically significant. In this section, my intention is to discuss briefly those who were the principal figures in mainstream jazz in the sixties. In any case, I have tried to treat the most controversial figures elsewhere in this book, as well as those involved in creating a jazz not yet acceptable to the general jazz public.

The Modern Jazz Quartet (John Lewis, piano; Milt Jackson, vibraphone; Percy Heath, bass; and Connie Kay, drums), whose formation and early music were touched upon in the previous chapter, was perhaps the most popular small jazz group during the sixties. In 1969 Whitney Balliett wrote for *The New Yorker* what was certainly the best short biographical piece on the Modern Jazz Quartet. "The Quartet," he wrote, ". . . is tintinnabulous. It shimmers, it sings, it hums. It is airy and clean. Like any great mechanism, its parts are as notable as their sum." John Lewis, he goes on to say, "is an emotional pianist—in a transcendental way," while "Jackson is more than a consummate foil. He is profuse, ornate, affecting, and original." [1] By 1969 the Quartet had been together for seventeen years. "The Quartet will never break up," Jackson said at the time. "The only way we'd break up would be somebody getting sick." The Quartet gave its final concert on November 25, 1974; happily, no one was sick. Their last performance together may be heard on *The Last Concert* (Atlantic).

In the middle sixties, the Quartet toured extensively in Europe, Japan, and Australia. They continued to release record albums regularly, and this work was consistently well received. As a group, they climbed to near the top in almost every jazz poll here as well as abroad; their principal competition came from Dave Brubeck and Miles Davis. Milt Jackson, however, won everything in sight. Milt Jackson and vibes, for most jazz buffs of the time, were an inseparable association. Some of the Quartet's best efforts may be heard on recordings resulting from their tours; of particular note is *European Concert* (Atlantic). And for an interesting survey of the Quartet's capabilities, a good selection may be found in their *Classics,* on the Prestige label.

In surveying the mainstream as jazz approached the seventies, we should note the following considerations: A number of mainstream jazzmen will be recognized as crossovers from other categories; some of the post-bop and post-cool groups of the fifties will have continued into the sixties; others will have gained and then lost ground during the period. Finally, and for some readers, it is likely that certain jazz figures will be conspicuous by their absence; these will include those who got their start probably from the middle to the late sixties (Freddie Hubbard, Jeremy Steig, and Herbie Hancock are names that come to mind easily), but did not become prominent until·the seventies and will therefore be treated in the chapter on the seventies.

Here, then, follows a representative sampling of the most popular mainstream jazzmen and jazz groups across the sixties, in a concordance of the most widely read jazz polls. Trumpet: Dizzy Gillespie, Miles Davis, Al Hirt. Trombone: J. J. Johnson, Kai Winding, Bob Brookmeyer. Alto saxophone: Cannonball Adderley, Paul Desmond, Johnny Hodges. Tenor saxophone: John Coltrane, Stan Getz, Sonny Rollins. Baritone saxophone: Gerry Mulligan. Clarinet: Buddy De-Franco, Pete Fountain. Flute: Herbie Mann, Frank Wess. Vibraphone: Milt Jackson, Bobby Hutcherson. Piano: Oscar Peterson, Bill Evans, Dave Brubeck. Guitar: Wes Montgomery, Charlie Byrd, Jim Hall. Bass: Ray Brown, Charlie Mingus, Richard Davis. Drums: Elvin

Jones, Joe Morello, Shelly Manne. Miscellaneous instruments: Roland
Kirk (African reed instruments). Organ: Jimmy Smith. The favorite
big bands included Duke Ellington's and Count Basie's. (Although
Stan Kenton made a valiant effort to re-establish his popularity with
the creation of his Neophonic Orchestra in 1965, his efforts were not
well met.) The most popular small jazz groups (in the sixties called
"combos") were: The Modern Jazz Quartet, Dave Brubeck's group,
Miles Davis' group; and, for a time, Ramsey Lewis and his trio.

There were, of course, a number of fancies, some passing and others
that continued to hang on. Latin American rhythms and instruments
and percussionists were being used more widely, not only in groups
whose specialty this was, but in mainstream jazz. From the early sixties
on, the sounds of Indian music, brought to the attention of the American public by the Beatles' association with Ravi Shankar, one of
India's foremost sitar players, began to infiltrate if not mainstream
jazz then certainly a number of pop-rock-blues groups with jazz pretensions, and later showed up in the work of a number of avant-garde
jazzmen. The most significant new influence, however, as jazz approached the seventies, must be sought in what we may call the rock
phenomenon.

Rock, according to rock historian Carl Belz in his definitive *The Story
of Rock,* emerged in the middle fifties "from sources in the Pop, Country and Western, and Rhythm and Blues traditions," and is characterized by the style of Elvis Presley. Between 1957 and 1963 there was
a "gradual expansion of rock and its ability to subsume a variety of
sub-styles and innovations." Among the best-known performers of
this period were Presley, of course; Fats Domino; Bill Haley; Jerry
Lee Lewis; Chuck Berry; Buddy Holly; Ray Charles; The Everly
Brothers; Ricky Nelson; Chubby Checker; Sam Cooke; and a hundred
others, including vocal groups with such soft-sell names (in contrast

to the hard-sell names to come) as The Shirelles, The Contours, The Crystals, The Beach Boys, and The Marvelettes.

From 1964 on, rock moved in a new direction which included, Belz said, "a combination of self-evident worldliness with an artistic sophistication . . ." characterized particularly by the music of the Beatles. The success of the Beatles brought a wave of British groups to the United States, among which were the Rolling Stones, a group with a curious attraction to the old and new blues of black America. From San Francisco, the citadel of hippie culture in the mid-sixties, came the sounds of The Grateful Dead, Jefferson Airplane, Big Brother and The Holding Company, and others, and always the blues; city blues and country blues—white groups singing and playing black blues.[2]

From rock's beginnings, jazzmen and jazz writers thought if they ignored it, it would go away. At the outset it certainly seemed to be a fad—something for the kids, like bubble gum and hula hoops. But as the years rolled on, a bitterness grew. Rock, the street talk had it, was giving jazz a bad name; rock and roll performances were being palmed off as "jazz" festivals, and at the beginning of the sixties the press, it was claimed, associated the nation's social upheaval not with those hippie types, but with jazz—giving jazz a bad name. And worse still, people were not buying jazz records as they had in the past. The young, traditionally buyers of jazz records, were now buying pop, rock, rhythm and blues, everything *but* jazz records, and the result was unprecedented economic pressure on those engaged in jazz as a business. In 1966, in an article for *Seattle* magazine, I wrote: "During a two-week period last November, *Billboard* received from record manufacturers 281 single records for review purposes. . . . During the same two-week period, the following record albums were reported to have sold a million or more copies: One album each by The Monkees, the Dave Clark 5, The Rolling Stones, The Animals, The Four Seasons,

Herman's Hermits, Roger Miller, and The Mama's and The Papa's (watch those apostrophes); three albums by the Beatles; and five albums by Herb Alpert. . . . And if we use three dollars as an average album price after discount, the sale of albums alone in a relatively short time came to a minimum of $48,000,000." [3]

By 1967, small cracks had appeared in the rock dam. The Gary Burton Quartet, with Burton on vibraphone, Larry Coryell on guitar, Steve Swallow on bass, and Stu Martin on drums, were experimenting with a blend of jazz and rock. Burton had worked with Stan Getz just the year before, and earlier with George Shearing. Coryell's roots were in rock, and before he joined Burton, he had worked with a rock band called Free Spirits. Now, together, they made a provocative combination. Robert Christgau, one of the most important rock reporters (*Esquire, The Village Voice, Newsday,* the *New York Times*) later said, "Coryell is the white hope of jazz-rock." (We will meet Coryell again later.)

At the same time, the Blues Project, a rock group, was making passes at jazz. Arnold Shaw, in *The Rock Revolution,* could write: ". . . jazz and rock are beginning to go together in an exploratory courtship." Jeremy Steig, a young jazz flutist, formed The Satyrs, clearly as a rock group. Other rock groups were beginning to discover joy and excitement in their attempts at jazz improvisation. And when *Time* magazine published a piece in August 1967 entitled "A Way Out of the Muddle," full of optimism and hope for the marriage of jazz and rock and wishing the newlyweds "bon voyage," the merger took on a sort of bourgeois respectability. In January 1968 *Life* magazine published a review of Cream—a rock group with British blues guitarist Eric Clapton, in which Richard L. Saltonstall, Jr., told *Life* readers that "The healthiest development in popular music these days is the extraordinary convergence of jazz and rock."

What was it, then, that the two saw in each other, as it were? Jazz saw, of course, a potential revival of lost popularity, and certainly an opportunity to share in rock's booming financial success. To rock, already popular and rich, jazz offered little except respectability. While rock saw jazz as barely a cut above rock socially, in the beginning jazz as *music* bore the same relationship to rock as Claude Debussy to Jelly Roll Morton. Jazz had become a music worthy of the most serious study; one could speak of jazz theory, counterpoint, orchestration, form and analysis. As for rock, its chief musical virtues were, in Christgau's words, ". . . its stubborn simplicity—the stupid beat, the changeless changes . . ." Was there more? Perhaps an objective laying-out of rock's musical elements might uncover something more, some special quality, some minor appeal. (Of course, there is no adequate substitute for listening to the music itself.)

Melodically, rock, being blues-oriented, uses frequent blue notes; modal tunes (a great favorite of the Beatles) are quite common, particularly in ballads and other slow-moving tunes—a favorite mode is the Mixolydian (at the keyboard, the scale from G to G, using the white keys only). The harmonies used depend, of course, on the type of melody to be harmonized; in blues-oriented melodies the chord changes are never far from the traditional twelve-bar blues progression; and modal tunes take modal harmonies—moving from the triad C E G to the triad B flat D F, and back again, is a common rock chord progression. At the maximum, the harmonies of rock can be as charming and engaging as any to be heard in most music of the Renaissance, when modal harmonies were the order of the day. At the minimum, the use of one or two chords only—particularly after a minute or two—will enforce the impression that, harmonically, the music is poverty-stricken. (In the hands of a first-rate improviser, however, the lack of changes is not necessarily a handicap.) The rock rhythm section usually provides a steady, propulsive, generally "square" beat made up of steadily moving eighth-notes (da-da-da-da-da-da-da-da); as rock approached the seventies, rock rhythms became nearly indistinguishable from those used in mainstream jazz. The musical structures of rock were, for the most part, essentially those of early jazz, with occasional modifications. (Much was made in the sixties of a seven-bar phrase in the Beatles' "Yesterday.")

The size and makeup of rock groups varied, but the combination of five young men appeared to have a slight edge over any other, and everyone played, or sang, or both. Mainly they played guitars—hollow-body electric guitars; solid-body electric guitars; cutaway guitars with true vibrato tailpieces, adjustable reinforcing truss rods, straightline ovalled rosewood fingerboards, all in solid or shaded walnut and cherry-red sunbursts. Rock groups played six-string, flat-top classic guitars, four-string tenor guitars, twelve-string folk guitars, and the four- and eight-string electric bass guitar sometimes called a Fender bass, after inventor Leo Fender. (There were many other brands of bass guitar, but Fender seemed to be the generic name, like calling all fruit gelatine Jell-O.) The old-fashioned bass fiddle—by the seventies this was called an "acoustic" bass—was temporarily out and the electric bass guitar was in. Electric organs, electric pianos, and electric harpsichords became commonplace. Electronic equipment produced instruments which, in turn, were capable of making sounds at a degree of loudness never before associated with music, and this amplification became one of rock's most singular characteristics. Electronic feedback, for example, once regarded both as noise and an intrusion, became for rock musicians a legitimate rock sound. The high-level volume was considered essential by rock groups and devotees alike, and an integral part of the rock experience. The booming sounds were considered to be most intensely experienced and appreciated when accompanied by the split-second, on-and-off flashing of strobe lights. The experience was said to be psychedelic.

The nearly standard instrumental makeup was: lead guitar, rhythm guitar, electric bass, drums, and some sort of keyboard instrument. For special occasions, rock groups would add to their regular ensemble such nonrock instruments as the French horn, harmonica, recorder, cello, tambourine, jew's harp, and sitar. Later, those with jazz pretensions added (or started with) the standard brass-reed instruments of jazz.

In 1975 Don Asher, former nightclub pianist, in a memoir in *Harper's,* remembers what it was like to be a lover of jazz in the early sixties, at the outset of the rock phenomenon, and the subsequent gritting of teeth, endless frustration, and pessimistic view of life in general. As the sixties progressed, there were changes for the better. And here—representing the feelings of many in 1975, myself included —is Asher's summation: "Those of us who survived the shattering of the thirty-two-bar icon are better for it. We are able to recognize the freshness of the new melody, the utility of the rock bassist's propulsive rhythmic figures, and the drummer's churning drive. The practicability of the electric keyboard is unquestionable, although many a pianist will miss the sweet sound of good wood. There has been an inevitable merging of boundaries. A jazz flavor now spices the improvisational lines of rock groups, and a boiling pulse powers the jazz rhythm section." [4] Sometimes the remembrance of things past forces us back to the present.

For most of its history, jazz had been a symbol of protest, sometimes mild, sometimes strong, but never manifested more fiercely than during the sixties. Jazz, of course, came out of the South, from an oppressed black people. This oppression and sense of aloneness found its voice first in work songs, spirituals, and above all the blues—often bitter, resentful, defiant. And so it has remained.

When jazz left the South and arrived in the big cities, it soon ran head on into the dominant Puritan morality of established society and the general American culture. And it was not long before those members on the fringe of America's white society who believed they had reason to protest against the values of the Establishment, found in jazz an immediate and satisfying appeal. David Riesman, whose 1950 book title *The Lonely Crowd* expresses so touchingly that paradox of our time, said that "jazz lovers are protesters. They are individualists who reject contemporary majority conformities."

For our purposes, the protesters may be split into three groups: intellectuals, youth, and the black community—all those who in one way or another see themselves as isolated from the general society. (There will, of course, be some overlap: there are young intellectuals and young blacks.) The intellectual feels trapped between the insecure joy of free response and the predictable rewards of philistine conformity. The rebellious young are disgusted with society's strictures, tired of the burdensome responsibilities thrust upon them by parents, school, government, justly frightened and confused at the inevitability of growing up, of having to accept conventions and standards of a society they had no part in shaping; and, like blacks, and with various styles of expression—some smoldering, some fiery—the young protest. To be a white jazz-lover, let alone a jazz performer, requires some psychological degree of identification with black America.

For blacks, jazz as protest is, of course, something special. From the forties through the sixties, the black jazz scene was closely related to the black social scene, and at this point a brief survey of that social scene may be useful toward an awareness and understanding of that relationship. At the same time, for example, that Charlie Parker was on the threshold of revolutionizing jazz in 1942, concert singer Roland Haynes went to jail in Rome, Georgia, because his wife had taken a "white place" in a local shoe store, and he had supported her position —an item not much discussed in white circles at the time, but sufficiently important to be listed in *The Chronological History of the Negro in America.* Among other significant events in the fifties, special mention must be given to Martin Luther King, Jr., and his fight against segregation, and the passage of the Civil Rights Act of 1957. By 1960 black college student sit-ins were spreading rapidly, eventually encompassing more than 70,000 blacks and whites in classrooms, libraries, beaches, and churches. The Congress of Racial Equality (CORE) and the Student Nonviolent Coordinating Committee (SNCC) were in the press almost daily, and those hoping to break down segregation in public transportation were called Freedom Fighters. At the same time, a wave of black nationalism—with black Africa as the nation—spread across America's black ghettoes; in addition, by 1961 there were fifty-one Black Muslim temples and missions. Jazz musicians composed and performed "African" pieces—Randy Weston's *Uhuru Afrika,* and Oliver Nelson's *Afro-American Sketches,* for example—and many took Mohammedan names: saxophonist Edmund Gregory, for example, became Sahib Shabab; drummer Art Blakey became Abdullah Ibn Buhaina; and, perhaps of corollary interest, Cassius Clay, heavyweight boxing champion, who refused to enter military service in 1967, became Muhammad Ali. It was not until 1969, however, that Roland Kirk became Rahsaan Roland Kirk.

The year 1964, a presidential election year, was a time of riots in Florida, New Jersey, Illinois, Pennsylvania, and New York's Harlem. It also saw the creation of the all-black Freedom Now Party, and a substantial increase in the membership of the Black Panther Party. The following year brought the assassination of Malcolm X, then leader of the Organization of Afro-American Unity; and the most terrible riots in Watts, on the outskirts of Los Angeles, where thirty-four persons were killed, over a thousand injured, and property damage was estimated at $40 million. By 1966 both SNCC and CORE began to advocate Black Power, and their audiences included the roughly five and a half million blacks who between 1950 and 1965 had left the South and spread both north and west. In addition to the foregoing, by the end of the sixties, black community members—many of whom saw in black jazzmen not only cultural heroes of a sort but social leaders as well—had been forced to assimilate the assassinations of Martin Luther King, Jr., Medgar Evers, Malcolm X, and President John F. Kennedy and his brother Robert, both of whom had shown special consideration to the plight of America's black community. Finally, American troop involvement in the Vietnam war—starting with the commitment of combat troops in 1965 and turning into the longest if not the most agonizing war in United States history—gave protesters, black and white alike, a common cause.

The events of the sixties raise three important questions: How were black jazzmen affected by these events? What did they do about them? How was their response manifested in the jazz they played? What they said or did privately does not concern us. On the record, we have only what they said and did publicly, and the press provided considerable coverage. To begin with, let us consider briefly the black jazzmen's efforts at organization, where we find two kinds of action: jazzmen banding together in the interest of new "black" jazz, and jazzmen lending themselves to support of nonjazz organizations for the welfare of blacks in general. Here, then, follows a brief but nonetheless characteristic list of activities of the jazzmen publicly most concerned with the new music and with jazz as a symbol of social protest.

In 1961, pianist Randy Weston organized the Afro-American Musicians Society; in 1961 and 1963 Weston made two trips to Nigeria. In 1963 the Jazz Arts Society, a New York organization, arranged to open an operating branch in Nigeria. In October 1964, in a series of programs provocatively entitled "The October Revolution in Jazz," some twenty groups and soloists—black and white—presented new music and panel discussions ("Jim Crow and Crow Jim"), all organized by Bill Dixon, a trumpeter-composer. Those performing included Paul Bley, John Tchicai, Roswell Rudd, and David Izenzon; the panelists included Cecil Taylor, Archie Shepp, and Sun Ra—all jazzmen in the forefront (along with pioneers Ornette Coleman and John Coltrane) of what was becoming known as "the new thing." Shortly after, Dixon organized the Jazz Composers Guild, whose charter members included, among others, the October Revolution people mentioned above. In a *Down Beat* interview with Robert Levin, Dixon said that two of the Guild's main goals were "to awaken the musical conscience of the masses of people to that music which is essential to their lives; to protect the musicians and composers from the existing forces of exploitation," in language as stereotyped as the slogans of the archetypal October Revolution.

In 1965, LeRoi Jones (who later became Amiri Baraka) headed a Black Arts group that brought mobile jazz performances, by Archie Shepp and others, to the streets of Harlem. Frank Kofsky, an ardent supporter of the "new thing" and related social issues, in his *Black Nationalism and the Revolution in Music,* tells of a concert he attended in 1966 featuring Archie Shepp and others, after which a short speech was made by Stokely Carmichael, of SNCC, and a leading figure in black nationalism. Kofsky pointed out that "One could hardly ask for a more vivid instance of the relationship that joins the two."

(As a footnote to the account of jazzmen supporting the freedom

273

movement, it is necessary to remember that many mainstream jazz performers, black and white, donated their services to numerous benefit performances for civil rights organizations during this very same period. A Freedom Jazz Festival, a benefit for CORE, included the Gerald Wilson band and the Chico Hamilton Quintet; the Artists Civil Rights Assistance Fund included on its board of directors Dizzy Gillespie and Quincy Jones. The star of the NAACP fund-raising Freedom Spectacular was the Duke Ellington Orchestra. Space will not allow listing all those in jazz who had contributed their services over the decade of the sixties. While the list is not endless, it is nonetheless substantial.)

While there may have been differences in the way the "new thing" leaders viewed questions of instrumental technique, say, or the value of music theory, they all agreed, in accordance with their individual opinions, on jazz as a *social* phenomenon. A composite of the views of the leaders and the followers, a kind of general credo, may be summed up as follows: True jazzmen were black jazzmen; the best jazzmen had always been black; the "new thing" was a historically inevitable musical revolution, as was the work of Charlie Parker; jazz is black protest music, always was and always will be, and whites who join in are in the role of Mailer's white negro; black jazzmen have always been exploited by the white jazz Establishment; and the only viable answer to this exploitation is black nationalism; finally, the idea of black jazz by black people for black people may be more important than whether what is being played and heard is art, or is good in any musical sense.

The strongest and most vocal supporter of avant-garde jazzmen was the playwright and critic LeRoi Jones. In 1961 he saw the principal figures as Ornette Coleman, Eric Dolphy, Don Cherry, Freddie Hubbard, Billy Higgins, Ed Blackwell, Wilbur Ware, Charlie Haden, Cecil

Taylor, and Wayne Shorter. A cut below these, perhaps as lesser innovators, Jones suggested Archie Shepp, Oliver Nelson, Dennis Charles, Earl Griffith, Scott LaFaro, Buell Neidlinger, Chuck Israels, George Tucker, "and others." Coleman eventually moved into a class of his own, constantly flanked by Cherry; Dolphy, who became a bass clarinet specialist, made some contributions until he died in 1964; Hubbard eventually moved into the mainstream. Higgins was Coleman's early drummer; LaFaro died in 1961. Later, two others joined the ranks: saxophonist Albert Ayler and a pianist-composer calling himself Sun Ra. Ayler, like Shepp, got his start playing with Taylor. Unlike Shepp, however, Ayler revealed little technique. His interests appeared to alternate between the occult and fundamental religion, and a good sampling of his curious, primitive sophistication may be heard on his 1964 *Vibrations,* on Arista; the 1968 *Love Cry,* on Impulse; and, before he died in 1970, the relentlessly primitive *Music Is the Healing Force of the Universe,* on Impulse, with Muhammad Ali on drums.

Sun Ra's function in the sixties may be compared with Dizzy Gillespie's public function in the forties, although there would be little comparison musically. Gillespie had his beret, his goatee, his leopardskin vest, and his awry horn—what I will call the put-on of paraphernalia. Sun Ra was the leader of an "arkestra"—the Sun Ra Myth–Science Arkestra—complete with silky tunics, rich priestly head coverings, a dozen players caught up in a sort of African-Egyptian-cosmic haze, all of which is available on the Saturn album, *Sun Ra and His Solar Arkestra Visit Planet Earth.*

Ultimately, Shepp and Taylor, the two most admired for their ability, courage, and outspokenness, became spokesmen for the "new thing" on both musical and social issues. Cecil Taylor was the most technically proficient member of the group and, in the view of many, the most artistically significant; we will discuss his career at greater length when we deal with the seventies. For the present, it is enough to say that in the early days it was Taylor's proven musical ability within the movement that gave pause to those with little regard for the musical ability of the majority of new thing-ers, and who saw the jazz of protest as a passing fancy. Archie Shepp—no Coltrane or Rollins—was, however, the talker, frequently the group's voice, the phrase-maker, and the jazz press gave him good space. Born in 1937 in Florida and growing up in Philadelphia, he came to New York where in 1960 he worked with Taylor; later he worked with Coltrane. An excellent introduction to Shepp's playing may be heard on his 1968 *Magic of Ju-ju* (Impulse), which includes several tracks in which he plays relatively "straight," and a side in which he builds up the characteristically long, intense shriek of the "new thing." In December 1965, for *Down Beat*, he wrote, "Give me leave to state this unequivocal fact: jazz is the product of the whites—the ofays—too often my enemy. It is the progeny of the blacks—my kinsmen. By this I mean: you own the music, and we make it." [5]

Can the music of the "new thing" jazzmen be described? Of course. It can be described metaphorically, as it usually is, or it can be described technically, as a number of jazz theorists have done (Don Heckman and Don Ellis, among others). For the average jazz buff, however, neither metaphor nor analysis adds very much to a single hearing of, say, such a stylistically established new thing work as *Magic of Ju-ju*. Technically speaking, little of what is found in the new thing had not already been used, in part, in earlier jazz. What distinguishes the use in new thing music is special prominence and proportion to the rest of its elements. The protracted lack of steady rhythm or pulse, for one thing; and, for another, the disproportionate use of extreme instrumental registers over inordinately long periods of time. (An interesting comparison of some of the new thing techniques may be made with serious composer LeMonte Young's *The Tortoise, His Dreams and Journeys,* composed in 1964 and consisting entirely of a single chord held for a number of hours, with occasional slight changes in timbre and quality. Not a piece one would care to try on one's piano.)

There is, of course, the matter of emotional intensity. Bringing the listener's emotional intensity to a high pitch can frequently be accomplished by the simple act of repetition plus that old musical stand-by, crescendo (Ravel's *Bolero* is a good example of what can be done with repetition and crescendo). These techniques, though old-hat to experienced listeners, apparently were not old-hat to new thing jazz-men, and we must not leave this question without noting that the repetition of musical idea with simultaneous increase in volume also served to heighten the emotional intensity of the *performer.* And in this sense the performance was as much for the performer himself as it was for anyone who happened to be listening. In Balliett's *Ecstasy at the Onion,* Percy Heath, of the Modern Jazz Quartet, laid out this point neatly. "You have to know how it feels to be miserable," he said, "how it feels to be sad, how it feels to be in the dumps before you can project it. When that slave cried out in the field, he wasn't just making music, he *felt* that way." [6]

On the other hand, Hampton Hawes, a black jazz pianist, who in the late fifties was generally acknowledged to be one of the most promising jazzmen of his generation, said in an interview in *Down Beat* (October 17, 1968), "There are a whole bunch of cats who can't run changes, but they can play a lot of far-out stuff. When you ask them, 'What was that?'—they say, 'Well, I'm out there.' Now what is that crap? That don't mean nothing. *Music* is what's happening. Man, I don't care about 'out there.'" And Hawes had his share of supporters.

277

the
seventies

(Overleaf) Cecil Taylor and Bill Evans

BEFORE WE GO ANY FURTHER, we should say something about the thorny question of women in jazz. In the seventies women are increasingly finding opportunities to be recognized and accepted in all areas previously considered male bastions, jazz included. In this book the almost exclusive use of masculine terms in describing jazz and its development has been a matter of grammatical convenience as well as a reflection of the fact that, indeed, most jazz people *have* been men. Although women have been associated with jazz from its very inception, the majority—particularly in the early years—were singers. While the general public has always assumed that singers, especially those who sang the blues, were jazz singers, jazz writers and critics still debate the question of whether there is such a thing as jazz singing, male *or* female. Space forbids a lengthy discussion of this debate. My own position was summed up in *The Anatomy of Jazz* (Seattle: University of Washington Press, 1960) twenty years ago, when I wrote, "Jazz singing of course has not developed and advanced in the same sense instrumental jazz has; and in the past twenty years—since the death of the incomparable Bessie Smith—there has been no development of jazz singing. For this reason I believe the subject of jazz singing will eventually, and properly, come under the classification of folk music studies." My position in the mid-seventies remains relatively unchanged; however, I can see considerable merit in the views of those who wish to place Ella Fitzgerald, for example, in the halls of jazz, or Bessie Smith, Billie Holiday, Mildred Bailey, Sarah Vaughan, or Dinah Washington, to name only a few who come to mind quickly.

The key to the question of jazz singing, I suppose, is whether there is an attempt on the part of the singer to do a creative improvisation (the goal of any jazz musician, man or woman), or whether what we are hearing is a studied performance, musical ideas worked out in the woodshed and then repeated in public performances time and again with little or no effort at variation. One way to determine the matter of degree of creativity in a jazz singer is to be present at consecutive performances during which the singer performs the same program of songs. We should ask, To what degree do the performances differ from each other, and to what degree are they the same? That is the basic question, not how a singer advertises himself or herself.

On another level, there are those singers who have enjoyed long-time associations with bona fide jazz musicians, singers who chose (or were chosen) to be accompanied by jazz musicians providing backgrounds of solo improvisation or arranged accompaniments of jazz ensemble ideas. These singers would include a number who made their marks as big-band vocalists—singers like Anita O'Day, June Christy, Chris Connor (all Stan Kenton alumnae of the forties and fifties); and Maxine Sullivan, who worked with John Kirby's band in the late thirties and who enjoyed a New York revival in 1976.

To classify is risky. One who makes up categories runs the risk of being belabored by all factions. Making lists is somewhat easier, and while the basic problem is invariably comprehensiveness or inclusiveness, the classifier can always add "and others" as a disclaimer. Making lists is an interesting game for the compiler, if not always for the reader, but at this stage, lists of women in jazz, however tangentially involved, may be of some value. In 1974, the action of a colloquium organized by the Committee on the Status of Women, to discuss Women in Music, was reported by Jean Bowen in *Hi Fidelity and Musical America,* August 1974. Ms. Bowen, Assistant Chief of the Music Division of the New York Public Library and a member of the panel, reported that "there was general agreement that in the jazz and pop field there seem to be few women performers other than singers or pianists but that no figures exist to *back up this hunch."* (My italics)

Whitney Balliett, jazz writer for the *New Yorker,* provides one point of departure with a short list of first-rank men and women singers of popular songs, still singing in the seventies, whose models are Mabel Mercer, Frank Sinatra, Mildred Bailey, and Billie Holiday. "They include," he wrote, "Anita Ellis, Sylvia Sims, Maxine Sullivan, Helen Merrill, Johnny Hartman, Matt Dennis, Bobby Short, Nancy Harrow, Susannah McCorkle, Marlene VerPlanck, Hugh Shannon, Bobby Troup, Irene Kral, Jackie Cain, Barbara Lea, David Allyn, Blossom Dearie, Teddi King, and Thelma Carpenter."

As we scan these names, we see several whose performances regularly elicit the word "jazz." Sylvia Sims, for one; Helen Merrill, for another; and Irene Kral, whose brother Roy Kral, and Jackie Cain, popularized bop vocal duets in the forties and fifties. In any case, singers sing whatever pleases them at a given time in their careers, and some singers may enjoy being shown on more than one list. Here, for example, are a number of blues singers, some of whom might appear on still another list. Women: La Vern Baker, Ida Cox, Barbara Dane, Julia Lee, Lizzie Miles, Chippie Hill, Ma Rainey, Bessie Smith, Mamie Smith, Big Maybelle Smith, Kay Starr, and Linda Hopkins, who in the mid-seventies made a temporary career of imitating Bessie Smith in the Broadway show *Me and Bessie.* Men: Louis Armstrong, Jimmy Rushing, Jack Teagarden, Joe Turner, Muddy Waters, and a legion of folk singers.

A list of singers past and present who certainly *cared* about jazz and whose performances were usually described as jazz-oriented, jazz-tinged, jazz-inflected, or who thought of themselves as *jazz* singers, would surely include the names of Ernestine Anderson, Mildred

Bailey, Pearl Bailey, Betty Carter, Chris Connor, Blossom Dearie, Urszula Dudziak, Ella Fitzgerald, Helen Humes, Peggy Lee, Carmen McRae, Helen Merrill, Mary Ann McCall, Marilyn Moore, Annie Ross, Nina Simone, Carrie Smith, Phoebe Snow, Dakota Staton, Sarah Vaughan, Dinah Washington, Ethel Waters, Lee Wiley, and Nancy Wilson. And among the men: Ray Charles, Jon Hendricks, Eddie Jefferson, Roy Kral, Dave Lambert, King Pleasure, Buddy Stewart, Mel Tormé, and Leo Watson.

Those women in jazz about whom there can be no equivocation, who have asked to be judged as jazz musicians and who have attempted to provide us with creative improvisations (sometimes successfully, sometimes not) but always made the *attempt* on the spur of the moment, before our very ears as it were, must be sought among the instrumentalists.

I wish to establish, first, the unequivocal position in jazz history of Lil Hardin Armstrong—a woman in jazz whose sensitivity to changing jazz styles and her subsequent musical and marital involvement with Louis Armstrong helped change the course of jazz history. As a member of King Oliver's band playing in Chicago in 1923, she recognized the potentiality of young Armstrong, who seemed satisfied to play second cornet to Oliver's first, and persuaded him to leave Chicago to play with Fletcher Henderson's band in New York. Upon his return to Chicago, which she may well have planned (they were married upon his return), she encouraged him to strike out on his own, as a leader, and to form the Hot Five and, later, the Hot Seven —two historically significant groups in which Lil Hardin played piano. These groups then went on to play an essential role in jazz history by gradually de-emphasizing the collective improvisation of the New Orleans style and contributing to the pre-swing development of solo improvisation. It is my considered opinion that Lil Hardin was heavily involved in all the moves that made Armstrong one of the most significant figures in jazz history.

The majority of women instrumentalists in jazz have always been pianists. The reasons for this are not complicated, but simply traditional: While young boys took lessons on such "masculine" instruments as trumpet, trombone, and drums, young girls took piano lessons or studied such acceptably "feminine" instruments as violin, flute, or harp. Although the late sixties and seventies saw greater opportunities for women in jazz, as well as in many other fields, the piano (or, at least, keyboard instruments) remains the jazzwoman's main instrument.

Those pianists with longtime standing in the world of jazz would have to include, in addition to Lil Hardin Armstrong, Cleo Brown and her boogie-woogie piano of the thirties; Una Mae Carlisle; Barbara Carroll; Dorothy Donegan; Lorraine Geller; Julia Lee; Marian McPartland; Hazel Scott; and Mary Lou Williams, who has been called "The Queen of Jazz" and "The greatest female in the world of jazz." In the fifties, Beryl Booker had a swinging trio with Bonnie Wetzel on bass and Elaine Leighton on drums. Both Dorothy Ashby and Alice Coltrane started on piano, switched to harp, and in the seventies dominated the field.

Other seventies entries include Toshiko Akiyoshi, Japan's leading jazz pianist since the middle fifties (despite her U.S. residency since then); in 1976 jazz critics voted her band as the one most deserving of wider recognition and, in addition, placed her among the most promising composers. In the same poll, Carla Bley did as well as Akiyoshi among composers deserving wider recognition, a position she held in 1971 and 1972 as well. Additional jazzwomen of the seventies, deserving of wider recognition, are Urszula Dudziak, keyboards;

Rhoda Scott and Shirley Scott, organ. Special mention must be made of Patrice Rushen who, in 1976 at age 21, was being favorably compared with Herbie Hancock and Chick Corea; her keyboard work may be heard to good advantage on *Before the Dawn* (Prestige).

The roster of jazzwomen, other than those playing keyboard instruments, has never been long. Most of these women, of course, are relatively unknown to the general public and include Norma Carson, a trumpet player of the fifties in the Gillespie mold; Margie Hyams, vibraphonist, who had her own trio in the forties; Terry Pollard, who was on vibes in the fifties; Mary Osborne, a first-rate jazz guitarist of the forties and fifties; Elsie Smith, who played tenor saxophone and clarinet in the mid-fifties; Melba Liston, trombonist and composer, who worked with Gillespie, Basie, and Quincy Jones in the forties and fifties, and was long considered to be the only female trombonist in jazz (in the seventies, the sound of Janice Robinson's trombone seriously challenges the position Melba Liston held for nearly thirty years). Additional jazzwomen of the seventies who warrant special attention are percussionist Sue Evans and vibraphonist Ruth Underwood, both of whom have shown a remarkable capacity for creative improvisation.

While women in jazz have had to battle old myths about their status in society, many black jazzmen have had similar difficulties. In the fall of 1975, for example, the *New York Times* published a story about three black jazzmen:[1] bass player Ron Carter, pianist Harold Mabern, and trumpeter Jimmy Owens. The headline read, "Jazzmen in City Still Battle Old Myths." Carter, who was thirty-eight, spoke about the problems of being a jazz musician—one of them being the general public's impression of jazzmen: "The jazz player can't read music," Carter said. "He comes to rehearsals late or drunk or high on narcotics. He cannot or will not do commercial jingles." Many jazzmen have found that this misconception affects their ability to function as average Americans, so they avoid, when they can, telling anyone they play jazz. "It makes it harder," Carter said, "to get credit cards, bank loans, good housing, and the other things most working people have."

Harold Mabern, thirty-nine, had worked with Cannonball Adderley, Art Farmer, Miles Davis, J. J. Johnson, and had, besides, appeared on forty-some jazz recording dates. He made the point that jazz musicians who can't accept the fact that music is a business are in great difficulty. "A musician who only has talent, and no head for business," Mabern said, "will starve." However, even for those aware of this, making a career in jazz is still difficult. Mabern would have liked to work with the groups that provide the background for commercial jingles because the pay is excellent, but only once in his career had he done so. "I would like to get commercial work," he said, "but evidently you have to know somebody."

Jimmy Owens, at thirty-two, had worked with Charlie Mingus and Lionel Hampton, and was now obsessed with the economic plight of all musicians, jazz and classical alike. "Even the best-trained graduates of Juilliard can't find their way to the stage door at the New York Philharmonic," he said. And as for the jazz stars, "Some of the best musicians in the world still go out on the road for $200 a week, trying to pay hotel bills, buy food, clothing, and maintain families here in New York." Owens became a prime mover in organizing Creative Black Artists, Inc., whose principal aim was to improve the economic position of black jazzmen.

The economic plight of most jazzmen throughout the history of jazz is too well known to need recounting here. For jazz musicians under forty, and others as well, to be concerned with such mundane affairs as food, clothing, shelter, and the welfare of their families is surely not unusual. The public has always thought of jazz, when they think of it at all, as a young person's fancy, and while jazzmen approaching "old" age might properly have economic concerns, it has been the accepted view that the young should care only for their art. It is therefore interesting to compare the views expressed by "old-timers" Carter, Mabern, and Owens with the views of a number of jazzmen somewhat younger.

In an article in the March 1975 *Esquire* (page 86) "Prime Chops and Fresh Licks," subtitled "Presenting the Jazz Stars of Tomorrow," Gary Giddens, one of the brightest jazz critics of the mid-seventies, chose, along with others, saxophonist Azar Lawrence, who said, "Jazz doesn't bother me, but I don't consider myself playing jazz, I play music." Earl McIntyre, tuba and trombone player, told Giddens, "Jazz means that I can play four sets with Mingus for twenty-five dollars or one set with The Band [a pop group] for three hundred." Drummer Buddy Williams said, "Economically, jazz is a stigma. If you're a musician, you play music." Drummer Thelonious Monk, Jr., said, "I consider myself a *musician*." Giddens noted what these men have in common: All are in their twenties, all have had formal training, and "most stoutly deny any identification as jazz musicians . . . and, above all, they know that *Down Beat* reviews don't pay the rent."

The money that comes with popularity pays the rent, the argument goes, and it is safer to say you're *not* playing jazz if you hope to achieve popularity and, in due course, money. The irony of this situation is that Cecil Taylor, the jazzman who probably made as much contribution to jazz in the late sixties and into the seventies as anyone, *says* he plays jazz, while his detractors claim he doesn't. Furthermore, no jazzman of the seventies can claim to be a stronger proponent of black music (and everything it represents) than the pianist and com-

poser Cecil Taylor. Since the popularity of the black music Taylor
represents is extremely limited, he would appear to have found a way
to draw something from jazz that his younger colleagues don't comprehend. Taylor has been called one of the most inventive musicians
of our time, a prophet, a genius. From the late fifties on he has moved
further and further out of the mainstream until he became by the
seventies, in Gary Giddens' phrase, "the outermost concentric circle
of the avant garde." His influence among those first-rate musicians,
black and white alike, who have no difficulty in acknowledging that
they play jazz, has been strong and pervasive. Despite his openness
and desire to share his views with others, the forbidding quickness
and depth of his musical thought and his uncompromising spirit have
made him a sort of island. As one jazzman put it, "Taylor's mind is
a nice place to visit, but I wouldn't want to live there."

Taylor was born in New York in 1933. He was graduated from the
New England Conservatory of Music, where, despite his protests
against conservative faculty members with little or no interest in non-
European musical traditions, he received a solid classical musical education from which in the mid-seventies (some twenty years after
graduation) he still continued to draw. What he chose to select from
his formal training, together with the "vocabulary" he absorbed from
his close relationship with jazzmen in the street, as it were, resulted
in jazz improvisations and compositions of a special sort of curious
originality. While his classical influences range from Debussy to Bartók (I have even heard Samuel Barber in Taylor's music), his jazz
influences include pianist Erroll Garner, a wonderfully and awkwardly
romantic original, whose own work in the late fifties was always full
of Lisztian surprises; and early Ellington. (It is sometimes said that
Taylor has also been influenced by the craggy harmonies of early
Monk, but I doubt it. Monk used these harmonies, of course, but

Taylor undoubtedly had heard them earlier, during his four years at the conservatory.)

What, then, does Taylor's music sound like? In *Down Beat,* in 1971, Taylor told John Litweiler, "We in black music think of the piano as a percussive instrument: we beat the keyboard, we get inside the instrument." Does that mean that Taylor bangs on the piano? Well, yes—sometimes. But on other occasions he is lyrical or angular or simply muscular. Moreover, Taylor's experiments have extended over many years, and we must consider whether we're talking about the Taylor of 1957, 1967, or 1977. Clearly, the most satisfactory answer to the question, What does Taylor's music sound like? is to play his recordings from several different periods. A good start can be made with *Looking Ahead* (Contemporary), *Unit Structures* (Blue Note), and *Silent Tongues* (Arista), which span much of the best of his creative years from 1958 to 1974. For those interested in the technical and theoretical aspects of Taylor's early work, Gunther Schuller's analysis of two Taylor works in *The Jazz Review,* January 1959, is a model of what such analysis should be. Many of the technical terms used by Schuller and others to describe Taylor's music have been referred to in our sections on third stream and the "new thing."

If Cecil Taylor is aware of the work of any white jazz piano player in mid-seventies America, it is that of Bill Evans, whom Balliett once called "the premier pianist of his generation." Since there is only a four-year difference in age between Taylor (born 1933) and Evans (born 1929), it is reasonable to assume that Taylor is included in Evans' generation. Taylor would not like that. On occasion, he has characterized Evans' way of playing the piano—Evans' concern with touch—as a nonblack approach to the instrument. Evans has said, ". . . to say that only black musicians can be innovative is so utterly ridiculous I can hardly consider the question." And during his long career in jazz, he has to a large extent affirmed this position.

For twenty years, whenever creative jazzmen, black or white, came together with a wish to try something new, fresh, original, experimental, they called Bill Evans. For whatever reasons—his quick musical grasp, his sight-reading ability, his near-perfect ear, his flawless rhythmic sense—Evans was called and in the end chosen. He has collaborated with Miles Davis, Scott LaFaro, Jim Hall, Oliver Nelson, Gunther Schuller, Percy Heath, and Gary Peacock, to mention a few. Evans no doubt received something from these and other jazzmen (his earliest influences came from Bud Powell and Lennie Tristano), but he also gave something in return. Miles Davis once said, "I sure learned a lot from Bill Evans. He plays the piano the way it should be played." And in the jazz community Davis was never known for giving compliments, let alone for giving them lightly.

Evans was born in New Jersey. He was graduated from Southeastern Louisiana College and later studied at the Mannes School of Music in New York. Like a number of other jazzmen—Sonny Rollins, particularly—Evans has wandered back and forth between the jazz world and the workaday world, no doubt seeking to fulfill his personal, perhaps emotional goals, but always with a strong commitment to jazz. Whether his playing or creative ability have been dampened by his outside explorations is, of course, a debatable point, and we must note here not what his musical position might have been, but what in the mid-seventies it is. And it is formidable. When he is right his fingers can spin silk or shatter icicles. He doesn't play as rapidly as, say, Art Tatum did, but few pianists ever have (Cecil Taylor does, for one, and so does Oscar Peterson). In ballads, however, and in slow tempos, he has no match; the sounds linger and move and linger as in a windchime. Few can match his sense of shifting harmonies, displaced modulations, harmonic nuance; and in his accompaniments his sensitivity to those with whom he is playing is incomparable.

Evans is among the last of his generation to continue to base a certain amount of his improvisational work upon standard or well-known popular songs, which, I would like to think, is one reason for his continued popularity with middle-aged jazz buffs, who bought jazz records in their youth and continue to do so. After scanning record jackets of various seventies groups for a familiar song title—looking for something with which to compare the improvising ability of one soloist with that of another where both had started with the same harmonic foundation, the same material—and finding such titles as "Vibrations" or "Eighty-First Street" or "Abyss," what a pleasure it is to see Evans' selections: "I'll See You Again," "Dancing in the Dark," "Green Dolphin Street," and even that Rodgers and Hart near-hit "My Romance." While Evans' work in the sixties and seventies also has its "Vibrations," the inclusion of a standard or two is his way of coming to the mark, as it were, as if he were unafraid and welcomes competition and challenge and comparison.

For a sampling of Evans' work between 1964 and the middle seventies, listen to *Bill Evans: The Tokyo Concert* (Fantasy), particularly his "T.T.T.T." (Twelve Tone Tune Two), full of marvellously fresh and surprising sequences, and the interesting support of Eddie Gomez on bass and Marty Morell on drums. Evans' version of Steve Swallow's "Hullo Bolinas" on the same album reflects a good deal of Evans' harmonic quirkiness; it opens like a curious sort of Mendelssohn-Chopin salon piece with occasional "wrong" notes in the right places, followed by a little characteristic jazz rat-tatatat figure here, there, everywhere, finally returning to the three-four Chopin opening—this time with Erik Satie overtones—and ending in the tinkly highest reaches of the piano keyboard. Or his *Intuition* (Fantasy) with Evans and Gomez alone, during which Evans takes on the electric piano in an exciting bop-oriented "Are You All the Things," and a clean, waltzy, sparkly "A Face Without a Name"—in three-four. (No one in jazz seems more at home in waltz-time than Evans.) Finally, his work in *Trio 64* (Verve) includes a bouncing "Little Lu-Lu," a suave "I'll See You Again," and a dashing "Santa Claus is Coming to Town"—all of which indicates Evans' constant search for fresh and provocative material. Two albums containing his earliest recordings have been reissued by Milestone. They are *The Village Vanguard Sessions* and *Peace Piece and Other Pieces*.

Until the middle and late sixties, few critics or jazzmen could have predicted that the trickling infusion of the rock spirit into the body of jazz would by the mid-seventies become part of the mainstream. Jazz people refused to accept the idea that a squalling music recently arrived on the scene could affect or influence a music as mature as jazz. As rock continued to infiltrate jazz, jazz stalwarts liked to think that the rock industry was at last showing some sense by allowing itself to come under the influence of jazz. Ironically, rock advocates had diagnosed jazz as debilitated, if not already dead.

By the mid-seventies rock elements in mainstream jazz had become a commonplace. The rhythms of the rock drummer were everywhere. The ground bass, or *ostinato* as it is sometimes called, was also ubiquitous. "Ground bass" does not refer to bass instruments, but is a simple bass line played by anyone in the group. It may also be a melodic pattern, phrase, or theme repeated over and over (*ostinato* also means "obstinate") that pervades the musical atmosphere of the piece. It comes in as an introduction, accompanied or not by the percussion, and continues underneath as the basis for improvisation. Usually two or four bars long, the *ostinato* frequently serves as the jazz improviser's entire harmonic orientation; in its most obstinate form, it becomes the piece's *raison d'être*—hypnotizing by sheer repetition. Whether one accepts or rejects the melodic, harmonic, rhythmic, textural, and orchestrational influences of rock on jazz is irrelevant here; the influence remains and, in mainstream jazz at any rate, seems to grow stronger. There are few jazzmen in the mid-seventies, either major or minor figures, who are not aware of rock's relation to jazz and of those young people for whom rock is nostalgia and who continue to be the greater part of the record-buying public. For those jazzmen who seek popularity, who wish to be in close relation to the money-flow, to be in the mainstream, the spirit of rock has become a fact of their economic lives—a force to be reckoned with.

Here, then, are those jazzmen and jazz groups most popular or best known through the mid-seventies, presented according to the instruments they play. Our list will not include major figures we have already discussed elsewhere; nor will it necessarily include those who flourished earlier but continued to perform through the mid-seventies (such men as Milt Jackson, say, or Zoot Sims, Kenny Burrell, Charlie Mingus, Lee Konitz, and others). Space forbids comment on these jazzmen individually, however worthy their past accomplishments, except in those instances where a jazzman has continued to maintain high visibility. Here, then, are the seventies figures, not necessarily in any order of importance:

Trumpet: Freddie Hubbard, Miles Davis, Dizzy Gillespie, Jon Faddis. Trombone: Bill Watrous, Garnett Brown, Roswell Rudd. Soprano saxophone: Wayne Shorter, Steve Lacy, Bob Wilber. Alto saxophone: Ornette Coleman, Phil Woods, Anthony Braxton. Tenor saxophone: Sonny Rollins, Stan Getz, Dexter Gordon. Baritone saxophone: Gerry Mulligan, Pepper Adams, Cecil Payne. Clarinet: Rahsaan Roland

Kirk. Flute: Hubert Laws, James Moody, Jeremy Steig. Piano: Oscar Peterson, Chick Corea, Keith Jarrett, McCoy Tyner (and, of course, Taylor and Evans). Guitar: Joe Pass, John McLaughlin, Jim Hall, George Benson, Larry Coryell, Jeff Beck. Acoustic bass: Richard Davis, Ron Carter, Charlie Haden, Charlie Mingus. Electric bass: Stanley Clarke, Miroslav Vitous, Bob Cranshaw. Drums: Billy Cobham, Elvin Jones, Buddy Rich. Percussion: Airto Moreira, M'tume. Vibraphone: Gary Burton, Bobby Hutcherson, Karl Berger, Dave Friedman. Organ: Jimmy Smith. Miscellaneous instruments: Kirk for African or non-Western reed instruments: Howard Johnson, tuba: Jean-Luc Ponty, violin; Toots Thielemans, harmonica. Big bands: Thad Jones/Mel Lewis, Count Basie, Gil Evans. Small groups: Weather Report, McCoy Tyner, Miles Davis. Rock-pop-blues groups: Mahavishnu Orchestra; Earth, Wind and Fire (in 1974); Frank Zappa and Mothers of Invention (in 1973). Synthesizer: Herbie Hancock, Sun Ra, Joe Zawinul. (Nearly all mid-seventies pianists have had a go at the electric piano, with Chick Corea in the lead; those involved with synthesizers are former piano men, and it is likely that eventually there will arise a single category to encompass all the keyboard men.)

A comparison of mainstream jazzmen of the sixties with those of the seventies may be useful in identifying the mainstream forces during those periods. For example, Dizzy Gillespie and Miles Davis remain high in both periods while Al Hirt, a Dixieland trumpeter and television phenomenon with one foot in the swing era, appears to have been a shooting star. The trombonists of the sixties who were leading exponents of the post-bop and post-cool styles were replaced in part by Watrous, an incredible technician, and Rudd, of the "new thing." The soprano saxophone, a sometime, oldtime instrument considered in the sixties only a "miscellaneous" curio associated with jazz-master of the past Sidney Bechet and, later, John Coltrane, gained widespread use in the seventies, usually as a characteristic new thing sound by Wayne Shorter.

Of the sixties saxophonists, Cannonball Adderley, John Coltrane, and Johnny Hodges were dead, and Paul Desmond, the exponent of cool jazz and a star of the Dave Brubeck group, was no longer among the stars; Ornette Coleman, however, remained constant, as did Sonny Rollins and Stan Getz. Mulligan, who had been pre-eminent on the baritone saxophone, was joined by Adams and Payne, who were interested in new perspectives. The clarinet, a major jazz instrument of all previous periods, fell into relative disuse in the seventies (except, of course, among those jazzmen still playing in a traditional or Dixieland style). The flute, on the other hand, generally unused in the sixties, became quite common in the seventies. The piano, important throughout jazz history, appears to dominate the seventies; of further significance is the widespread use of the word "acoustic" (as in acoustic piano, acoustic bass, acoustic guitar, to distinguish them from their electric counterparts).

In the seventies one does not simply say "piano." (In an advertisement for a McCoy Tyner album in 1975, part of the copywriter's encomium said, "Perhaps the last of the great all-acoustic keyboard artists . . .") It is a safe generalization to say that the work of the major pianists of the seventies shows the influence of rock, with the work of Cecil Taylor and Oscar Peterson being the principal exceptions. The influence of pop and rock is especially evident in the guitar, again with Joe Pass and Jim Hall as the principal exceptions. Drummers in the seventies found themselves distinguished from percussionists—those men who specialize in playing a variety of non-Western noisemakers—and many seventies jazz groups employed both; it was not considered especially ambiguous to have a percussionist beat out, say, a Brazilian rhythmic pattern against a straightforward rock pattern beat out by an everyday drummer.

Big bands remain big bands. Those that remain as mainstream favorites are made up generally of interchangeable sections of first-rate readers, two or three good soloists, a stratospheric trumpet or two, three or four good arrangers, and a name leader. Ellington, of course, is sorely missed. It is in the most popular smaller groups that the important changes from the sixties to the seventies are most evident. Jazz-pop-rock-blues groups, like Weather Report, Mahavishnu Orchestra, Blood Sweat and Tears, Chicago, and others simply did not exist in the early sixties; by the seventies their record albums sold in the millions.

A group of musicians whose records do not sell in the millions but who nevertheless are highly esteemed in certain quarters of the jazz community are those who consider themselves to be in the avant garde or on its fringes. Space forbids discussing all those involved in experimental jazz activities in the seventies, but listing a handful of these jazz players, and where they can be heard, may be useful. Let us start with Keith Jarrett's *El Juicio—The Judgement* (Atlantic), which provides us not only with some representative leanings of an important member of this unofficial group, but includes as well the backup support of still other important avant-garde jazzmen: Dewey Redman on tenor saxophone, Paul Motian on drums, and Charlie Haden on bass. Haden may be heard leading his own group in *Liberation Music Orchestra* (Impulse), which includes Carla Bley on piano, Paul Motian on drums, Howard Johnson on tuba, Dewey Redman and Gato Barbieri on an assortment of reed instruments, and Roswell Rudd on trombone. Rudd may be heard leading the Jazz Composers Orchestra in *Numatik Swing Band* (JCOA). Barbieri is leader on *In Search of the Mystery* (ESP). Anthony Braxton, playing various reeds, shows well on *Five Pieces 1975* (Arista), with Kenny Wheeler on trumpet, Dave Holland on bass, and Barry Altschul on drums. The electric violin work of Michal Urbaniak on *Fusion III* (Columbia) is provocative, and so is LeRoy Jenkins' violin in *For Players Only* (JCOA); as is Sam Rivers' saxophone work on *Hues* (ABC), and Paul Bley's piano on *Open, To Love* (ECM). The keyboard work of Lonnie Liston Smith is easily available in several albums; Pharaoh Sanders has a dozen albums ranging through the sixties and seventies; and the sounds of Rahsaan Roland Kirk's reeds —manzella and stritch—seem ubiquitous. Worthy of more attention than he has received is saxophonist Roscoe Mitchell; for those seriously interested in the avant garde, his *Solo Saxophone Concerts* (Sackville) is essential.

The abundance of prevailing jazz styles in the seventies, along with the flashing fads and fancies, shows if not always an abundance of creativity then at least the bubbling vitality essential to robust life. And while there are secret and not-so-secret places where a special sort of tinkering with the elements of jazz goes on—Harlem, Los Angeles recording studios, the lofts in New York's Lower East Side— the one place where whatever is happening in jazz is brought out into the open, as it were, is the jazz festival. It is here—at Montreux, and Newport at New York—that we are likely to receive in one massive dose a heavy sampling of whatever jazz is on the way out, currently in, or coming up. And for those fearful souls unable or unwilling to battle crowds, noise, bad food and drink, questionable sanitation facilities, and the like, it is comforting to know that nearly everything that takes place will be recorded (and, on occasion, even televised). One need only wait.

The word "jazz" in connection with "festival" is deemed by festival producers and promoters to be an okay word. Whether all the participants will, in fact, be playing jazz has not always been a primary concern of festival business interests. Although the inclusion of folk singers with a rock beat, say, or pop singers with jazz-rock groups has not always been well-met by jazz buffs on the scene, occasionally the juxtaposing of such groups with bona fide jazz groups would expose the basic musical characteristics of the various groups and clarify to some extent who was borrowing what from whom. The word "jazz" attracted those who were interested in jazz, and others, frequently the majority, were drawn by the heavily advertised magical names of their favorite pop or rock group. Eventually, elementary borrowings between groups became commonplace, and the lines—for some, anyway—became blurred. (When Weather Report, a group made up of longstanding jazzmen, won a *Down Beat* popularity poll, a reader wrote to the editor stating that Weather Report doesn't play jazz, but does play rock, and that he had heard that those who contributed to *Down Beat* polls were between eighteen and twenty-two, implying, of course, that the connection between jazz and young people was so weak that young people couldn't be trusted to make judgments.)

Rock had moved into pop, or vice versa, and elements of both deeply penetrated mainstream jazz. For young people—those who in the past had been the prime market for jazz—rock was all-encompassing. It had its magazines, its writers, its classifiers, its promoters—in short, its industry. At its peak, jazz players could choose to be influenced by proponents of white rock or black rock. Under the heading of white rock they could choose from hard rock (late Beatles, Buffalo Springfield); acid rock (Rolling Stones, Mothers of Invention); psychedelic rock (Jefferson Airplane, Led Zeppelin, The Who); folk rock (The Band; Crosby, Stills and Nash). Under black rock, they could choose from two kinds of soul: new soul (Little Stevie Wonder, The

Supremes) or old soul (B. B. King, James Brown, Aretha Franklin, Booker T. and the M.G.'s).

The forward guard in the late sixties was Blood, Sweat and Tears, a nine-piece organization with an eclectic but engaging approach to the entire jazz/pop/rock/blues/third-stream configuration. From these ingredients, including a little jazz improvisation, they stirred up what turned out to be a strikingly popular musical recipe. With the help of the press, disk jockeys, word-of-mouth reports, and the subsequent heavy record sales, Blood, Sweat and Tears was soon joined by others intent upon riding the newest and hottest bandwagon—Jethro Tull, for example, and Chicago, for another.

Enter Larry Coryell, a young guitarist with a rock foundation and a penchant (and talent) for jazz improvisation. Soon he was in the company of highly respected jazz drummer Elvin Jones and bass player Jimmy Garrison—the same Jones who had been an indispensable part of the John Coltrane Quartet and who many believed to be among the most influential jazz drummers of the sixties. The dam opened wide. Big-band jazzmen old and new rushed in. A key figure was trombonist-arranger-composer-conductor Don Sebesky who by 1970, when he was thirty-three, had spent the better part of his career swimming in the big-band mainstream (he had played with Claude Thornhill, Kenton, and similar groups). His work on *The Jazz-Rock Syndrome* (Verve) at the outset of the seventies helped open the floodgates and proved to the jazz world that the vigor of rock was just as easily absorbed into the big band as it was into the combos. In fact, many thought rock and big-band jazz made the more exciting combination. Mounting a big band posed an economic problem, of course, but whenever that problem could be solved the result was likely to be a big band in the image of Don Sebesky. Or Quincy Jones.

And the jazz-rock sounds arranged by Sebesky and Jones became more or less the big-band sound of the seventies.

The pop-rock people were in one sense more fortunate than jazz people. They saw their music as new and exciting and capable of absorbing ideas and sounds from any source. When in the late sixties the mystique of Eastern religions and philosophies made its way to New York, Los Angeles, and points between, with the vibrant sound of the sitar and the droning of *om,* the sound, if not the spirit, of Ravi Shankar's music began to be heard in pop-rock-jazz groups. Little did it matter that Coltrane had recorded *Om* (Impulse) in 1965, a work for Coltrane fanciers only. Besides, anything as long ago as 1965 was already old hat and needed refurbishing. And, the thesis went, black jazzmen were into the black thing, the African thing, with jungle sounds and weird instruments and drummers named M'tume. John McLaughlin, then an eminently successful rock-pop-blues-jazz guitarist, and some of his friends produced The Mahavishnu Orchestra, which in *Birds of Fire* (Columbia) presented its version of Miles Davis' "Miles Beyond" immediately adjacent to "Celestial Terrestrial Commuters," thus showing their ability to move easily between the two worlds.

Which leads us to "space" jazz, and the attempts of jazz players to imitate electronic composer Gyorgy Ligeti and the manner in which his electronic sounds were used for the motion picture *2001,* with small beeps, soft chirps, gentle sighs, and long oscillating bands of electronic sound. You may wish to hear the blending of these sounds and their jazz connection in Lonnie Liston Smith's *Astral Traveling* (Flying Dutchman). Or perhaps you prefer African jazz, with the authentic sounds of Africa, in Dollar Brand's *Sangoma* (Sackville). On the other hand, you might prefer having these influences on jazz, plus a number of others, all under one roof, so to speak, where they can be heard in one place. If so, they are all available, and more—space sounds, jungle sounds, champagne bubble noises, rock rhythms, modal harmonies, synthesizer sounds—all in Grover Washington, Jr.'s *Mister Magic* (Kudu)—on *one* track. And very popular, too, in 1975.

The seventies saw another extraordinary phenomenon: the literal re-creation of the jazz sounds of the past. Several jazz groups, including the National Jazz Ensemble founded by Chuck Israels, and the New York Jazz Repertory Company founded by George Wein, working with scores and parts laboriously and carefully copied from old recordings, or working with the original scores, managed to provide interested listeners with fresh live and recorded versions of classic jazz performances without the interference of shellac and the surface noises of old 78 rpm records. Audiences could enjoy re-creations of performances by Armstrong, Parker, Ellington, Jelly Roll Morton, and others. Enthusiastic arrangers, going a step further, transcribed classic solo improvisations and then arranged these solos for brass *sections,* saxophone sections, or both. Perhaps the most startling example of this practice may be heard on *Supersax Plays Bird* (Capitol), during which a number of famous Charlie Parker solos are heard harmonized for the entire saxophone section. The record jacket notes, by Leonard Feather, say, "This, in effect, is how Charlie Parker would have sounded had he been able to play five saxophones at once, in harmony."

Another re-creation worth mentioning is the Time-Life series of records covering the years 1937 to the early fifties, entitled *The Swing Era* and released in 1972. With the help of heavy advertising and the merchandising expertise of Time-Life, the re-created sounds of Benny Goodman, Harry James, Tommy Dorsey, Glenn Miller, and Artie Shaw were heard throughout the land. Swing had another revival with the unprecedented popular success of French jazz violinist Stephane Grappelly, who teamed up with concert violinist Yehudi Menuhin in a number of delightfully bouncy swing versions of songs of the thirties. Listen to *Fascinating Rhythm* (Angel) and try to guess who's who. Traditional jazz continued to be played of course in many clubs in New York, Chicago, and San Francisco—wherever the crowds of Dixieland buffs could noisily gather. A ragtime-flavored score in the motion picture *The Sting* made Scott Joplin a household word, and untold numbers of piano players bought sheet music rags and ragtime records and almost everyone else listened to the jaunty ragtime rhythms, and some thought that this, too, is jazz. And it was all to the good.

And there was more. In 1974, Flying Fish Records, of Chicago, released *Hillbilly Jazz*, with an accompanying booklet by Rick Ulman, from which we learn of the influence of jazz on folk and Country & Western music, and of the categories (new to most jazz buffs) of Okie jazz, Tex-Mex music, Southwestern Swing, Western Swing, Honky Tonk, and Switched-On Nashville, all of which apparently belong to the generic Hillbilly Jazz. According to Ulman, Charlie Christian and Django Reinhardt influenced some guitar players; Joe Venuti influenced some country fiddle players; and the piano style "comes from a combination of barrel house, Baptist and honky tonk with the boogie woogie of Pinetop Smith and the blues of Leroy Carr." If you question any of this, listen to *Hillbilly Jazz* and you may be persuaded. And even a hurried listening to the popular combination of African rhythm, Caribbean rhythm, Spanish melodies, and a dash of the big-band Afro-Cuban jazz of the fifties, all together called *Salsa,* will uncover another fertile field in which jazz may grow. Listen to Joe Bataan's *Afrofilipino* (Epic). Whitney Balliett made the point succinctly in his *New York Notes*—when he said, "The music appears to be in good health. Indeed there are probably more people of all ages playing jazz than ever before, and, even more, the young are listening again." [2] And that, too, is all to the good.

The electronic keyboard instruments of the seventies revived the notion of what used to be called the "one-man band." With one keyboard directly in front of the player, and two flanking left and right, electric keyboard champions like Herbie Hancock or Chick Corea became copiously self-sufficient. A 1975 advertisement by Hohner, a principal manufacturer of keyboards (their specialty in the 1920s was harmonicas) illustrates several of their keyboard instruments, and informs the reader, "You're looking at 4 guitars, a harp, 2 basses, a zither, 2 harpsichords and a tuba. And 5 different kinds of piano." The last word, however, in the jazz of the seventies, is the synthesizer, as operated by such synthesizer stars as Hancock and Joe Zawinul. The key names are ARP and Moog, the best-known synthesizer makers.

A synthesizer creates sounds and shapes sounds. It can bend sounds, twist them, and turn them inside out. From 1963 on, Robert Moog (rhymes with rogue), a physicist interested in music, put together an instrument for the synthesis of sound—combining a number of separate electronic devices to form a single instrument. The components include audio generators, processors, controllers, oscillators, filters, and articulators, each with its special function. In *Contemporary Keyboard,* September 1975, Moog told Dominic Milano that "a synthesizer should have at least one audio oscillator to produce pitched sound, one filter to shape the sound spectrum, an articulator which would produce and shape the overall loudness, and at least two control devices—one of which would be a keyboard, the other, an envelope generator which shapes the overall contour."

Synthesizers come in all sizes and all prices, depending (like automobiles) on the number of "accessories"—from a portable one for

$1,500 to a studio one that starts at $50,000; in addition there are synthesizers that specialize in string sounds and symphony orchestra sounds. Still other devices, like the Mellotron, duplicate the actual sound of any instrument or voice by a series of tape machines enclosed in a pianolike case; each tape has three tracks which include a variety of instrumental sounds, and the whole can be mixed and controlled by the switches alongside the keyboard. Cost: about $3,000. A good example of how various synthesizer sounds are manipulated by a first-rate jazz musician may be heard on Herbie Hancock's *Thrust* (Columbia) in which he uses in addition to a Fender Rhodes Electric Piano and a Hohner D-6 Clavinet, an ARP Odyssey Synthesizer, an ARP Soloist Synthesizer, an ARP 2600 Synthesizer, and an ARP String Synthesizer.

Never before in the history of jazz was there as much interest shown in what presumably were nonjazz instruments as in the late sixties and seventies. Earlier, we alluded to the new jazz sounds of the time. It may be valuable now to take a closer look at the proliferation of these nonjazz instruments or devices and their principal, or at least representative, exponents.

The brasses were the instruments least affected. Electronic gadgets attached to a trumpet enabled the trumpeter to bend tones, produce echoes, fuzz up a clear tone, make wa-wa noises, or sound like a trombone. Miles Davis preferred these effects (or, at least, used them in a performance I attended). Similar electronic devices have been used to alter the sound of the various standard saxophones—soprano, alto, tenor, and baritone. Yusef Lateef has made a specialty of the oboe; Benny Maupin has played something called a Saxello; and Keith Jarrett revived the sound of a recorder. Rahsaan Roland Kirk, however, has ranged far and wide, blowing into anything he thought might produce an interesting sound, and favoring what he called a manzello and a stritch. (He also has called this last a stritchophone, but I wouldn't look for it in a lexicon of musical instruments—neither would I look for his "black mystery pipes" or his "black puzzle flute.")

Electronic devices gave stringed instruments added power. Jean-Luc Ponty and Michal Urbaniak made violin sounds jazz had never known. Electric violas and cellos came into big-band string sections. Stanley Clarke and Miroslav Vitous explored the electric bass; Ron Carter favored a piccolo bass. The sitar, so far nonelectrified, became a jazz instrument in the hands of Colin Walcott; and Emmett Chapman made interesting music on an unusual guitar called a stick. The harp was favored by Dorothy Ashby and Alice Coltrane; Toots Thielemans proved the harmonica was a legitimate jazz instrument; and Rufus Hartley became a bagpipe specialist.

On the use of percussion instruments in the seventies, an entire chapter may be written without exhausting the subject. Perhaps it will suffice simply to show the percussion instruments used by Bill Summers on *Survival of the Fittest* (Arista). Here they are, in no particular order: djembe, log drum, cow bells, sleigh bells, guiro, maracas, quica, balafon, tamborim, caxixi, shehere, gankoqui, agogo, berimbau, pandeira, hindewhu, cabasa, marimbuls, and Balinese gongs. These percussion instruments, and others, are also the workaday tools of Mongo Santamaria and Airto Moreira—percussionists whose use of characteristic Latin rhythms leads directly to the Latin dance vogue of the mid-seventies.

After several years of social dancing during which dancing partners worked ever so hard to remain independent of each other, dancers in the seventies rediscovered body-contact dancing. And they apparently liked what they found. The dances, many of which originated in New York's Spanish-speaking communities, were now being performed in some seven hundred discotheques around the country. These dance halls, called discos, provided their customers with articulate, jiving disk jockeys spinning disco-beat music, soul music, and occasional jazz-tinged music, along with flickering lights and shadows and, in some discos, the heady experience of body-contact, cheek-to-cheek dancing in the artificial fog. Add to these the excitement of mixing hetero-sexuals and homosexuals (some discos, in New York at any rate, were former gay bars) and we have most of the ingredients comprising the disco phenomenon. For a good idea of what a typical disco dance number sounds like, you may wish to try drummer Hamilton Bohannon's *Keep On Dancing* (Dakar).

New dance steps arrived regularly at the discos, held their brief sway and moved on, to be replaced by newer fancies. The common denominator, however, remained: a rock-steady rhythm with a Latin beat. The Detroit Shuffle came and went; so did the Time Warp, the Bump, the Skate, and the Chicago Bus Stop. The most popular dance, however, was the Hustle, first displayed in the early seventies in New York by what has been called the Latino-Italian Hustle con-spiracy. Danced to a pattern of 1-2, 1-2, 1-2-3 (the 1-2-3 moving into a sort of shuffle), against a background of rhythms borrowed from the rhumba, samba, and old-fashioned swing music, the Hustle became the dance that couples performed *tête-à-tête*.

Disco dancers were ever ready to learn the new dances popping up here and there, and schools of dance instruction were ever ready to provide the necessary know-how. Dance studios in the major cities, particularly New York and Los Angeles, offered lessons in the Hustle, the Rope, and in what they called Afro-jazz and Latin Soul, Afro-Cuban and Primitive Haitian, along with jazz dancing, tap dancing, rock 'n' roll dancing, Flamenco dancing, and belly dancing. Since jazz is our main concern, it may be of value here to point out what the nation's major dance schools have in mind when they offer "jazz" dancing.

Lessons in "jazz" are generally lessons in how to move to music that *sounds* jazzy, that is, music with some of the traditional rhythmic characteristics of jazz. The music may be played by any instrumental ensemble and may even include attempts at improvised jazz solos, but these solos are not considered essential. What *is* essential are the steady rhythms of the type most often found in big-band jazz. The movements of "jazz" dancing include bold striding, rocking from side to side, bouncing up and down, hula-style arm and hand movements, deep knee bending, swiveling the hips, and, for contrast and punctuation, occasional sudden freezes while the beat goes on.

Perhaps the most significant dance movements of the seventies with a jazz orientation were the popular phenomena called *salsa* and *reggae*. Salsa (hot, piquant sauce) is a combination of sounds and rhythms: Latin, Afro-Cuban, rock, soul, and jazz, with special allusions to the mambo, rhumba, and other Cuban dance music of the fifties and sixties. The fusion of musical elements from diverse styles became in the mid-seventies so intricate that Robert Farris Thompson, chairman of the Yale University Council on African Studies, in discussing the Coco recording *Cortijo and His Time Machine* in the June 1975 *Saturday Review*, was able to write matter-of-factly of the "Afro-Cubanized, jazz-flavored Puerto Rican folk music of Rafael Cortijo."

The typical salsa sound is derived from two old-fashioned Cuban ensembles: the *conjunto*, based on the sounds made by the traditional street festival band; and the *charanga*, specializing in flute and string sounds. When the sounds are essentially purist (with the roots bared, as it were) the salsa is *tipico;* when the sounds have jazz inflections and appear to have been conceived in a commercial spirit, the salsa is

Americano. Whether the music is purist or commercial, or (as John Storm Roberts, a leading salsa critic put it) salsa by established performers, young-band salsa, new wave salsa, or Latin-jazz-rock, many non-Latins find it to be just the right music for the new body-contact dancing combined with spinoff steps.

In 1976 Columbia Records released a series of recordings under a new label called "Salsoul." At that moment, and on other labels, the salsa superstars included Carlos Santana, percussionist; Cal Tjader, vibraphonist; Eddie Palmieri, pianist; Ray Barretto, conga drummer; Johnny Pacheco, flutist; Tito Puente, timbale player; and Willie Colon, trombonist. *Sondo Nuevo* (MGM) combines Tjader with Palmieri, and Barretto can be heard to good effect on *Carnaval* (Fantasy).

In the mid-seventies, reggae, a local pop style originating in Jamaica, came into the international scene. Advertisements urged dancers to "Dance to 'jah' music," and those who cared knew that 'jah' means God. The roots of reggae are to be found in Jamaican pop music of the fifties and sixties, when tough Jamaican kids imitating basic British and American rock noises brought about styles variously called ska, bluebeat, rocksteady, and finally, reggae.

In 1976 the most widely advertised exponent of reggae was Bob Marley and the Wailers, a native group from Kingston. For true believers, reggae is a manifestation of Rastafari (Head Creator); Rastafarians see Africa as their promised land, and Haile Selassie, former Emperor of Ethiopia, as their spiritual leader. Marley's 1976 album *Rastaman Vibration* sings of this spirit. The sound of reggae is at once primitive, earthy, funky, and recalls rock 'n' roll; it is the sound of the ghetto, the barrio, the sound of protest, of black nationalism, black power. When asked where his music came from, Bob Marley said, "It just happen. Natural music. Nobody show us how to play, understand? I-and-I listen funky music, soul. This our soul." Add rhythm and blues, soul, heavy *heavy* electric sounds, Jamaican dance rhythms with faint allusions to the Caribbean calypso and rhythms pounded out on used Standard Oil steel drums, and we have some idea of the makeup of Marley's natural music. In the mid-seventies it appeared that with the continued heavy promotion of reggae generally and Bob Marley and the Wailers specifically, reggae stood on the threshold of widespread popular acceptance.

Clearly, there is much to know about jazz in the sixties and seventies that our jazz pioneers never dreamed of, and informal attempts to educate the general public on this point have not always been welcome. In times past, even greater resistance was shown by the professional educators. The connection between jazz and American education was a curious one indeed—one that some saw as an unnatural conjunction, an incongruity; others saw organized education as the highest embodiment of respectability, and jazz as one of the lowest. Happily, jazz eventually attained the degree of respectability it now enjoys, and in the sixties and seventies the paths of jazz and American education finally converged.

In October 1969, the Music Educators National Conference (MENC), the most prestigious and respectable organization concerned with music in the public schools, officially endorsed the use of rock in the nation's public schools. This action was followed by a supplement to the *Music Educator's Journal* (the official publication read by MENC's 58,000 members) pushing rock, and including such provocatively titled articles as "Roll Over, Beethoven," and "Give Bach a Sabbatical." School administrators throughout the land, never much on distinguishing rock from jazz, could now officially embrace what had come to be called the stage band—a type of band which, in fact, had been around unofficially, in many instances, for over a decade.

(In 1957, a high school dance band from Farmingdale, Long Island, played at the Newport Jazz Festival, and was featured in the national press.) Drawn from the marching and concert bands, stage bands were easily formed, highly popular with the students, and reflected the taste of the band leaders, most of whom favored the big-band sound of the late forties and fifties. To sound like Stan Kenton's band was the perhaps possible dream. By 1973, a compilation of several surveys showed that the American educational system supported over 15,000 high school stage bands and 2,000 junior high school stage bands. Public and private institutions of higher learning came in with 800 stage bands (some of which were now called jazz bands). If we reckon a mere fifteen students to each band, we arrive at a minimum number of 267,000 students engaged in playing jazz or jazz-oriented music, or what they *thought* was jazz, at least once a week throughout the school year. And if we add the number of students merely listening to these bands, the total number becomes very large indeed.

Among institutions of higher learning, the stage was set in 1947 when North Texas State College offered jazz arranging and performing and, finally, a jazz major. Twenty-five years later the school had seventy-five dance-band majors and eleven "lab" bands. During that time North Texas State was joined by colleges and universities in all parts of the nation. In the sixties one could hear stage or lab or workshop or jazz bands at such institutions as Indiana University, Michigan State University, and Stanford University, to name only a few of the best known. In 1972 the University of Miami graduated its first jazz majors; the same year, the summer National Music Camp at Interlochen—a bastion of classical music training—offered its students a choice of jazz courses, ending the session with a jazz concert.

(These offerings were no doubt made in self-defense. Kenton stage-band clinics and summer camps, frequently staffed by North Texas

State faculty and graduates, had for years been on the campuses of a number of major universities, and what had begun as a Kenton influence had become a Kenton industry. As late as 1976, Gunther Schuller, then president of the New England Conservatory of Music, told Robert Palmer in *Down Beat* that "sometimes I'm shocked by the inanity of the whole stage band thing. Even my good friend Stan Kenton, with his whole thing of smothering the country with these bands and these arrangements that all sound alike. . . . It's a terrible, pernicious, insidious thing, because all these kids are being fooled into thinking that they are involved with jazz in some way." The Kenton summer clinics and camps attracted some students, at least, who were potential Interlochen campers.)

The year 1973 saw the formation of the National Association of Jazz Educators, affiliated with the MENC, complete with committees, subcommittees, and an annual convention. A year later, the Rutgers Institute of Jazz Studies published its first issue of the *Journal of Jazz Studies,* and the following year the Eastman School of Music in Rochester, New York, announced it would offer a master of music degree in Jazz Studies and Contemporary Media. In 1975, Harvard University initiated a "Learning from Performers" series during which jazz historian Leonard Feather lectured on "The Be-bop Era," trumpeter Nat Adderley directed a jazz workshop, and trumpeter Freddie Hubbard's workshop attracted 350 Harvard-Radcliffe students. In 1976, *The Christian Science Monitor* did a full-page story on the Berklee College of Music, an institution "with the nation's most comprehensive program in American jazz," and its 2,300 students and its new $5 million Boston performance center. "Step inside," Steward Dill McBride wrote, "and you will find that behind this quiet facade in Boston's Back Bay some of the best sounds in contemporary music are being produced"—a far cry from the *Down Beat* items of Chapter 1.

As I write these words, jazz has reached a high point of development. Not only does it offer jazz musicians with virtuosity beyond the conception of the pioneers, but it has produced dedicated jazz teachers, historians, theorists, concerned critics, and a vast audience. One group that will help determine the future of jazz will unquestionably include a number of formally trained jazz players; this is not a prophecy but a fact. On the other hand, I am certain that the nation's back streets will continue to produce their share of jazz players who, attracted by jazz the symbol—the social significance of jazz—will continue to make their strong marks in jazz history, and this, too, is all to the good. Jazz is a boundless receptacle.

notes

CHAPTER 1

1. Nat Hentoff, "Reading the Blues," *Nation,* 186 (March 15, 1958), 240.

2. *Down Beat,* 22 (February 9, 1955).

3. *Down Beat,* 21 (February 19, 1954).

4. André Hodeir, *Jazz: Its Evolution and Essence* (New York: Grove Press, 1957), p. 32, translated by David Noakes from Hodeir's *Hommes et problèmes du jazz* (Paris: Au Portulan, chez Flammarion, 1954); Part VI, a section on contemporary jazz, was added for the English version.

5. Winthrop Sargeant, *Jazz: Hot and Hybrid* (New York: E. P. Dutton and Co., 1946), p. 25.

6. Morroe Berger, "Jazz Pre-History, and Bunk Johnson," in *Frontiers of Jazz,* ed. Ralph de Toledano (New York: Oliver Durrell, 1947), p. 103.

7. Orrin Keepnews and Bill Grauer, *A Pictorial History of Jazz* (New York: Crown Publishers, 1955), p. 1.

8. Jacques Barzun, *Music in American Life* (New York: Doubleday and Co., 1956), p. 85.

9. Nat Shapiro and Nat Hentoff, eds., *The Jazz Makers* (New York: Rinehart and Co., 1957), p. 232.

10. Nicolas Slonimsky, *Music since 1900* (Boston: Coleman-Ross Co., 1949), pp. 170–71.

11. Harold E. Spender, *A Briton in America* (London: Heinemann, 1921), as quoted in *The Jazz Age Revisited,* p. 120.

12. G. H. Knoles, *The Jazz Age Revisited* (Stanford: Stanford University Press, 1955), p. 120.

13. Aldous Huxley, *Jesting Pilate: An Intellectual Holiday* (New York: George H. Doran and Co., 1926), p. 297.

14. H. O. Osgood, *So This Is Jazz* (Boston: Little, Brown, and Co., 1926), p. 103.

15. Gilbert Seldes, *Dial,* August 1923.

16. Ibid.

17. Ibid.

18. P. F. Laubenstein, "Jazz—Debit and Credit," *Musical Quarterly,* 15 (October 1929), 606.

19. Slonimsky, *Music since 1900,* pp. 359, 397.

20. Ibid., p. 449.

CHAPTER 2

1. Sidney Finkelstein, *Jazz: A People's Music* (New York: Citadel Press, 1948), p. 25.

2. André Hodeir, *Jazz: Its Evolution and Essence* (New York: Grove Press, 1957), p. 46.

3. Both quotes from Sam Morgenstern, ed., *Composers on Music* (New York: Pantheon Books, 1956), pp. 359, 392.

4. In Barry Ulanov, *A History of Jazz in America* (New York: Viking Press, 1952), p. 5.

5. Hodeir, *Jazz,* pp. 3, 6.

6. In Morgenstern, *Composers on Music,* p. 512.

7. In Ulanov, *A History of Jazz in America,* p. 196.

8. Wilder Hobson, *American Jazz Music* (New York: W. W. Norton and Co., 1939), p. 54.

9. Virgil Thomson, "Swing Music," *Modern Music,* 13 (May 1936), 17.

10. Ulanov, *A History of Jazz in America,* p. 195.

11. Robert Goffin, *Jazz, from the Congo to the Metropolitan* (New York: Doubleday and Co., 1944), p. 243.

12. Paul Eduard Miller, "An Analysis of the Art in Jazz," *Esquire's 1946 Jazz Book* (New York: A. S. Barnes and Co., 1946), pp. 139–40. Italics in original.

13. Ulanov, *A History of Jazz in America,* p. 7.

14. Marshall Stearns, *The Story of Jazz* (New York: Oxford University Press, 1956), pp. 260, 282. Italics in original.

15. Hodeir, *Jazz,* p. 197.

16. Miller, *Esquire's 1946 Jazz Book,* p. 134.

17. Stearns, *The Story of Jazz,* p. 304. Italics in original.

18. Hodeir, *Jazz,* p. 159.

19. Ibid., p. 197.

20. Ibid., p. 205.

21. Ibid., p. 143.

22. Stearns, *The Story of Jazz,* p. 108.

23. Hodeir, *Jazz,* p. 139.

24. Ibid., p. 240.

25. Albert Upton, *Design for Thinking* (Stanford: Stanford University Press, 1961), p. 30.

26. Richard A. Waterman, *Journal of Ethnomusicology,* No. 2, 1962, p. 132.

CHAPTER 3

1. In Morton White, *The Age of Analysis* (New York: New American Library, 1945), p. 225.

2. Jerry Coker, *Improvising Jazz* (Englewood Cliffs, N.J.: Prentice-Hall, Inc., 1964), p. 3.

3. Barry Ulanov, *A History of Jazz in America* (New York: Viking Press, 1952), p. 239.

4. Béla Bartók, *Hungarian Folk Music,* trans. M. C. Calvocoressi (New York: Oxford University Press, 1931), pp. 2–3.

5. Gustave Reese, *Music in the Middle Ages* (New York: W. W. Norton and Co., 1941), see pp. 48, 263, 353, 401.

6. Gustave Reese, *Music in the Renaissance* (New York: W. W. Norton and Co., 1954), p. 42.

7. See Manfred F. Bukofzer, *Music in the Baroque Era* (New York: W. W. Norton and Co., 1947), p. 371.

8. Alexander Wheelock Thayer, *The Life of Ludwig van Beethoven*, 3 vols. (New York: Beethoven Association, 1921), II, p. 10.

9. Casimir Wierzynski, *The Life and Death of Chopin*, trans. Norbert Guterman (New York: Simon and Schuster, 1949), pp. 83–84.

10. Nat Shapiro and Nat Hentoff, eds., *Hear Me Talkin' to Ya* (New York: Rinehart and Co., 1955), p. 19.

11. Ibid., p. 36.

12. Ibid., p. 22.

13. Ibid.. pp. 77, 78.

14. André Hodeir, *Jazz: Its Evolution and Essence* (New York: Grove Press, 1956), p. 144.

15. Robert U. Nelson, *The Technique of Variation* (Berkeley: University of California Press, 1948), pp. 31–32.

16. Shapiro and Hentoff, *Hear Me Talkin' to Ya*, p. 20.

17. Ibid., pp. 46, 47.

18. Eric Larrabee, "Jazz Notes," *Harper's* 216 (May 1958), 96.

19. Ethel Waters and Charles Samuels, *His Eye Is on the Sparrow* (New York: Doubleday and Co., 1951), pp. 146–47.

20. Ralph J. Gleason, "Brubeck," *Down Beat*, 24 (September 5, 1957), 16.

21. Sam Morgenstern, ed., *Composers on Music* (New York: Pantheon Books, 1956), p. 554.

CHAPTER 4

1. Willi Apel, *The Notation of Polyphonic Music 900–1600*, 4th ed.

2. Béla Bartók, *Hungarian Folk Music*, trans. M. D. Calvocoressi (New York: Oxford University Press, 1931), p. 195.

3. Bartók, *Hungarian Folk Music*, p. 9.

4. Walter Piston, *Harmony* (New York: W. W. Norton and Co., 1941; rev. ed., 1948), pp. 52–53.

5. Piston, *Harmony,* p. 227.

6. Marshall Stearns, *The Story of Jazz* (New York: Oxford University Press, 1956), p. 8.

CHAPTER 5

1. Aaron Copland, "A Modernist Defends Modern Music," *New York Times,* December 25, 1949.

2. Barry Ulanov, *History of Jazz in America* (New York: Viking Press, 1954), pp. 338–39.

3. Guido Adler, "Style-Criticism," *Musical Quarterly,* 20 (April 1934), 172.

4. Leonard Feather, "Duke Ellington," in *The Jazz Makers,* ed. Nat Shapiro and Nat Hentoff (New York: Rinehart and Co., 1957), p. 190.

5. Arnold Schoenberg, *Style and Idea* (New York: Philosophical Library, 1950), p. 183.

CHAPTER 6

1. John Philip Sousa, *Marching Along* (Boston: Hale, Cushman, and Flint, 1941), p. 175.

2. Richard Franko Goldman, *The Concert Band* (New York: Rinehart and Co., 1946), p. 56.

3. Louis C. Elson, *The History of American Music* (New York: Macmillan Co., 1925), pp. 157–60.

4. Alan Lomax, *Mister Jelly Roll* (New York: Duell, Sloan and Pearce, 1950), p. 72.

5. Ibid., p. 78.

6. Henderson H. Donald, *The Negro Freedman* (New York: Henry Schuman, 1952), p. 153.

7. Ibid., p. 145.

8. Lomax, *Mister Jelly Roll,* p. 61.

9. Rudi Blesh, *Shining Trumpets* (New York: Alfred A. Knopf, 1946), pp. 156–57.

10. Lomax, *Mister Jelly Roll,* p. 86.

11. Frederic Ramsey, Jr., and Charles Edward Smith, eds., *Jazzmen* (New York: Harcourt, Brace and Company, 1939), p. 70.

12. Sidney Finkelstein, *Jazz: A People's Music* (New York: Citadel Press, 1948), p. 155.

13. Larry Gara, "Baby Dodds," *Jazz Journal,* May–December, 1955.

14. Ernest Borneman, "Jazz Cult," Part II, *Harper's,* 194 (March 1947), p. 262.

15. Blesh, *Shining Trumpets,* pp. 22, 187.

16. W. L. Grossman and J. W. Farrell, *The Heart of Jazz* (New York: New York University Press, 1956), p. 75.

17. Charles Delaunay, *New Hot Discography,* ed. Walter E. Schaap and George Avakian (New York: Criterion Music Corp., 1948), pp. 2–3.

CHAPTER 7

1. Charles Edward Smith, *New Republic,* 94 (February 16, 1938), p. 39.

2. Nat Shapiro and Nat Hentoff, eds., *Hear Me Talkin' to Ya* (New York: Rinehart and Co., 1955), p. 203.

3. Shapiro and Hentoff, *Hear Me Talkin' to Ya,* p. 225.

4. Leonard Feather, "Duke Ellington," in *The Jazz Makers,* ed. Nat Shapiro and Nat Hentoff (New York: Rinehart and Co., 1957), p. 189.

5. Orrin Keepnews and Bill Grauer, *A Pictorial History of Jazz* (New York: Crown Publishers, 1955), p. 103.

6. Shapiro and Hentoff, *Hear Me Talkin' to Ya,* p. 223.

7. Hugues Panassié, *Le jazz hot* (Paris: Éditions Corrêa, 1934). English ed. *Hot Jazz* (New York: Witmark Music Publishers, 1936); (London: Cassell, 1936). Reprinted by Negro University Press, 1970.

CHAPTER 8

1. Benny Goodman and Irving Kolodin, *The Kingdom of Swing* (Harrisburg, Pa.: Stackpole Co., 1939), p. 146.

2. Gilbert Millstein, "Apostle of Swing," *New York Times Magazine,* April 19, 1953.

3. Eddie Condon and Richard Gehman, eds., *Eddie Condon's Treasury of Jazz* (New York: Dial Press, 1956), p. 272.

4. Wilder Hobson, *American Jazz Music* (New York: W. W. Norton and Company, 1939), pp. 150–51.

5. Paul Bowles, "Once Again, le Jazz Hot," *Modern Music,* 20 (January 1943), 140.

6. Nat Shapiro and Nat Hentoff, eds., *Hear Me Talkin' to Ya* (New York: Rinehart and Co., 1955), p. 322.

7. Condon and Gehman, *Eddie Condon's Treasury of Jazz,* pp. 273–74.

8. Goodman and Kolodin, *The Kingdom of Swing,* p. 161.

9. Marshall Stearns, *The Story of Jazz* (New York: Oxford University Press, 1956), p. 191.

10. George T. Simon, *Glenn Miller and His Orchestra* (New York: Thomas Y. Crowell Company, 1974), p. 289.

11. Leonard Feather, *The Encyclopedia of Jazz* (New York: Horizon Press, 1955), p. 26.

12. Shapiro and Hentoff, *Hear Me Talkin' to Ya,* p. 303.

13. Sidney Finkelstein, *Jazz: A People's Music* (New York: Citadel Press, 1948), p. 210.

14. Shapiro and Hentoff, *Hear Me Talkin' to Ya,* p. 305.

15. Ulanov, *A History of Jazz in America* (New York: Horizon Press, 1952), p. 190.

16. Paul Eduard Miller, ed., *Esquire's 1945 Jazz Book* (New York: A. S. Barnes and Co., 1945), caption opposite p. 50.

CHAPTER 9

1. Richard Boyer, "Bebop," *The New Yorker*, 24 (July 3, 1948), 28.

2. Ted Hallock, *Down Beat*, 16 (July 1, 1949), 13.

3. "Louie the First," *Time*, 53 (February 21, 1949), 52.

4. Nat Hentoff, "The Post-Bop Legitimacy of Modern Jazz," *Reporter*, 18 (February 6, 1958), 39.

5. Ross Russell, "Be-Bop Instrumentation," *Record Changer*, 7 (November 1948), 23.

6. John Mehegan, "The ABC of the New Jazz," *Saturday Review*, 39 (November 10, 1956), 34.

7. Ellison, "The Charlie Christian Story," *Saturday Review*, 41 (May 17, 1958), p. 43.

8. Nat Shapiro and Nat Hentoff, eds., *Hear Me Talkin' to Ya* (New York: Rinehart and Co., 1955), p. 337.

9. Ellison, "The Charlie Christian Story," p. 42.

10. Leonard Feather, "John 'Dizzy' Gillespie," in *The Jazz Makers*, ed. Nat Shapiro and Nat Hentoff (New York: Rinehart and Co., 1957), pp. 332–33.

11. Aaron Copland, "A Modernist Defends Modern Music," *New York Times*, December 25, 1949.

12. *Newsweek*, 36 (September 4, 1950), 76.

13. Whitney Balliett, "The Measure of 'Bird,'" *Saturday Review*, 37 (March 17, 1956), 34.

14. Wilder Hobson, "The Amen Corner," *Saturday Review*, 41 (January 25, 1958), 59.

15. Ross Russell, *Bird Lives!* (New York: Charterhouse, 1973), p. 366.

16. Shapiro and Hentoff, *Hear Me Talkin' to Ya*, pp. 348–49.

17. Dave Dexter. Jr., *Jazz Cavalcade* (New York: Criterion Music Corp., 1946), p. 233.

18. John S. Wilson, *High Fidelity Magazine*, 7 (August 1957), 70.

19. John Lewis, *The World of Music* (Information Bulletin No. 4 of the International Music Council, Unesco House, Paris, May 1958).

CHAPTER 10

1. Whitney Balliett, *Such Sweet Thunder* (New York: The Bobbs-Merrill Company, Inc., 1966), p. 132–36.

2. Ralph Gleason, *Down Beat,* July 18, 1974, p. 17.

3. Mimi Clar, *The Jazz Review*, April, 1959.

4. John Tynan, *Down Beat,* November 23, 1961, p. 40.

5. Pete Welding, *Down Beat,* April 26, 1962, p. 29.

6. P. Rivelli and R. Levin, eds., *The Black Giants* (New York: World Publishers, 1970), p. 1.

7. Martin Williams, "Jazz Since 1938," in *International Cyclopedia of Music and Musicians* (New York: Dodd, Mead, and Co., 1964), p. 1071.

8. John Tynan, *Down Beat,* January 19, 1962, p. 28.

9. Shelly Manne, *Down Beat,* November 2, 1967.

10. Bill Cole, *Down Beat,* October 14, 1971, p. 16.

11. Don Ellis, *Down Beat,* September 28, 1961, p. 66.

12. Nat Hentoff, "Jazz's Third Stream," *Metronome,* January, 1961, p. 11.

13. Robert Palmer, *Down Beat,* February 12, 1976, p. 12.

14. Gunther Schuller, "Jazz and Classical Music," in Leonard Feather's *Encyclopedia of Jazz* (New York: Horizon Press, 1960), p. 497.

15. John S. Wilson, "Is Jazz Too Respectable?" *Hi Fi,* May, 1960, p. 37.

16. Martin Williams, *Jazz Masters in Transition*—1957–69 (New York: The Macmillan Company, 1970), p. 65.

17. Gene Lees, "View of the Third Stream," *Down Beat*, February 13, 1964, p. 16.

CHAPTER 11

1. Whitney Balliett, *Ecstasy at the Onion* (New York: The Bobbs-Merrill Company, Inc., 1971), p. 161.

2. Carl I. Belz, *The Story of Rock*, 2nd ed. (New York: Oxford University Press, 1972).

3. Leroy Ostransky, "An Ear for Music," *Seattle*, April, 1967, p. 10.

4. Don Asher, "Nocturne in B-Flat Minor," *Harper's*, November, 1975, p. 41.

5. Archie Shepp, *Down Beat*, December 16, 1965, p. 11.

6. Whitney Balliett, *Ecstasy at the Onion*, p. 183.

CHAPTER 12

1. George Goodman, Jr., "Jazzmen in City Still Battle Myths," *New York Times*, September 1, 1975, Section C, p. 6.

2. Whitney Balliett, *New York Notes—A Journal of Jazz, 1972–1975* (Boston: Houghton Mifflin Company, 1976), p. 1.

a selected
jazz bibliography

ALLEN, WALTER C., AND BRIAN A. L. RUST. *King Joe Oliver.* Belleville, N.J.: Allen and Rust, 1955. Reprinted in London: Sidgwick and Jackson, 1958.

ARMITAGE, MERLE. *George Gershwin.* New York: Longmans, Green, 1938.

ARMSTRONG, LOUIS. *Satchmo.* New York: Prentice-Hall, 1954. Paperback ed., New York: Signet Books, 1955.

——. *Swing that Music.* New York: Longmans, Green, 1936.

BAKER, DAVID. *Jazz Improvisation.* Chicago: Music Workshop Publications, 1969.

BALLIETT, WHITNEY. *Dinosaurs in the Morning: 41 Pieces on Jazz.* Philadelphia: Lippincott, 1962.

——. *New York Notes—A Journal of Jazz, 1972–1975.* New York: Houghton Mifflin, 1976.

——. *The Sound of Surprise.* New York: Dutton, 1959. Paperback ed., London: Penguin Books, 1963.

——. *Such Sweet Thunder.* New York: Bobbs-Merrill, 1966.

BELZ, CARL I. *The Story of Rock.* New York: Oxford University Press, 1972.

BERENDT, JOACHIM E. *The New Jazz Book: A History and Guide.* Translated by Daniel Morgenstern. New York: Hill & Wang, 1962.

BERTON, R. *Remembering Bix: A Memoir of the Jazz Age.* New York: Harper, 1974.

BLACKSTONE, ORIN. *Index to Jazz.* 4 vols. New Orleans: Gordon Gullickson, 1947.

BLESH, RUDI. *Combo: USA.* New York: Chilton Books, 1971.

——. *Shining Trumpets: A History of Jazz.* New York: Alfred A. Knopf, 1946. Rev. ed. 1958. Reprinted in New York: Da Capo Press, 1972.

BLESH, RUDI, AND HARRIET JANIS. *They All Played Ragtime.* New York: Alfred A. Knopf, 1950. Reprinted in London: Sidgwick and Jackson, 1958; in New York: Grove Press, 1959.

329

BOULTON, DAVID. *Jazz in Britain*. London: W. H. Allen, 1958.

BROONZY, WILLIAM, as told to YANNICK BRUYNOGHE. *Big Bill Blues*. London: Cassell, 1955.

BRUNN, H. O. *The Story of the Original Dixieland Jazz Band*. Baton Rouge: Louisiana State University Press, 1960.

BUERKLE, J. V., AND DANNY BARKER. *Bourbon Street Black*. New York: Oxford University Press, 1973.

BURLEY, DAN. *Dan Burley's Original Handbook of Harlem*. New York, 1944.

CAREY, DAVE, AND ALBERT McCARTHY. *The Directory of Recorded Jazz and Swing Music*. 6 vols. Fordingsbridge, Hampshire, Eng.: Delphic Press, 1949.

CARMICHAEL, HOAGY. *The Stardust Road*. New York: Rinehart, 1946.

CERULLI, DOM, BURT KORALL, AND MORT NASATIR. *The Jazz World*. New York: Ballantine Books, 1960.

CHARTERS, SAMUEL B. *The Country Blues*. New York: Rinehart, 1959.

———. *Jazz: New Orleans, 1885–1957*. Belleville, N.J.: Walter C. Allen, 1958. Rev. ed., paperback, New York: Oak Publications, 1963.

CHARTERS, SAMUEL B., AND L. KUNSTADT. *Jazz: A History of the New York Scene*. New York: Doubleday, 1962.

CHILTON, JOHN. *Who's Who of Jazz*. New York: Chilton Books, 1972.

COKER, JERRY. *Improvising Jazz*. Englewood Cliffs, N.J.: Prentice-Hall, 1964.

———. *The Jazz Idiom*. Englewood Cliffs, N.J.: Prentice-Hall, 1975.

COLE, BILL. *Miles Davis: A Musical Biography*. New York: Morrow, 1974.

CONDON, A. E., AND H. O'NEAL. *The Eddie Condon Scrapbook of Jazz*. New York: St. Martin's, 1973.

CONDON, EDDIE, AND RICHARD GEHMAN, eds. *Eddie Condon's Treasury of Jazz*. New York: Dial Press, 1956.

CONDON, EDDIE, as told to THOMAS SUGRUE. *We Called It Music*. New York: Henry Holt, 1947. Paperback ed. in London: Corgi Books, 1962. Reprinted in Westport, Conn.: Greenwood Press, 1970.

CONNOR, DONALD RUSSELL. *B.G.—Off the Record*. Fairless Hills, Pa.: Gaildonna Publishers, 1958.

DANCE, STANLEY. *The World of Duke Ellington.* New York: Scribner, 1970.

———. *The World of Swing.* Vol. 1. New York: Scribner, 1974.

DELAUNAY, CHARLES, AND eds. WALTER E. SCHAAP AND GEORGE AVAKIAN. *New Hot Discography.* New York: Criterion Music Publishers, 1948. Reprinted in New York: Wehman, 1963.

DE TOLEDANO, RALPH, ed. *Frontiers of Jazz.* New York: Durrell, 1947. Second ed. in New York: Ungar, 1962.

DEXTER, DAVE, JR. *Jazz Cavalcade.* New York: Criterion Music Corp., 1946.

DODDS, WARREN, as told to LARRY GARA. *The Baby Dodds Story.* Los Angeles: Contemporary Press, 1959.

ELLINGTON, DUKE. *Music is My Mistress.* New York: Doubleday, 1973.

Esquire's Jazz Book. New York: Smith and Durrell, 1944–47. Rev. ed. in New York: Crowell, 1975.

EWEN, DAVID. *Panorama of American Popular Music.* New York: Prentice-Hall, 1957.

FEATHER, LEONARD. *The Book of Jazz.* New York: Horizon Press, 1957. Paperback ed. in New York: Meridian Books, 1959. Rev. ed., Horizon, 1965.

———. *The Encyclopedia of Jazz.* New York: Horizon Press, 1955. Rev. ed., 1960.

———. *The Encyclopedia of Jazz in the Sixties.* New York: Horizon Press, 1967.

———. *The Encyclopedia Yearbook of Jazz.* New York: Horizon Press, 1957.

———. *Inside Be-bop.* New York: J. J. Robbins, 1949. Reissued as *Inside Jazz.* New York: Consolidated Music, 1955.

FINKELSTEIN, SIDNEY. *Jazz: A People's Music.* New York: Citadel Press, 1948. Reprinted in New York: Da Capo Press, 1975.

GARFIELD, JANE. *Books and Periodicals on Jazz from 1926 to 1932.* New York: Columbia University School of Library Science, 1933.

GELATT, ROLAND. *The Fabulous Phonograph: From Edison to Stereo.* Rev. ed. New York: Appleton, 1966.

GITLER, IRA. *Jazz Masters of the Forties.* New York: Macmillan, 1966. Reprinted in New York and London: Collier Books, 1974.

GLEASON, RALPH. *Celebrating the Duke.* . . . Boston: Atlantic Little, Brown, 1975.

GLEASON, RALPH, ed. *Jam Session: An Anthology of Jazz.* New York: Putnam, 1958.

GOFFIN, ROBERT. *Horn of Plenty: The Story of Louis Armstrong.* New York: Allen, Towne and Heath, 1947.

———. *Jazz, from the Congo to the Metropolitan.* New York: Doubleday, 1944. Reprinted in New York: Da Capo Press, 1975.

GOLD, ROBERT S. *Jazz Lexicon.* New York: Alfred A. Knopf, 1964. Reissued in rev. ed. as *Jazz Talk.* New York: Bobbs-Merrill, 1975.

GOLDBERG, ISAAC. *George Gershwin: A Study in American Music.* New York: Simon & Schuster, 1931.

———. *Jazz Masters of the Fifties.* New York: Macmillan, 1965.

GOODMAN, BENNY, AND IRVING KOLODIN. *The Kingdom of Swing.* Harrisburg, Pa.: Stackpole and Co., 1939. Reprinted in New York: Ungar, 1961. Paperback ed. in London: Constable, 1962.

GREEN, BENNY. *Drums In My Ears.* New York: Horizon Press, 1973.

———. *The Reluctant Art.* New York: Horizon Press, 1963.

GROSSMAN, WILLIAM, AND JACK W. FARRELL. *The Heart of Jazz.* New York: New York University Press, 1955. Reprinted in London: Vision Press, 1958.

HADLOCK, RICHARD. *Jazz Masters of the Twenties.* New York: Macmillan, 1966. Reprinted in New York and London: Collier Books, 1974.

HALL, STEWART, AND PADDY WHANNEL. *The Popular Arts.* London: Hutchinson Educational, 1964.

HANDY, WILLIAM C. *Father of the Blues: An Autobiography.* New York: Macmillan, 1941.

HANDY, WILLIAM C., AND ABBE NILES. *A Treasury of the Blues.* New York: C. Boni, 1949. Reprinted in London: Sidgwick and Jackson, 1957.

HARRIS, REX. *Jazz.* Harmondsworth, Middlesex: Penguin Books, 1952. Reprinted in New York: Grosset & Dunlap, 1955.

HARRIS, REX, AND BRIAN RUST. *Recorded Jazz: A Critical Guide*. Baltimore: Penguin Books, 1958.

HENTOFF, NAT, AND ALBERT MCCARTHY, eds. *Jazz*. New York: Rinehart, 1959. Reprinted in New York: Da Capo Press, 1974.

HENTOFF, NAT. *Jazz Country*. New York: Harper & Row, 1965.

———. *The Jazz Life*. New York: Dial Press, 1961. Reprinted in New York: Da Capo Press, 1975.

HOBSON, WILDER. *American Jazz Music*. New York: W. W. Norton, 1939.

HODEIR, ANDRÉ. *Jazz: Its Evolution and Essence*. New York: Grove Press, 1956. Paperback ed., 1957. Reprinted in New York: Da Capo Press, 1975.

HOLIDAY, BILLIE, as told to BILL DUFTY. *Lady Sings the Blues*. New York: Doubleday, 1956. London: Barrie Books, 1958. Paperback ed. in New York: Popular Library, 1958.

HORRICKS, RAYMOND. *Count Basie and His Orchestra*. London: Gollancz, 1957. Reprinted in New York: Citadel Press, 1958.

HORRICKS, RAYMOND, and others. *These Jazzmen of Our Time*. London: Gollancz, 1959.

HUGHES, LANGSTON. *The First Book of Jazz*. New York: F. Watts, 1955.

JAMES, MICHAEL. *Miles Davis*. London: Cassell, 1961. New York: Barnes, 1961.

JONES, LEROI. *Black Music*. New York: Morrow, 1967. Paperback ed., 1971.

———. *Blues People*. New York: Morrow, 1963. Paperback ed., 1971.

KAMINSKY, MAX. *My Life in Jazz*. New York: Harper, 1963.

KEEPNEWS, ORRIN, AND BILL GRAUER. *A Pictorial History of Jazz*. New York: Crown Publishers, 1955. New ed. in New York: Spring Books, 1968.

KEIL, CHARLES. *Urban Blues*. Chicago: Chicago University Press, 1966.

KENNINGTON, DONALD. *The Literature of Jazz*. Chicago: American Library Association, 1971.

KMEN, HENRY A. *Music in New Orleans: The Formative Years, 1791–1841*. Baton Rouge: Louisiana State University Press, 1967.

KOFSKY, FRANK. *Black Nationalism and the Revolution in Music.* New York: Pathfinder Press, 1970.

LEONARD, NEIL. *Jazz and the White Americans.* Chicago: Chicago University Press, 1962.

LOMAX, ALAN. *Mister Jelly Roll.* New York: Duell, Sloan and Pearce, 1950. Paperback ed. in New York: Grove Press, 1956. Reprinted in New York: Grosset & Dunlap, 1959; in London, Pan Books, 1959.

LONGSTREET, STEPHEN. *The Real Jazz Old and New.* Baton Rouge: Louisiana State University Press, 1956.

MCCARTHY, ALBERT J. *Big Band Jazz.* New York: Putnam, 1974.

———. *Coleman Hawkins.* London: Cassell, 1963.

MCCARTHY, ALBERT J. and others. *Jazz on Record: A Critical Guide to the First 50 Years, 1917–1967.* London: Hanover Press, 1968.

MEHEGAN, JOHN. *Jazz Improvisation.* 4 vols. New York: Watson-Guptill Publications, 1958–1965. Paperback ed. in New York: Simon & Schuster, 1968.

MELLERS, WILFRED. *Music in a New Found Land.* London: Barrie and Rockliff, 1964. In New York: Alfred A. Knopf, 1965.

MERRIAM, ALAN P., with ROBERT J. BANFORD. *A Bibliography of Jazz.* Philadelphia: American Folklore Society, 1954. Reprinted in New York: Da Capo Press, 1970.

MEZZROW, MILTON, as told to BERNARD WOLFE. *Really the Blues.* New York: Random House, 1946. Paperback ed. in London: Transworld Publishers, 1961; in New York: Doubleday, 1972.

MINGUS, CHARLES. *Beneath the Underdog: His World as Composed by Mingus.* New York: Alfred A. Knopf, 1971.

MORGAN, ALUN, AND RAYMOND HORRICKS. *Modern Jazz.* London: Gollancz, 1956.

NEWTON, FRANCIS. *The Jazz Scene.* London: Macgibbon and Kee, 1959. Reprinted in New York: Da Capo Press, 1975.

OLIVER, PAUL. *Blues Fell This Morning: The Meaning of the Blues.* London: Cassell, 1960. Paperback ed. in New York: Collier Books, 1963.

OSGOOD, HENRY. *So This Is Jazz.* Boston: Little, Brown, 1926.

OSTRANSKY, LEROY. *The Anatomy of Jazz*. Seattle: University of Washington Press, 1960. Reprinted in Westport, Conn., Greenwood Press, 1973.

PANASSIÉ, HUGUES. *Le Jazz hot*. English ed., *Hot Jazz*. New York: Witmark Music Publishers, 1936. London: Cassell, 1936. Reprinted by Negro University Press, 1970.

———. *The Real Jazz*. New York: Smith and Durrell, 1942.

PANASSIÉ, HUGUES, AND MADELEINE GAUTIER. *Guide to Jazz*. Boston: Houghton Mifflin, 1956. Reprinted in Westport, Conn.: Greenwood Press, 1973.

PAUL, ELLIOT H. *That Crazy American Music*. New York: Bobbs-Merrill, 1957. London: F. Muller, 1957.

RAMSEY, FREDERIC, JR. *A Guide to Longplay Jazz Records*. New York: Long Player Publications, 1954.

———. *Been Here and Gone*. Brunswick, N.J.: Rutgers University Press, 1960.

RAMSEY, FREDERIC, JR., AND CHARLES EDWARD SMITH, eds. *Jazzmen*. New York: Harcourt, Brace, 1939. Paperback ed., 1959.

REISNER, ROBERT G. *Bird: The Legend of Charlie Parker*. New York: Citadel Press, 1962.

———. *The Jazz Titans*. New York: Doubleday, 1960.

———. *The Literature of Jazz: A Preliminary Bibliography*. New York: New York Public Library, 1954. Rev. ed., 1959.

RIVELLI, P., AND R. LEVIN, eds. *The Black Giants*. New York: World Publications, 1970.

ROBERTS, JOHN STORM. *Black Music of Two Worlds*. New York: Praeger Publishers, 1972.

ROSE, AL, AND EDMOND SOUCHON. *New Orleans Jazz; A Family Album*. Baton Rouge: Louisiana State University Press, 1967.

RUSSELL, ROSS. *Bird Lives! The High Life and Hard Times of Charlie (Yardbird) Parker*. New York: Charterhouse, 1973.

———. *Jazz Style in Kansas City and the Southwest*. Berkeley: University of California Press, 1971.

SARGEANT, WINTHROP. *Jazz: Hot and Hybrid*. New York: Arrow Editions,

1938. Rev. ed. in New York: Dutton, 1946. Rev. ed., *Jazz: a History,* in New York: McGraw-Hill, 1964.

SCHULLER, GUNTHER. *Early Jazz: Its Roots and Early Development.* New York: Oxford University Press, 1968.

SCOTT, ALLEN. *Jazz Educated, Man.* Washington, D.C.: American International Publishers, 1973.

SELDES, GILBERT V. *The Seven Lively Arts.* New York: Harper, 1924. Reprinted in New York: Sagamore Press, 1957.

SHAPIRO, NAT, AND NAT HENTOFF, eds. *Hear Me Talkin' to Ya.* New York: Rinehart, 1955. Paperback ed. in London: Penguin Books, 1962. Reprinted in New York: Dover, 1966.

SHAPIRO, NAT. *The Jazz Makers.* New York: Rinehart, 1957. Paperback ed. in New York: Grove Press, 1958.

SHAW, ARNOLD. *The Rock Revolution.* New York: Crowell-Collier Press, 1969.

SHAW, ARTIE. *The Trouble with Cinderella.* New York: Farrar, Straus & Young, 1952.

SIMON, GEORGE T. *The Big Bands.* New York: Macmillan, 1967. Rev. ed., 1971. Reprinted in New York and London: Collier Books, 1975.

―――. *The Feeling of Jazz.* New York: Simon & Schuster, 1961.

―――. *Glenn Miller and His Orchestra.* New York: Crowell, 1974.

SIMOSKO, V., AND B. TEPPERMAN. *Eric Dolphy.* Washington, D.C.: Smithsonian Institute Press, 1974.

SMITH, WILLIE THE LION, AND GEORGE HOEFER. *Music on My Mind: The Memoirs of an American Pianist.* New York: Doubleday, 1964.

SPAETH, SIGMUND. *A History of Popular Music in America.* New York: Random House, 1948.

SPELLMAN, A. B. *Four Lives in the Bebop Business.* New York: Pantheon Books, 1966.

STEARNS, MARSHALL. *The Story of Jazz.* New York: Oxford University Press, 1956. Paperback eds. in New York: New American Library, 1958; Oxford University Press, 1970.

STEWART, REX. *Jazz Masters of the Thirties.* New York: Macmillan, 1971.

STODDARD, T. *Pops Foster, the Autobiography of a New Orleans Jazzman.* Berkeley: University of California Press, 1971.

SUDHALTER, R. M., AND P. R. EVANS. *Bix, Man and Legend.* New York: Arlington House, 1974.

TERKEL, STUDS. *Giants of Jazz.* New York: Crowell, 1957. Reprinted, 1975.

THOMAS, J. C. *Chasin' the Trane: The Music and Mystique of John Coltrane.* New York: Doubleday, 1975.

ULANOV, BARRY. *Duke Ellington.* New York: Creative Age, 1946.

———. *Handbook of Jazz.* New York: Viking Press, 1957. Paperback ed., 1959. Reprinted in Westport, Conn.: Greenwood Press, 1975.

———. *A History of Jazz in America.* New York: Viking Press, 1952. Reprinted in New York: Da Capo Press, 1972.

WAREING, CHARLES H., AND GEORGE BARLICK. *Bugles for Beiderbecke.* London: Sidgwick and Jackson, 1958.

WATERS, ETHEL, as told to CHARLES SAMUELS. *His Eye Is on the Sparrow.* New York: Doubleday, 1951. Paperback ed. in New York: Bantam Books, 1952.

WELLS, DICKIE. *The Night People.* New York: Crescendo, 1971.

WHITEMAN, PAUL, AND MARY MARGARET McBRIDE. *Jazz.* New York: J. H. Sears, 1926.

WILLIAMS, MARTIN, ed. *The Art of Jazz: Essays on the Nature and Development of Jazz.* New York: Oxford University Press, 1959.

———. *Jazz Masters in Transition, 1957–69.* New York: Macmillan, 1970.

———. *Jazz Masters of New Orleans.* New York: Macmillan, 1967.

———. *Jazz Panorama: From the Pages of Jazz Review.* New York: Crowell-Collier, 1962. Paperback ed., 1964.

———. *The Jazz Tradition.* New York: Oxford University Press, 1970.

———. *Where's the Melody?* New York: Pantheon Books, 1966. Paperback ed. in New York: Minerva Books, 1967.

WILSON, JOHN S. *The Collector's Jazz: Traditional and Swing.* New York: Lippincott, 1958.

———. *The Collector's Jazz: Modern.* New York: Lippincott, 1959.

———. *Jazz: The Transition Years, 1940–1960.* New York: Appleton-Century-Crofts, 1966.

index

361

TURNER, JOE, 283
Twelve-bar blues form, 56-57, 58,
 193
"Twelves, The," 252
"Twelve Tone Tune Two," 252, 292
TYNAN, JOHN, 242-43, 246-47
TYNER, MCCOY, 242, 295, 296

Uhuru Afrika (Weston), 271
ULANOV, BARRY, 27, 29, 30, 32, 33-
 34, 35-36, 37, 105
ULMAN, RICK, 303
UNDERWOOD, RUTH, 286
Unit Structures (Blue Note), 290
UPTON, ALBERT, 41
URBANIAK, MICHAL, 298, 306

Variations, 37-38, 58-59, 141-42
VAUGHAN, SARAH, 281, 284
VENTURA, CHARLIE, 225
VENUTI, JOE, 156, 303
VERPLANCK, MARLENE, 283
"Vibrations," 292
Vibrations (Arista), 275
Vibrato, 80, 141
"Victory Parade of Spotlight Bands,"
 201
Village Vanguard Sessions, The (Mile-
 stone), 293
VITOUS, MIROSLAV, 295, 306
VITRY, PHILIPPE DE, 78
Vo-de-o-do style, 167

Wabash Dance Orchestra, 156
WAGNER, RICHARD, 87
Wailers, 309
WALCOTT, COLIN, 306
WALLER, FATS, 157, 159
WALLINGTON, GEORGE, 215
"Wall Street Wail" (Ellington), 14
WARD, HELEN, 182, 183
WARE, WILBUR, 274
WARREN, EARL, 195
WARRINGTON, JOHNNY, 88-89
WASHINGTON, DINAH, 284
WASHINGTON, GROVER, JR., 302
WASHINGTON, JACK, 195
WATERMAN, RICHARD A., 41-42
WATERS, ETHEL, 65-66, 152, 284
WATERS, MUDDY, 283
WATROUS, FREDDIE, 294, 295
WATSON, LEO, 284
Way Out West (Contemporary), 222
Weather Report, 295, 297, 299
WEBB, CHICK, 25, 151, 180, 190
WEBERN, ANTON, 235
WEBSTER, BEN, 157, 158, 182, 210
WEILL, KURT, 249
WEIN, GEORGE, 302
WEISS, SID, 195
WELLS, DICKIE, 158, 191, 195
WESS, FRANK, 263
"West End Blues," 136-37, 171
WESTON, RANDY, 271, 272-73
WETTLING, GEORGE, 144, 154, 182
WETZEL, BONNIE, 285
"What Is This Thing Called Love,"
 203